THE LOST FRONTIER

THE LOST FRONTIER

Momentous Moments in the Old West
You May Have Missed

ROD MILLER

TWODOT®

GUILFORD, CONNECTICUT
HELENA, MONTANA

*This book is dedicated to Dale Walker,
James Crutchfield, and Will Bagley
—my favorite Old West historians*

A · T W O D O T® · B O O K

An imprint of Rowman & Littlefield

Distributed by NATIONAL BOOK NETWORK

Copyright © 2015 by Rod Miller

British Library Cataloguing-in-Publication Information Available

Library of Congress Cataloging-in-Publication Data Available

ISBN 978-1-4930-0735-6 (paperback)
ISBN 978-1-4930-1520-7 (e-book)

♾™ The paper used in this publication meets the minimum requirements of American National Standard for Information Sciences—Permanence of Paper for Printed Library Materials, ANSI/ NISO Z39.48-1992.

CONTENTS

INTRODUCTION

How many young Americans grew up believing, and believe yet, the story about George Washington chopping down the cherry tree and other claptrap conjured up by Parson Weems? There is a good deal of historical "knowledge" out there based on things that never happened. There are many, many more things we all know that are based on real history but stretched and twisted and exaggerated and embroidered to the point they might as well be wrong.

Debunking "history" is a noble calling, and hats off to those who take on the mantle. While setting misconceptions straight played a role in the making of this book—and I hope it will clear up a few things for a few people—it has another purpose.

Besides all the history we think we know but don't, there are all kinds of people and places and events in the Old West that were important in their time, and even had lasting ramifications, that are largely lost to history. The reasons are many; sometimes their disappearance is deliberate, sometimes they are simply victims of circumstance. Many historians, of course, know about these things, but they never get the exposure they deserve and so are not common knowledge. Our store of history is limited, and it takes a lot of telling and retelling to uproot the tale of a cherry tree and plant a genuine memory in its place.

Each chapter in this book tells a story that deserves to be remembered—either because of its importance or its intrigue, or just because it's interesting. From cowboys and Indians to explorers and electricity to warfare and gunfights to royalty and rogues, the stories here cover a frontier West your education may have missed.

If there seems to be a disproportionate number of chapters dealing with Utah and Mormon history, there are reasons for it. For one thing, I am a Utah Mormon with a lifelong interest in the history of my state and people. Then there's the undeniable fact that except, perhaps, for the hundreds of thousands who came west during the California gold rush, no other group of people affected the settlement and development of our wide-open spaces as much as the tens of thousands of Saints who populated broad swaths of the West. Then there's the relative lack of knowledge about much that happened in frontier Utah. Back then, and for decades afterward, tenuous relations between the Mormons and the people of the United States meant few Americans cared much about what happened to the Saints. It also meant the Mormons, an already insular bunch made more so by repeated doses of persecution and paranoia, had little interest in publicizing what went on in their Zion and, in fact, were as likely to cover it up as talk about it.

But a lot happened to the Mormons back then, and they made a lot of things happen. Some of those obscure stories are told in these pages.

This is not scholarly or academic history. It is written for the ordinary reader. And while it is backed by considerable research in both primary and secondary sources, as well as background and commentary by scholars and academic historians, these pages are not weighted down with footnotes or citations or other references to source material. It is a book meant to be enjoyed, not studied; and while it is meant to be informative, it is not meant to be exhaustive.

Also, since many of these events are relatively obscure, information about them in the historical record is sometimes scant, and what is written occasionally differs from account to account, even to the point of being contrary. So, what you'll find in these pages is not always documented beyond contradiction. Then again, nothing we know about history is ever as clear cut and definitive and infallible as we like to believe.

All that said, these stories are true. I think.

Head 'Em Up and Move 'Em Out: Trail Driving

1546–1865—North America

Everyone knows the story. It is indelibly branded into American myth. It has become so iconic it defines, in many ways, our nation to the world. It has spawned mountains of books and movies and television shows and songs and poems. Reenacting the adventure permeated playgrounds for generations of young boys and filled the imaginations of authors and filmmakers who carried the adventure into outer space.

It is the story of the cowboy—the horseback hero whose trail-driving adventures tested his mettle in myriad ways and proved his pluck in every crisis he encountered.

Many of us know how he came to be: During the Civil War unattended cattle herds in Texas increased dramatically. And when the boys came home from the fighting, lacking any other means of support, they rounded up the semi-wild beasts and drove them north to the railheads whence they were shipped east to feed a nation hungry from years of wartime deprivation.

Thus, the cowboy, and all he stands for, was invented. For a period of, say, twenty years, the cowboy rode his way into the hearts and souls of America. This new thing, this trail drive, and these cowboys who accompanied and controlled the herds affected our national consciousness like nothing had before and nothing has since.

And that's the way it happened. Sort of.

But, in fact, by the time Texas cowboys hit the trail for Kansas and other points north, trail driving was already centuries old on the North American continent, and mounted men had long since been pushing cattle north. And east. And west.

Christopher Columbus and other explorers brought the first cattle to the Caribbean islands of the New World as early as 1494, but it was not until 1519 that the first of the four-footed bovines set hooves on the mainland, when Gregorio de Villalobos offloaded a small herd of cattle near present-day Tampico, Mexico (then New Spain). Following a spat with monopolistic stock raisers on the islands, settlers on the mainland were finally allowed to keep and raise cattle after 1524 and vast herds soon grew, through both imported stock and breeding. Coronado and other adventurers took cattle herds along as they explored the country, but these cattle—along with other animals—were meant to feed the troops, so those were not trail drives in the traditional sense.

But when the silver mines in Zacatecas, Mexico, attracted settlers in 1546, vaqueros drove herds of cattle there from the south and established ranches in the area to provide a steady supply of beef to the then-remote settlements. These drives, arguably, set the pattern for trail drives that would continue for centuries, culminating—but not ending—with the post–Civil War drives out of Texas. That, however, is far into the future.

Throughout the sixteenth century ranchers in New Spain hired vaqueros to tend cattle on expansive ranches and drive vast herds to open new grazing land or to markets. Records show some ranches carried herds of more than one hundred thousand cattle and raised tens of thousands of calves each year. In addition to being a source of food, many cattle were slaughtered for their hides, but faraway markets in Europe were as yet hard to reach, so trading in hides did not flourish until later.

At the end of that century, Juan de Oñate opened a settlement near where El Paso, Texas, is today, and the cattle he brought with him may have been the first in what is now the United States. It is certain that by 1598 his people had driven thousands of cattle north to a new settlement called San Gabriel, north of Santa Fe, in present-day New Mexico.

Oñate's original settlement on the Rio Grande near present-day Texas did not survive, but in 1659 Mission Nuestra Señora de la Guadalupe del Paso set up shop in the same area and opened the way for expansion into Texas. Expansion from there was relatively slow, with San Francisco de la Espada between the Trinity and Red Rivers established in 1689, San Francisco de los Tejas in 1690, and then several others in a broad swath across the south-central region of what would later become the state of Texas. Cattle were driven to and herds established at most Spanish missions in Texas, and the animals multiplied. There are reports of herds driven from central Texas southward to markets in Coahuila by 1770 and, with official sanction of an already prevalent practice coming in 1779, eastward to Louisiana.

Cattle ranching started in Arizona when Father Eusebio Francisco Kino drove herds from his ranches in Mexico and established ranches near the Gila River, training his Indian converts in the vaquero arts. Over the years his ranching interests spread to a number of river valleys in what is now southern Arizona.

During the same period, cattle ranching made its way to California, with herds driven hundreds of miles overland to reach San Diego in 1769. Missions—and their attendant cattle herds—marched their way northward to San Antonio, San Gabriel, San Luis Obispo, Monterey, San Francisco, and other places. Here, the vaqueros became Californios and developed their own modifications to cattle-handling and horse-training techniques, which later evolved into the buckaroo cowboy subculture that still exists.

Fertile California was soon overrun with cattle, and the Spaniards and Indians could eat only so much beef. Dried meat—carne seca, charqui, jerky—from California cattle supplied many a sailing ship at the ports of call up the coast, but it was the hide and tallow trade that herds from the coastal region and inland valleys supplied.

The hide and tallow trade flourished on the sly during most of the years of Spanish rule, and thrived openly following Mexican independence in 1821. "California banknotes," as the hides were called, paid for gunpowder, cloth, clothing, sugar, spices, tea, coffee, kitchen implements, tools, furniture, boots, shoes, jewelry, and all manner of consumer goods freighted in on ships that traveled the world. The largest ships might sail from California with more than fifty thousand hides aboard.

Things changed when Americans started taking a serious interest in California. As the missions broke up and ranchos declined in the face of Yankee intrusion, and with the market for hides in the eastern states and Europe glutted, the hide and tallow trade dwindled.

Cowboys and trail drives neither originated nor disappeared in America during the post–Civil War era. LIBRARY OF CONGRESS

The land that would become the southwestern United States wasn't the only place Spaniards established ranching and cattle herding—the same thing happened in the southeast, particularly Florida. Some believe remnants of cattle herds carried as a food source by Juan Ponce de León, who colonized Florida in 1521, and Don Diego de Maldonado, who came in 1540, established the presence of bovine ungulates on the peninsula.

There is no doubt that ranching was well underway in Florida after 1565, when the city of Saint Augustine took root, as cattle were raised on ranches in the area. As in the southwest, Indians—Seminoles and Creeks, in this case—were often employed to tend the herds, which flourished there and on other ranches to the point that cattle were exported to Cuba by the end of the century.

According to records, there were some twenty thousand head of cattle on more than thirty Florida ranches by 1700. When the British forced the

Spanish out of the area in 1763, cattle raising continued, but this time it was the Seminole who owned, tended, and traded the herds. Creek Indians also kept cattle, as did English settlers who came to Florida. Spain regained control of Florida after the American Revolution but handed it over to the infant United States in 1819.

It was still largely wilderness, with wild cattle wandering at will. Cowmen, or "cracker" cowboys, gathered herds from the swamps and scrub and lush plains to drive them hundreds of miles north to markets at Jacksonville, Savannah, and even Charleston. Later, in the 1830s, seaports on the Gulf Coast at Punta Rassa, Punta Gorda, and Tampa became the terminus for cattle drives, where the herds were loaded on ships for export, often to Cuba.

Halfway across the continent, Texas cattle continued to multiply and as Americans migrated there, beginning in earnest in 1822, cattle raising occupied many of the settlers. The immigrants disliked Mexican control, declared independence and formed the Republic of Texas in 1836, and joined the United States in 1845. Through it all, cattle ranches grew and spread, forcing out Mexicans and Spaniards who had occupied the land for hundreds of years, as well as Indian tribes who had lived there for thousands of years.

The cattle didn't care. Then again, it is unlikely they cared when forced out of the country themselves. Louisiana seems to have been the first market for Texas cattle, and a trail east to New Orleans was traveled by herds from at least 1836 on. The Shawnee Trail—or Sedalia Trail, Kansas Trail, or Texas Road if you prefer—opened up in the 1840s, and significant numbers of cattle crossed the Red River and were driven north to markets in Sedalia, Westport, Independence, Kansas City, and St. Louis in Missouri, as well as towns in eastern Kansas. In 1853 farmers fearing that Texas fever would infect their own herds turned back thousands of Texas cattle, and use of the trail dwindled.

Out in California an enterprising mountain man named Ewing Young assembled a herd of eight hundred cattle in 1837 and in July hit the trail for Oregon, where cattle were scarce. About four months later he reached the Willamette Valley with 630 head left in the herd. He sold about five hundred of the cattle for more than two and a half times his purchase price and used the rest to set himself up on an Oregon farm and ranch.

Westbound cattle drives also originated in Texas, Missouri, Arkansas, and elsewhere. Emigrants on the California and Oregon trails sometimes drove herds of cattle as seed stock for their new homes on the frontier. Entrepreneurial cattlemen also drove herds west to sell to settlers. While few formal records exist, newspaper reports from communities along the way report herds of cattle passing through on the way to California or Oregon, adding up to several thousand animals over the course of a season.

Herds originating in Texas blazed or followed trails across the southland, with the Gila River showing the way for many drovers. Once across the deserts and in the coastal regions of southern California, herds were moved north to Sacramento and San Francisco, where, in those days, you would find most of California's population.

The most traveled emigrant routes along the Platte River and over South Pass also saw herds moving west, as did other trails. One notable example is the Fancher party, traveling from Carroll County, Arkansas, to California. Their failure to arrive there constitutes one of the darkest days in American history.

The leader of the group, Alexander Fancher, had been to California before. He and his older brother John journeyed there around 1850. John started ranching near Fresno—an expected occupation, as the Fancher family had been in the horse and cattle business in Arkansas for many years. Fancher's brand was the first registered by the newly organized Tulare County in 1852.

At some point Alexander returned to Arkansas, intending to move more of the Fancher family west to join John. By 1857 he was ready to go. Along with wagons to move household goods and supplies, he assembled a herd of cattle. The size of the herd is difficult to pin down. Fancher himself may have been responsible for two hundred to three hundred head, and combined with cattle owned by others in the party, the herd may have numbered close to a thousand. There are reports that the wagon train employed nine men as drovers to move the cattle, which would indicate a fairly large herd.

The Fancher family's route, along the Cherokee Trail out of Arkansas and through what are now northern Oklahoma, southern Kansas, eastern Colorado, and southern Wyoming, entered Utah Territory at an unfortunate time. Feuding with the federal officials over control of the government, the Mormons were on the brink of a shooting war with the US Army. More than two thousand soldiers were on the march against the Saints, who were, at once, rebellious, frightened, belligerent, paranoid, and hostile toward outsiders.

Wending their way south through the Territory to link up with the Old Spanish Trial, the Fanchers stopped over at Mountain Meadows, a verdant spot hanging over the rim of the Great Basin in southwestern Utah; travelers often camped there to rest up and refit themselves and their animals before pushing on across the Mojave Desert.

The Fancher train drove into Mountain Meadows but never drove out, murdered there by a contingent of Mormon militia who killed all but the youngest of them. The cattle, along with all the other wealth of the emigrants, ended up in the hands of Mormon settlers and Indians in the vicinity.

The Civil War upset the cattle business. Texas herds, for a time, continued to supply Confederate troops and the general population of the South after being driven to Louisiana. But those supplies were interrupted by blockades. Next to Texas in number of cattle in the Confederacy came Florida. When the war cut off the Cuban market for Florida cattle, cowmen and cracker cowboys drove animals north to supply Confederate armies, and the supply was so important to the rebels that the government organized a "Cow Cavalry" to gather and move herds to feed the soldiers. Even the Yankee army fed on Florida beef, as Union troops occupied several forts on the peninsula.

With war's end and the South defeated, Confederate soldiers from Texas returned home to find vast numbers of mostly wild, free-roaming cattle just waiting for a dinner plate to occupy. They rounded up herds and pointed them north, and, as we have all been taught, invented the cowboy and the cattle drive—an important and ongoing chapter in the American story, but one which did not begin there.

Alexander Mackenzie:
Crossing the Continent

1792–1793—North America

Schoolchildren in the United States of America grow up celebrating Lewis and Clark and the Corps of Discovery and their epic journey across North America to the Pacific coast. Many never outgrow the notion, implied if not expressed, that the expedition sent out by President Thomas Jefferson was the first to accomplish such a noble and adventurous journey to such a far-flung destination.

But by the time Lewis and Clark and their crew reached the shores of the Pacific, Spaniards had already established nineteen missions up the coast of what would eventually become the state of California, including Mission San Carlos Borromeo de Carmelo at Monterey by 1770.

Perhaps the first traveler of Old World origins to reach the west coast of North America overland was the Spaniard Alvar Nuñez Cabeza de Vaca. A member of the hapless Narváez expedition, turned to flotsam and jetsam by a Tampa Bay hurricane in 1527, de Vaca was one of only four (out of a total of six hundred) members of the expedition to survive attempts to get back to Mexico.

After floating along the coast of the Gulf of Mexico in makeshift boats from Tampa Bay to Galveston Island, Cabeza de Vaca set out overland through the American Southwest where, among other things, he recorded the first sighting of a buffalo by a European. Eventually stumbling onto the shores of the Gulf of California near the mouth of the Yaqui River in 1536, the refugees finally found refuge in the Spanish colony of Culiacán (established in 1531), after their eight-year journey.

Cabeza de Vaca's journey places Lewis and Clark second, at best. But Alexander Mackenzie bumps them to third with his cross-country passage to the Pacific Ocean more than a decade before the Corps of Discovery packed their bags.

Mackenzie was born on Scotland's Isle of Lewis in 1764 and sailed to America in 1774 to join his father, an officer in the King's Royal Regiment of New York. During the Revolutionary War in 1776, the young Mackenzie was sent to live with relatives in Canada, where he later became an apprentice with the fur-trading firm of Finlay, Gregory & Company of Montreal, which was eventually merged into the North West Company. In 1787 McKenzie went off to Lake Athabasca, and he helped establish Fort Chipewyan in 1788.

Locating the Northwest Passage across the continent was in the air in those days, and Mackenzie caught the fever to find a water route to the Pacific. Here's how he described it in his journals, later published in two volumes as *Voyages from Montreal*:

> *I was led, at an early period of life, by commercial views, to the country North-West of Lake Superior, in North America, and being endowed by Nature with an inquisitive mind and enterprising spirit; possessing also a constitution and frame of body equal to the most arduous undertakings, and being familiar with toilsome exertions in the prosecution of mercantile pursuits, I not only contemplated the practicability of penetrating across the continent of America, but was confident in the qualifications, as I was animated by the desire, to undertake the perilous enterprise.*

And so, on July 10, 1789, Mackenzie dipped a paddle into a river the natives called the Dehcho, but that he would come to call the Disappointment River, and that would later be named the Mackenzie River in honor of the present exploration. Mackenzie did reach the ocean—but it was the Arctic Ocean rather than his intended target, the Pacific Ocean at Cook Inlet, hence the disappointment.

Apparently, Mackenzie was also disappointed with his lack of skill in navigation, cartography, astronomy, and other pursuits helpful to the serious explorer. But, for Mackenzie, disappointment did not lead to despair. After meeting a Hudson's Bay Company surveyor in Saskatchewan during the summer of 1790, he learned what tools and training he should have and set out for London, where he spent six months (through the winter of 1791–1792) getting the necessary instruments and knowledge.

"These objects being accomplished," Mackenzie wrote, "I returned, to determine the practicability of a commercial communication through the continent of North America, between the Atlantic and Pacific Oceans."

On October 10, 1792, the explorer recorded:

Having made every necessary preparation, I left Fort Chepewyan, to proceed up the Peace River, I had resolved to go as far as our most distant settlement, which would occupy the remaining part of the season, it being the route by which I proposed to attempt my next discovery, across the mountains from the source of that river; for whatever distance I could reach this fall, would be a proportionate advancement of my voyage.

The travelers built what would come to be known as the North West Company trading post Fort Fork on a fork of the Peace River, and wintered over there. While paddling canoes would have been the most common means of locomotion on the way up the Peace River, apparently the wind sometimes helped. "On the morning of the 18th [October], as soon as we got out of the draught of the fall, the wind being at North-East, and strong in our favour, we hoisted sail, which carried us on at a considerable rate against the current," Mackenzie wrote.

Two days later, "We landed before the house [a fort called the Old Establishment] amidst the rejoicing and firing of the people, who were animated with the prospect of again indulging themselves in the luxury of rum." Apparently, they were welcome there.

Come spring, Mackenzie described preparations for the launch upriver and the continuation of the voyage:

On the 9th day of May [1793] . . . the canoe was put into the water; her dimensions were twenty-five feet long within, exclusive of the curves of stem and stern, twenty-six inches hold, and four feet nine inches beam. At the same time she was so light, that two men could carry her on a good road three or four miles without resting. In this slender vessel, we shipped provisions, goods for presents, arms, ammunition, and baggage, to the weight of three thousand pounds, and an equipage of ten people; viz. Alexander Mackay, Joseph Landry, Charles Ducette, Francois Beaulieux, Baptist Bisson, Francois Courtois, and Jacques Beauchamp, with two Indians, as hunters and interpreters.

Proud though he seems of the canoe, it soon became a problem. Mackenzie wrote the next day, "The canoe being strained from its having been very heavily laden, became so leaky, that we were obliged to land, unload, and gum it." More difficulties with the canoe came a day later, on May 11, this time owing to the inattention of the crew. "Several Indians kept company with us, running along the bank, and conversing with my people, who were so attentive to them, that they drove the canoe on a stony flat, so that we were under the necessity of landing to repair the damages, and put up for the night, though very contrary to my wishes," he wrote.

Mackenzie's journals reveal continuing problems with watercraft through the expedition. Besides needing numerous repairs for a variety of reasons, including rough water, canoes were broken sometimes beyond repair or abandoned when overland treks proved too long to portage, and new canoes of various sizes were built along the way. All of these difficulties required unloading and reloading—and often carrying great distances by main strength before reloading—tons of supplies and provisions. One more journal entry, from May 20, will serve to make the point:

We now continued our toilsome and perilous progress with the line West by North, and as we proceeded the rapidity of the current increased, so that in the distance of two miles we were obliged to unload four times, and carry every thing but the canoe: indeed, in many places, it was

*with the utmost difficulty that we could prevent her from being dashed
to pieces against the rocks by the violence of the eddies.*

The phrase "West by North" in that passage reveals another item of note
concerning Mackenzie's journals. While filled with interesting information,
the journalist sometimes—often—is so enamored with recording compass
points and distances that it becomes tedious. Here is but one example:

*We now steered East, in a line with the high lands on the right five
miles; North one twelfth of a mile, North-East by North one eighth
of a mile, South by East one sixteenth of a mile, North-East by North
one fourth of a mile, where another river fell in from the right; North-
East by East one sixth of a mile, East two miles and a half, South one
twelfth of a mile, North-East half a mile, South-East one third of a
mile, East one mile and a quarter, South-South-West one sixteenth
of a mile, North-East by East half a mile, East one mile and three
quarters, South and South-West by West half a mile, North-East half
a mile, South one third of a mile, North-East by North one sixth of a
mile, East by South one fourth of a mile, South one eighth of a mile,
South-East three quarters of a mile.*

You get the point.

Regardless of the direction traveled after leaving Fort Fork, Mackenzie and his entourage would not see another white man for the duration
of the journey out and back. They would, however, see numerous Indians
of many bands and tribes, many of whom had never seen a white man.
"They had heard, indeed, of white men, but this was the first time that
they had ever seen a human being of a complexion different from their
own," Mackenzie wrote of a June 9 encounter.

In most, if not all, early explorations of North America, Indians were
crucial to the success, even the survival, of the expedition and the explorers. And so it was with Mackenzie. Natives all along the way shared food,
provided guides, drew maps, contributed canoes, and offered other com-
forts. On June 22 Mackenzie reported a helpful meeting with a man he
assumed was a chief:

An old man also, who appeared to possess the character of a chief, declared his wish to see me return to his land, and that his two young daughters should then be at my disposal. I now proceeded to request the native, whom I had particularly selected, to commence his information, by drawing a sketch of the country upon a large piece of bark, and he immediately entered on the work, frequently appealing to, and sometimes asking the advice of, those around him. He described the river as running to the East of South, receiving many rivers, and every six or eight leagues encumbered with falls and rapids, some of which were very dangerous, and six of them impracticable. The carrying-places he represented as of great length, and passing over hills and mountains. He depicted the lands of three other tribes, in succession, who spoke different languages. Beyond them he knew nothing either of the river or country, only that it was still a long way to the sea.

In what may be a unique, and most certainly an unusual event in western exploration, Mackenzie employed the services of a blind guide. His journal entry of June 26 tells how they met the sightless scout.

At midnight a rustling noise was heard in the woods which created a general alarm, and I was awakened to be informed of the circumstance, but heard nothing. At one I took my turn of the watch, and our dog continued unceasingly to run backwards and forwards along the skirts of the wood in a state of restless vigilance. At two in the morning the centinel informed me, that he saw something like an human figure creeping along on all-fours about fifty paces above us. After some time had passed in our search, I at length discovered that his information was true, and it appeared to me that a bear had occasioned the alarm; but when day appeared, it proved to be an old, grey-haired, blind man, who had been compelled to leave his hiding-place by extreme hunger, being too infirm to join in the flight of the natives to whom he belonged. . . . He replied, that if he had not lost his sight, he would with the greatest readiness have accompanied us on our journey. He also confirmed the accounts which we had received of the country, and the route to the Westward.

Despite the old man's reluctance, Mackenzie coerced, even forced, him to show the way for several days. "Our blind guide was, however, so averse to continuing with us," he wrote, "that I was under the very disagreeable necessity of ordering the men to carry him into the canoe; and this was the first act during my voyage, that had the semblance of violent dealing." The guide was still with them on June 29 when they met two other Indians known to him. Mackenzie wrote, "The blind old man gave a very favourable account of us to his friends, and they all three were very merry together during the whole of the afternoon. That our guide, however, might not escape from us during the night, I determined to set a watch upon him."

Alexander Mackenzie made his way across North America to the Pacific Ocean long before Lewis and Clark's much more famous expedition.
WIKIMEDIA COMMONS

Then, on July 1, the blind man attempted escape:

About twelve, though the night was rather dark, I observed the old man creeping on his hands and knees towards the water-side. We accordingly followed him very quietly to the canoe, and he would have gone away with it, if he had not been interrupted in his design. On upbraiding him for his treacherous conduct, when he had been treated with so much kindness by us, he denied the intention of which we accused him, and declared that his sole object was to assuage his thirst. At length, however, he acknowledged the truth, and when we brought him to the fire, his friends, who now awoke, on being informed of what had passed, reprobated his conduct, and asked him how he could expect that the white people would return to this country, if they experienced such ungrateful treatment.

But, it seems, Mackenzie thought better of forcing his blind pathfinder's continued service. He wrote, "The old man having manifested for various and probably very fallacious reasons, a very great aversion to accompany us any further, it did not appear that there was any necessity to force his inclination."

While Mackenzie and his crew benefitted from most encounters with natives, the explorers were always wary and experienced a few close calls. This, on June 2:

The Indians [those in Mackenzie's party] were therefore certain, that the Knisteneaux must be in our vicinity, on a war expedition, and consequently, if they were numerous, we should have had no reason to expect the least mercy from them in this distant country. Though I did not believe that circumstance, or that any of the natives could be in possession of fire-arms, I thought it right, at all events, we should be prepared. Our fuses were, therefore, primed and loaded, and having extinguished our fire, each of us took his station at the foot of a tree, where we passed an uneasy and restless night.

Then, a week later:

Here we perceived a smell of fire; and in a short time heard people in the woods, as if in a state of great confusion, which was occasioned, as we afterwards understood, by their discovery of us. At the same time this unexpected circumstance produced some little discomposure among ourselves, as our arms were not in a state of preparation, and we were as yet unable to ascertain the number of the party. . . . Two men appeared on a rising ground over against us, brandishing their spears, displaying their bows and arrows, and accompanying their hostile gestures with loud vociferations. My interpreter did not hesitate to assure them, that they might dispel their apprehensions, as we were white people, who meditated no injury, but were, on the contrary, desirous of demonstrating every mark of kindness and friendship.

The party actually came under attack on June 21. "My interpreters, who understood their language, informed me that they threatened us with instant death if we drew nigh the shore," Mackenzie wrote, "and they followed the menace by discharging a volley of arrows, some of which fell short of the canoe, and others passed over it, so that they fortunately did us no injury."

No further violence ensued, and, in fact, Mackenzie got the Indians to talk. Their advice offered little reason for hope.

But besides the dangers and difficulties of the navigation, they added, that we should have to encounter the inhabitants of the country, who were very numerous. They also represented their immediate neighbours as a very malignant race, who lived in large subterraneous recesses; and when they were made to understand that it was our design to proceed to the sea, they dissuaded us from prosecuting our intention, as we should certainly become a sacrifice to the savage spirit of the natives.

Despite the many difficulties encountered, Mackenzie seems to have possessed a talent for rallying the troops, which he was forced to do on a few occasions according to his journals. He wrote of a particularly nasty canoe accident on June 13:

All held fast to the wreck; to which fortunate resolution we owed our safety, as we should otherwise have been dashed against the rocks by the force of the water, or driven over the cascades. In this condition we were forced several hundred yards, and every yard on the verge of destruction; but, at length, we most fortunately arrived in shallow water and a small eddy, where we were enabled to make a stand, from the weight of the canoe resting on the stones, rather than from any exertions of our exhausted strength. For though our efforts were short, they were pushed to the utmost, as life or death depended on them. . . .

The loss was considerable and important, for it consisted of our whole stock of balls, and some of our furniture; but these considerations were forgotten in the impressions of our miraculous escape. . . .

All the different articles were now spread out to dry. The powder had fortunately received no damage, and all my instruments had escaped. Indeed, when my people began to recover from their alarm, and to enjoy a sense of safety, some of them, if not all, were by no means sorry for our late misfortune, from the hope that it must put a period to our voyage, particularly as we were without a canoe, and all the bullets sunk in the river. It did not, indeed, seem possible to them that we could proceed under these circumstances. I listened, however, to the observations that were made on the occasion without replying to them, till their panic was dispelled, and they had got themselves warm and comfortable, with an hearty meal, and rum enough to raise their spirits. . . .

In short, my harangue produced the desired effect, and a very general assent appeared to go wherever I should lead the way.

Mackenzie himself was not immune to discouragement. But, according to his June 22 entry, while admitting to second thoughts he did not allow them to fester. "Such were my reflections at this period; but instead of continuing to indulge them, I determined to proceed with resolution, and set future events at defiance," he wrote. Once he had himself convinced, he turned his powers of persuasion toward the crew:

At all events, I declared, in the most solemn manner, that I would not abandon my design of reaching the sea, if I made the attempt alone, and that I did not despair of returning in safety to my friends.

This proposition met with the most zealous return, and they unanimously assured me, that they were as willing now as they had ever been, to abide by my resolutions, whatever they might be, and to follow me wherever I should go.

On July 15 Mackenzie and his men heard news that rallied their spirits. "They told us," Mackenzie wrote of some Indians they encountered, "we should be three days in getting to the end of our journey; which must be supposed to have been very agreeable information to people in our exhausted condition."

Even as the coast grew closer, the expedition met obstacles, some of which took their very breaths away. "Before us appeared a stupendous mountain, whose snow-clad summit was lost in the clouds; between it and our immediate course, flowed the river to which we were going. The Indians informed us that it was at no great distance," wrote Mackenzie on July 17. He then prepared for the final push by dining on venison, and, "To the comfort which I have just mentioned, I added that of taking off my beard, as well as changing my linen, and my people followed the humanising example."

Then, on July 19, the travelers arrived at an Indian village where, Mackenzie reported, "From these houses I could perceive the termination of the river, and its discharge into a narrow arm of the sea."

The next morning, Mackenzie, most likely eager to dip his hand in the waters of the Pacific, wrote, "We rose at a very early hour this morning, when I proposed to the Indians to run down our canoe, or procure another at this place. To both these proposals they turned a deaf ear, as they imagined that I should be satisfied with having come in sight of the sea." He was not, of course, satisfied. Mackenzie spent the next three days paddling about in a leaky canoe, exploring the inlet and the bay to which it led, wishing to visit the bigger waters beyond.

He also wanted to take readings of his position. "I had flattered myself with the hope of getting a distance of the moon and stars, but the cloudy weather continually disappointed me, and I began to fear that I should fail in this important object," he wrote, adding, "Our provisions were at a very low ebb, and we had, as yet, no reason to expect any assistance from the natives. Our stock was, at this time, reduced to twenty pounds weight of pemmican, fifteen pounds of rice, and six pounds of flour, among ten half-starved men, in a leaky vessel, and on a barbarous coast."

Clearing skies finally offered an opportunity to employ his navigation instruments. "While I was taking a meridian, two canoes, of a larger size, and well manned, appeared from the main South-West channel," Mackenzie wrote. "These Indians were of a different tribe from those which I had already seen, as our guide did not understand their language."

Rather than beating a hasty retreat in the face of approaching boatloads of seemingly hostile natives, Mackenzie said, "I now mixed up some vermilion in melted grease, and inscribed, in large characters, on the South-East face of the rock on which we had slept last night, this brief memorial—Alexander Mackenzie, from Canada, by land, the twenty-second of July, one thousand seven hundred and ninety-three."

Mackenzie and his men made their way back east and experienced additional adventures along the way. It is likely the biggest of those occurred on August 24:

At length, as we rounded a point, and came in view of the Fort, we threw out a flag, and accompanied it with a general discharge of our fire-arms; while the men were in such spirits, and made such an active use of their paddles, that we arrived before the two men whom we left here in the spring, could recover their senses to answer us. Thus we landed at four in the afternoon, at the place which we left on the ninth of May.

Here my voyages of discovery terminate.

Their toils and their dangers, their solicitudes and sufferings, have not been exaggerated in my description. On the contrary, in many instances, language has failed me in the attempt to describe them. I received, however, the reward of my labours, for they were crowned with success.

Unfortunately, the trail Mackenzie blazed to the Pacific was too rugged and difficult to serve any further purpose. He urged further exploration and encouraged the United Kingdom to strengthen its tenuous hold on the region—which, at the time, was contested by the United States and Spain.

Mackenzie published *Voyages from Montreal* in 1801. Among his readers was President Thomas Jefferson. The book, no doubt, encouraged

Jefferson to mount explorations of his own to establish a claim to the territory, resulting in the Lewis and Clark expedition in 1803.

In 1802 Alexander Mackenzie became a "Sir" when King George III knighted him for his adventures and accomplishments as an explorer. Mackenzie dabbled in politics with little enthusiasm, failed in his attempts to reestablish himself as a trader, and retired to Scotland in 1812. He died there on March 12, 1820.

Zebulon Pike: Lost in the Louisiana Purchase

1806–1807—Western Frontier

When President Thomas Jefferson spent $15 million and more than doubled the size of the United States of America and its territories with the 1803 Louisiana Purchase, some thought it a bad bargain. Few knew what was out there, no one was certain where the borders were, and there were competing claims for much of the land.

There were more questions than answers at the time, and the questions needed answers. Within a few years two expeditions went west to find the answers—or, at least, to sharpen the questions.

The most famous of these, of course, was the Corps of Discovery, led by Meriwether Lewis and William Clark. Carefully planned, organized, and outfitted by the president, the Lewis and Clark journey had specific marching orders. Leaving the populated places of the nation in 1804 and returning in 1806, the Corps traveled more than eight thousand miles from the banks of the Mississippi to the shores of the Pacific. Along the way the expedition added immeasurably to knowledge about the prairies and plains and mountains and valleys, as well as the plants and animals and people out there. Lewis and Clark and the handful of soldiers and civilians who went with them pioneered the way for westward expansion, provided the basis for further exploration as well as settlement, and laid the groundwork for adding the Oregon country (or Columbia, as the British called it) to the growing nation.

By any measure the Lewis and Clark expedition was a rousing success. Then there was the Pike Expedition.

Led by Zebulon Pike, this exploration of lands acquired in the Louisiana Purchase was sloppy in its planning, poorly outfitted, unauthorized by anyone with sufficient authority, uncertain in its purpose, at times comedic and other times tragic in its execution, and, all in all, of questionable value.

Why? And how?

The origins of the Pike Expedition are mired in theories of conspiracy, intrigue, even treason. Pike's role in the affair ranges from courage to ineptitude to being sent on a fool's errand to serving as sacrificial lamb in pursuit of a larger, more evil purpose.

Then again, perhaps not.

Zebulon Pike was a frontiersman from the time he was a boy. Born in New Jersey on January 5, 1778, to a military father of the same name, Pike was raised at a variety of posts and forts on the far reaches of the country, mostly in Ohio and Illinois. As a teenager he joined his father's regiment and later became a commissioned, career officer in the US Army. In 1803 he was stationed at Kaskaskia, Illinois, when Meriwether Lewis showed up recruiting men for his Corps of Discovery. Pike was not among his selections.

While Lewis did nothing for Pike's military career by overlooking him, James Wilkinson, commanding general of the army, soon took him under his wing. Wilkinson played a role in the culmination of the Louisiana Purchase, presiding over the transfer of title in New Orleans, after which Vice President Aaron Burr wrangled Wilkinson's appointment as governor of Upper Louisiana. He set up shop in St. Louis in 1805.

Wilkinson's military history is rife with controversy as far back as the Revolutionary War, when, as a young and ambitious officer, he participated in an underhanded effort to have George Washington replaced as head of the Continental Army by Horatio Gates and was forced to resign. He was later appointed to another position but forced to resign from that post for incompetence.

Wilkinson joined the Pennsylvania militia as a brigadier general, then left the military and moved to Kentucky and worked for years for its independence from Virginia—with the intention to ally Kentucky with Spain, to whom he had sworn allegiance and for whom he was a paid spy.

In 1791, during the Northwest Indian War, he again donned a uniform to lead a unit of Kentucky Volunteers and received a commission as a lieutenant colonel in the US Army; he later was promoted to brigadier general and, despite suspicions of his treasonous alliance with Spain, made his way to the top as commanding general of the US Army—which brings us back to his appointment as governor of Upper Louisiana. In that position he conspired with Aaron Burr to take over the western half of the United States and set up an independent nation. Eventually, Wilkinson, for whatever reason, turned against Burr and blew the whistle on the plot.

The Pike Expedition may well have been in service to that treasonous plan.

But before sending Pike west, Wilkinson sent him north to explore the origins of the Mississippi River, the far reaches of the Louisiana Purchase in that direction, and, theoretically, the border of Burr and Wilkinson's intended nation. Pike set out on a keelboat with twenty men and little else, including the kind of expertise required for such a journey. The expedition bogged down in the northern winter and Pike never found the headwaters of the Mississippi—although he wrongly claimed its origin was at Cass Lake. The maps he created were useless, and his negotiations with Indians and the British were of even less value.

Before even catching his breath upon returning to St. Louis in April 1806, Pike was ordered by Wilkinson to lead an even larger expedition to the West. Wilkinson had no authorization from the War Department or President Jefferson or anyone else in authority in Washington for Pike's journey.

Among other duties, Pike was to locate the headwaters of the Arkansas and Red Rivers, as those waterways helped define the limits of the Louisiana Purchase and the frontier with New Spain. Those were tenuous times so far as relations with Spain were concerned. Not only were the borders in question, the Spaniards feared encroachment into their possessions by the United States and all-out war was not out of the question. Which makes Wilkinson's double-dealing and conflicting loyalties between the United States and Spain even more intriguing and questionable.

And so within this cauldron of conflict, Pike set out for the West on July 15, 1806. The expedition was outfitted with fair-weather uniforms that would prove unsuitable, an insufficient number of horses, scant provisions and camp equipment, very few instruments for scientific observations and mapping, and inadequate knowledge of terrain and climate.

His first assignment on the journey was to return a group of Osage Indians who had been hostages among the Pottawattamie to their homeland. So, with about twenty soldiers and the freed hostages, he set out from Fort Bellefontaine near St. Louis and journeyed up the Missouri and Osage Rivers until reaching the present-day border between Missouri and Kansas, near the homeland of the Osage hostages.

Then it was northwest to the Republican River in today's southern Nebraska to inform the Pawnee tribe that it was now governed by the United States. Next, south across the plains to the Arkansas River, which they reached on October 14 near the apex of the stream's "great bend," in what is now Kansas. Pike sent part of his command downstream, with orders to reach the Mississippi River and then travel north to St. Louis. He would take the bulk of the soldiers upstream on the Arkansas into present-day Colorado. Pike's descriptions of the region led to its being considered the "Great American Desert."

Meanwhile, Nemesio Salcedo, commandant of the Spanish army and governor of Chihuahua (which included Santa Fe at the time), determined to keep the Americans at bay. It seems he mistrusted all Americans, including Wilkinson, despite the fact that Wilkinson had apparently sworn loyalty to the Spanish crown. Wilkinson had informed Salcedo of the Lewis and Clark expedition, and the governor sent troops to intercept and arrest the explorers, but the Spaniards missed the Corps on the Platte River and were unable to locate the fast-moving expedition thereafter. Wilkinson also let Salcedo know that Pike was on the way. Why he did so is unknown, with various theories wrapped in conspiratorial intrigue. Salcedo would have better luck capturing Pike and his people.

But that would come later. In fact, as Pike headed up the Arkansas on October 28, he was behind the Spanish cavalry—he was on their trail, instead of them on his. As winter approached, the American explorer pressed on until reaching the Rocky Mountains. In late November, from where Pueblo would later be located, Pike saw a mountain looming to the west and determined to scale it. Leaving most of his men in camp, Pike and three others spent days attempting to climb the mountain he named Grand Peak. Although he apparently reached the summit of a nearby mountain, he never made his destination. In fact, he wrote that no human being would be able to ascend the 14,110-foot mountain that, within a few years and forever after, would bear his name.

Pike gathered his troops and followed the Arkansas River into the mountains and wandered around, following its various tributaries for a time. Winter had well and truly arrived by then, and the expedition had run short of food, clothing, and other supplies. Meat was virtually their only source of food, and the weakened men were hardly able to harvest enough game to sustain themselves. Eventually, they stumbled into the steep and deep Royal Gorge and Pike realized he had gotten nowhere. He ordered construction of a small stockade, left a few men to inhabit it, and set out to find the Red River. Both the men left behind and the men who went with him nearly starved and froze to death.

Pike did locate what he believed to be the Red River, but it was, in fact, the Rio Grande. He built another small stockade near where Alamosa, Colorado, would be established, and forted up for a time. One of the party set out for and made his way to Santa Fe, which led to the rescue of the expedition—and the arrest of all involved—on February 26, 1807. Pike swore to his captors that he believed himself to be at the Red River, unaware he was in Spanish territory. The Spaniards were said to have offered mules to the Americans and an escort back to American soil, but Pike refused the offer. It took the Spaniards some time to gather Pike's other soldiers in their winter quarters, but eventually they were all taken to Santa Fe.

Soon, Spanish authorities escorted them south, through Albuquerque and El Paso and on to Chihuahua. Along the way Pike took every opportunity to talk with officials, kept a careful eye on the location of cities and towns and military establishments, and kept notes on anything and everything else that might prove useful to the United States. Salcedo held

Pike for a time, then escorted him to the border for release at Natchitoches, now in the state of Louisiana, on July 1, 1807. Eight members of his expedition remained imprisoned in Chihuahua. Spain demanded an apology from the United States for the incursion, which was not forthcoming. It took another two years to get the other prisoners released and returned.

Pike was accused of being a part of Burr and Wilkinson's conspiracy, but he claimed ignorance of its existence. The truth of the matter is likely forever unknown. Most believe Pike's papers from the expedition prove his innocence. Others think many of his actions on the expedition were suspicious, seeming to indicate he was more interested in spying on the Spanish strength in the area than fulfilling his purported mission—which may explain his choice in the Rockies of arrest and transportation deeper into New Spain, rather than escort back to his homeland.

In any case, his name was cleared.

Pike's career in the military afterward was routine, with promotions to major and later colonel. He wrote and published in 1810 *An Account of Expeditions to the Sources of the Mississippi and through the Western Parts of Louisiana*, much of it written from memory, as his papers from the westward expedition had been seized by the Spaniards. The book was a commercial failure.

The War of 1812 saw Pike promoted to brigadier general, in command of troops dispatched to capture York—Toronto, today—in Upper Canada. He launched the attack on April 27, 1813. The premature detonation of an explosive mine by British forces killed several of their own along with scores of Americans. A rock propelled by the blast crushed the life out of him. At age thirty-four Zebulon Pike died a war hero.

This engraving of Zebulon Pike as he appeared during the War of 1812 was published in *Analectic Magazine* in November 1814.

Maximilian and Bodmer:
Science and Art in the Old West

1833–1834—Missouri River

Consult any list of great artists of the western frontier and the name Karl Bodmer will almost certainly be on it. Charles M. Russell, Frederic Remington, Albert Bierstadt, Thomas Moran—all inhabit, with Bodmer, the pantheon of painters who portrayed the American West of the nineteenth century. But Bodmer saw it first. And his work, especially when compared to that of Bierstadt and Moran, reveals people and places as they were, rather than romanticized, overzealous creations whose artistic license, while magnificent, distorts reality almost beyond recognition.

Born February 6, 1809, in Zurich, Switzerland, Johann Karl Bodmer picked up an artist's paintbrush at age thirteen under the tutelage of an uncle, an experienced engraver. In Europe he created oil paintings, watercolors, wood engravings, drawings, illustrations, and aquatints of cities and landscapes in the style of the Barbizon School. In America he is remembered for his rich depictions of the Great Plains and American Indians.

But were it not for Prince Alexander Philipp Maximilian zu Wied-Neuwied, it is unlikely Karl Bodmer would ever have laid eyes on an American Indian.

Maximilian was born in Prussia on September 23, 1782. Grandson of a count and member of a family firmly entrenched in the aristocracy, the prince rubbed shoulders with men who carried the torch of the Enlightenment, and the great explorer and naturalist Alexander von Humboldt was something of a mentor to him. Like Humboldt, he set out to explore the New World—in 1815 the prince organized an expedition to learn something of the tribal people of Brazil. Maximilian's published account, *Travels in Brazil in the Years 1815, 1816, 1817*, gained him a reputation as a naturalist, but that was not enough for the young prince.

And so, years later, he mounted a second expedition to the Western Hemisphere, this time to North America, for which Maximilian employed the services of Bodmer.

For whatever reason, Maximilian believed the government of the young nation was not paying proper attention to the various cultures of its native people, and he was determined to provide the sort of scientific scrutiny the work required. He also hoped to give Europeans an eye-witness account of his travels, for purposes of both entertainment and information. Accompanying him on the journey would be the artist Karl Bodmer to make a visual record, and David Dreidoppel, who would act as hunter and taxidermist as well as servant to the prince.

The three adventurers landed in Boston Harbor on July 4, 1832, and immediately set out for the West, albeit on a meandering course. They visited New York City, Philadelphia, Pittsburgh, Cincinnati, and Louisville before running aground in New Harmony, Indiana. There, Maximilian and Dreidoppel were laid low by cholera or some similar ailment and ended up spending the winter. The time was not altogether wasted, however, as the prince became friends with and learned from two prominent naturalists in the area, Charles Alexandre Lesueur and Thomas Say. Bodmer kept his health through the winter and took the opportunity provided by the delay to journey to New Orleans to meet a friend of the New Harmony naturalists, Joseph Barrabino.

Back on the trail in March, the tourists made their way to St. Louis. Here, they first laid eyes on the Indians they had been seeking. Just as important, they met the famous American explorer William Clark, who shared advice and maps from his experiences with the Corps of Discovery, which, some twenty-six years earlier, had explored the route they intended to follow.

The trio boarded an American Fur Company river steamer, the *Yellow-Stone*, on April 10, 1833, and set out upriver. While relatively safe and comfortable compared to alternative means of travel, the steamboat offered its own set of difficulties for the expedition. Fires, running aground in storms, unloading the boat to clear shallow water then reloading upstream, losing supplies and specimens overboard or to water damage onboard, and a host of other hazards faced the expedition. But they pressed on. Visits to Fort Pierre and Fort Clark provided opportunities for Maximilian to gather information about Indians and their lives upon the plains, as well as learn of native plants and animals and gather specimens.

Fort Union, at the confluence of the Yellowstone and Missouri Rivers, near today's border between North Dakota and Montana, proved the end of the line for the steamboat. The travelers spent about two weeks there. Bodmer sketched and painted Indians and landscapes, the prince wrote about the same, and Dreidoppel gathered specimens of wild animals native to the region.

Although the *Yellow-Stone* would go no farther, Maximilian and his entourage would continue upstream to the Rocky Mountains. Loaded into a keelboat, the trio made their way to Fort McKenzie, an American Fur Company establishment situated near the mouth of the Marias River and built to trade with the Blackfoot Indians.

Maximilian spent some five weeks there and on August 29 witnessed what must have been a highlight of the journey. Throughout their visit the land around the fort was populated by Indians of various tribes, coming in to barter furs and robes for trade goods. On that fateful day at the end of August, a band of Blackfoot Indians camped at the fort were attacked by a hostile Assiniboine war party. With the help of whites at the fort, the Blackfoot visitors repelled the attack after a lengthy battle. It gave Maximilian the opportunity to experience frontier warfare and allowed Bodmer to witness, and sketch, an Indian battle firsthand.

On the other hand, Indian hostilities also prevented the prince from continuing upriver to the Rocky Mountains, making Fort McKenzie the terminus of the expedition. And so they packed up their collections and provisions and set out downstream in a small boat with American Fur Company men at the oars.

The travelers wintered at Fort Clark, near today's Bismarck, North Dakota. Once again, the Prussian prince, and most everyone else, was

A Karl Bodmer painting of Mandan Indians, from his westward journey with Prince Maximilian. LIBRARY OF CONGRESS

stricken with illness. This time, it was probably scurvy. As spring arrived an Indian remedy of herbs, plants, and bulbs cured the ailment.

And so it was downriver again. When the party reached St. Louis in April, rather than retrace their outbound route they turned to the north and east and made their way to New York by way of the Great Lakes, passing through Buffalo, then Albany, and reaching New York City in time to book passage on a ship for Europe that departed July 16, 1834. Prince Maximilian was back in Neuwied and sleeping in his own bed by late August.

The Prince turned his notes and records from the expedition into a two-volume work, *Maximilian, Prince of Wied's Travels in the Interior of North America, 1832–1834.* The books were published and sold by subscription from 1839 through 1842. A later, condensed version was also published. Both editions are rare.

Bodmer's work is less so. In fact, beyond their value as art, the images he created from the trip are widely considered among the best depictions of frontier landscapes, Indians, and Indian life in the nineteenth century in terms of accuracy and scientific value. The artist worked with several engravers and printers to create aquatints—an engraving process that produces images similar in appearance to ink and watercolor paintings. Several of these engravings introduced the chapters in Maximilian's book.

About eighty black-and-white engravings of Bodmer's works were bound separately, with a map, in an "atlas" to accompany the books. Several bound books of Bodmer's engravings and aquatints were printed over the years in various sizes and on assorted paper stocks, giving his work wide exposure and circulation.

Maximilian retained Bodmer's plates along with his own notes and other materials, all of which eventually made their way to the Joslyn Art Museum in Omaha, Nebraska.

Today, Karl Bodmer's name is recognized and honored for his association with America's frontier. Prince Maximilian's, less so. But without the prince, there would be no Bodmer—at least in the context of the Old West. Between them, they created a rich and memorable account of the people and places along the Missouri River. Without them—and let's not forget David Dreidoppel—our knowledge of the Mandan, Hidatsa, Omaha, Osage, Crow, Lakota, Assiniboine, Cree, Arikara, Gros Ventre, and Blackfoot in the nineteenth century would be lacking.

"Corralled for Defense":
Indian Attacks on Wagon Trains

1840–1860—Emigrant Trails

We've all seen it in the movies or read it as we turned the pages, wide-eyed and trembling: The wagon train with its weary pioneers slogs across the grassy plain under a thirsty sun. Without warning, an otherworldly shriek splits the air, followed by a cacophony of screeching and screaming and the pounding of hooves as hundreds or even thousands of painted Indians top a rise and stampede toward the wagons. So great in number they nearly blot out the sun, the fearsome savages in their feathered war bonnets come and keep coming as the desperate travelers circle the wagons and take up defensive positions to fend off the attack. Blasts of burning powder and blinding clouds of gun smoke and streams of hot lead fill the air as circling Indians and crouching emigrants fire away at one another. Bodies soon litter the ground both within and without the circled wagons.

This scene, or something very much like it, has, for a century and more, been a standby in the western, whether in print or on the screen.

But did it really happen like that?

Sometimes. Maybe. In the small town of Almo, Idaho, not far from where the trails to Oregon and California parted ways and near the well-known landmark along the trail, City of Rocks, there stands a monument to one such pitched battle and massacre of men, women, and children bound for the California settlements. The marker reads:

Dedicated to the memory of those who lost their lives in a horrible Indian massacre, 1861. Three hundred immigrants west bound. Only five escaped.

The trouble is, the massacre the monument memorializes never happened. And, according to the best research on the subject, nothing like it—at least on that scale—ever did. Certainly emigrants died on the trail, and some were killed in Indian attacks. But the danger of dying at the hands of marauding bands of Indians has been so overblown that it bears little resemblance to the reality of the time.

Most guidebooks from the day offer advice on dealing with Indians along the trail and advise caution. But, relative to other advice, little is said. *The Latter-Day Saints' Emigrants' Guide*, published by William Clayton in 1848, covers the trail almost inch by inch. Early on in the guide he mentions a landmark called "Indian Grave," but, as the editor of a reprint version of the guide notes, has nothing else to say about Indians: "Clayton refers to Pawnees five times in three pages and then never again gives advice about Indians. The Pioneers subsequently met many Sioux, Crow, Snake and Great Basin Indians. This is a serious omission in his guide."

An 1849 guidebook, *Accompaniment to the Map of the Emigrant Road from Independence, Mo., to San Francisco, California*, by T. H. Jefferson, advises caution in trading with Indians, but seems to downplay any danger.

You will probably meet but few Indians and not have much trade with them. Always be on your guard. Take but few articles of trade. The less you have to do with the Indians the better. . . . Listen to no tales of danger that you may hear upon the road, but move steadily onward, and be prepared to defend yourselves. An Indian values his life as much as you do, and thinks twice before he molests resolute men.

Randolph B. Marcy's 1859 book, *The Prairie Traveler*, advises that caution and preparation are usually sufficient to discourage attack.

A few men, well mounted, should constitute the advance and rear guards for each train of wagons passing through Indian country. Their duty will be to keep a vigilant look-out in all directions, and to reconnoitre places where Indians would be likely to lie in ambush. Should hostile Indians be discovered, the fact should be at once reported to the commander, who (if he anticipates an attack) will rapidly form his wagons into a circle or "corral," with the animals toward the centre, and the men on the inside, with their arms in readiness to repel an attack from without. If these arrangements be properly attended to, few parties of Indians will venture to make an attack, as they are well aware that some of their warriors might pay with their lives the forfeit of such indiscretion.

In one of the earliest—1845—and most verbose of the travel guides, *The Emigrants' Guide to Oregon and California*, Lansford W. Hastings gives advice on protecting a wagon train from Indians:

Nothing different from the foregoing, worthy of remark, occurs, from day to day, in reference to the method of traveling until the company arrives in the territory of hostile Indians, which commences at the Kansas river, and extends throughout the residue of the journey. Throughout all portions of the country, beyond the Kansas, emigrants are required to proceed with more caution, especially in the country of the Pawnees, Sioux, Shyanes, Eutaws, and Black-feet. Wherever there are evidences of hostile Indians being in the vicinity of the company, it is advisable, always, to enjoin upon all, to avoid a separation from the main body of the company, and, at the same time, to keep an advance and rear-guard out, as the company is on the march. Should the guards discover an approaching enemy, the safest course is, to throw the caravan, at once, into a defensive attitude, which is very readily done, by forming a "caral," in a manner, quite similar to that first described; the only difference being, that the teams of both cattle and horses occupy the interior, instead of the exterior, of the "caral," without being detached from the wagons. . . . Upon many portions of the route, it becomes necessary thus to form the wagons, several times each day, in order to dispose of various marauding and war parties, with whom emigrants, frequently come in contact.

While Hastings implies that circling the wagons into a defensive corral against warring Indians may be a regular occurrence, he says a few paragraphs later that dying from an Indian attack happens "seldom," and that accidental death from firearms is more likely.

In order to avoid the misfortunes which so frequently befall emigrants from the accidental discharge of firearms, guns should never be capped or primed; yet they should, always, be carried loaded, and otherwise in order for action, upon a moment's warning. More danger is to be apprehended, from your own guns, without the observance of the above precaution, than from those of the enemy; for we, very frequently, hear of emigrants being killed from the accidental discharge of firearms; but we very seldom hear of their being killed by Indians.

If careful studies of deaths along the trails are to be believed, Hastings is right in saying "we very seldom hear of [emigrants] being killed by Indians." There are historians who downplay the research, however. They claim violence against wagon trains by Indians was more frequent and severe than so-called politically correct scholars and their studies report. The studies, they say, cover only the Mormon, Oregon, and California Trails, which is true—but those trails were far and away the trails used by the most emigrants. And, they contend, the research doesn't cover all the years of western migration. That, too, is true—but the studies do cover the decades that were, by far, the busiest.

The oft-cited studies, in a nutshell, say that between 1840 and 1860, Indians killed 362 emigrants on the trails—only slightly more than the number said to be slaughtered in the mythical Almo Massacre. It is difficult to say how many deaths the average person today would assign to Indian attacks on wagon trains, but it would be a safe bet that, given the influence of books and movies, it is well beyond 362. It is also worth noting that of the Indian depredations against emigrant parties that did occur, the deadliest year was 1851, when sixty were killed, and throughout trail history no more than twenty pioneers were killed in any single incident.

Also, it was not the storied tribes of the Great Plains—the Sioux, the Arapaho, the Blackfeet, the Cheyenne—who were most likely to attack

Dangers were many for wagon train emigrants, but Indian attacks were low on the list. LIBRARY OF CONGRESS

wagon trains. Nearly all—90 percent—of the attacks occurred west of South Pass, in the lands of the Shoshoni, Bannock, Ute, and Paiute tribes. The most dangerous places to travel, as far as Indian attacks, were along the Humboldt and Snake Rivers and the Applegate Trail.

That is not to say that travel on the emigrant trails was safe or easy. There were many deadly dangers, and estimates of trail deaths range as high as sixty-five thousand. Accidents—such as the firearms mishaps Hastings cautioned against—took many lives. Drowning at the many river crossings was a deadly hazard, as were misfortunes with wagons and livestock.

But, far and away, disease was the biggest killer. Cholera was the most deadly, with many thousands dying of "the bloody flux." Mountain fever—most likely tick fever—killed many. Scurvy, smallpox, mumps, tuberculosis, and other afflictions also took their toll.

And, of course, Indians killed travelers along the trail. While the number may be much lower than what many might have imagined, no death can be dismissed. And those deaths were tragic beyond measure for the victims, as well as for their loved ones who survived.

Representative, perhaps, of these bloody incidents was the Utter-Van Ornum Massacre. The twelve-wagon train, with eighteen men, five women, twenty-one children, and about one hundred head of livestock, left Wisconsin in May 1860 and by September had reached Castle Creek in western Idaho. Indians, most likely Shoshoni and Bannock—some reports claim there were also a few white men involved—were spotted September 9. A roughhewn report, said to be from a survivor of the fight, appeared in the *Oregon Argus* on November 24, 1860. According to this excerpt,

> *The train immediately "corralled" for defense—had a favorable position, but no water. The Indians, finding they could accomplish nothing, threw down their arms and made friendly signs—came up, and made signs for something to eat. We fed many of them, and they appeared to be satisfied, and signs for us to go on to the water, that they were friendly. So we started toward the river. After we got out of our strong position they commenced on us, but we expected some kind of treachery, and were on the lookout for them. Before we got corralled and our cattle gathered, two of our men were shot down. . . . The attack commenced about 10 a.m. and lasted till the night of the 9th. . . . While they had us hemmed up, we killed not less than 25 or 30 of them; it was certain death to an Indian if he showed his head for we were all pretty good marksmen—but they were too many for us.*

The Indians kept the emigrants pinned down for two days and killed twenty of them in that and subsequent fighting. Three young children were kidnapped and kept by the Indians. The survivors abandoned the wagons and wandered off in groups. Some, including children, starved to death, and there were claims of cannibalism. Soldiers located and rescued some the survivors more than a month later.

Of the forty-four who started the journey, only sixteen completed it. But that number includes a young boy, said to be Reuben Van Ornum, taken by soldiers from a Shoshoni camp in Cache Valley, Utah Territory, more than two years later. It seems unlikely the ten-year-old boy was Van Ornum, as he did not speak English and was fluent in Shoshoni. The Indians claimed he was the son of a sister of Chief Washakie and a Frenchman. Still, the boy was given to Zachias Van Ornum, supposedly an uncle from Oregon.

Edward R. Geary, superintendent of Indian Affairs in Oregon, reported the deadly massacre to his superiors in Washington City, DC, on November 7, 1860.

> *It is at length in my power to communicate authentic information in regard to the heart-rending tragedy of the ninth of September, to which I referred in my letter to your office of the 4 ult. This terrible disaster occurred about fifty miles below Salmon Falls on the Immigrant route to Oregon. The company consisted of forty-four persons—seventeen men and twenty-seven women and children—of whom fifteen, after privations seldom paralleled in the annals of human sufferings, are known to survive and have been rescued.*
>
> *Of the others, the larger number are known to have fallen in their gallant defense, which lasted for thirty-four hours, against an over-whelming force, or in their efforts to escape when compelled to abandon the protection afforded by their wagons. . . . If any of the missing still survive, it is feared they are in captivity to the most cruel and brutal monsters that wear the human form, and are enduring indignities and tortures from which death would be a most welcome refuge.*

Tragic though such brutal killings were, it is well to remember that deaths after wagons were "corralled for defense" were a relative rarity on the emigrant trails. Indians were much more likely to steal than kill, and livestock were their prey much more than were emigrants. In many cases Indians aided in river crossings, put misguided travelers back on the trail, traded fresh livestock for worn-out draft animals, provided food, and otherwise assisted pioneers.

They also attacked, killed and raped and tortured, stole from, plundered, and otherwise harassed pioneers. And some of the tens of thousands of emigrants on the trails did the same to them.

Porter Rockwell: God's Gunfighter

1840–1878—Western Frontier

From the 1840s through the 1870s, Orrin Porter Rockwell cut a wide swath across the American frontier. Known from the banks of the Mississippi River to the shores of the Pacific Ocean, his fame—or notoriety, depending on who you asked—was described in stark terms of black or white. There were no shades of gray in Rockwell's reputation.

Gunfighter. Murderer. Horseman. Tracker. Scout. Lawman. Outlaw. Assassin. Guide. Protector. Enforcer. His contemporaries and biographers described Rockwell as all these things.

The eulogist at his 1878 funeral, Mormon apostle Joseph F. Smith, said, "He had his little faults, but Porter's life on earth, taken altogether, was one worthy of example, and reflected honor upon the Church. Through all his trials he had never once forgotten his obligations to his brethren and his God."

The Salt Lake Tribune took another view, describing Rockwell as one "of the long list of Mormon criminals whose deeds of treachery and blood have reddened the soil of Utah, and who have paid no forfeit to offended law," in editorializing on his demise. "He killed unsuspecting travelers. . . . He killed fellow Saints. . . . He killed Apostates who dared wag their tongues about the wrongs they had endured. And he killed mere sojourners in Zion merely to keep his hand in." The *Tribune* accused him of "at least a hundred murders for the Church."

Time did not dim judgments about the man. If anything, passing years further illuminated differences of opinion. Authors Charles Kelly and Hoffman Birney, writing in their 1934 biography *Holy Murder: The*

Story of Porter Rockwell, claimed "he murdered, robbed, and terrorized; he burned and scourged; he perjured and lied. He was, in deed and fact, the Terror of the Plains, the field of his infamy extending from the Mississippi Valley to the deserts of Nevada. He is variously credited with from a dozen to a hundred murders, but not once, so far as the record shows, did he draw a gun or dagger in self-defense."

Forty years later, Nicholas Van Alfen, in *Porter Rockwell: Mormon Frontier Marshal and Body Guard of Joseph Smith,* said, "Law-abiding citizens respected him; criminals hated and feared him. . . . As a peace officer, he unflinchingly faced the most dangerous criminals and desperadoes of his region and times. His name was seriously reckoned with in outlaw camps. . . . Rancher, frontiersman, lawman, and servant of the people was this unique character, Orrin Porter Rockwell."

Born in 1813 in Massachusetts, Rockwell lived as a boy in Manchester, New York, where he knew, and idolized, Joseph Smith Jr., eight years his senior. When the young prophet founded what would become the Church of Jesus Christ of Latter-day Saints—the Mormons—Porter Rockwell was a loyal follower from the first day. His association with Smith and his successor at the head of the church, Brigham Young, affected the course of Rockwell's life more than any other influence.

When Smith sent a vanguard of Mormons to western Missouri in 1831 to establish a Mormon Zion in Jackson County, young Rockwell was among them. With his father he operated a ferry on the Big Blue River some ten miles west of the bustling frontier outpost of Independence. He married a neighbor girl—still little more than a boy himself—in the first Mormon wedding in the state and set up housekeeping near the ferry.

For a variety of reasons—from incompatible views on slavery, to divergent views concerning Indians, to differing political aspirations and opposing economic attitudes—the pious Saints could not get along with their rough-and-tumble Missouri neighbors and by 1833 were harassed out of the area, forced across the Missouri River to try again in Clay County. That place, too, proved inhospitable and the Mormons, some ten thousand of them by now, were pushed farther north in 1837 into newly established Caldwell County, where neighbors were scarce.

The continuing conflicts with old Missouri settlers proved a baptism by fire for young Rockwell. Watching neighbors beaten, tarred and feathered, burned out, or even killed affected him deeply. Threats against his mother at the hand of a Missouri mobster, along with having the roof pulled off his own cabin and his household goods destroyed, planted seeds of revenge in his heart. By the time his people were pushed north into Caldwell County—created by the state legislature as an exclusive homeland for the Mormons—he determined to be pushed no more.

When vigilante mobs of angry Missourians continued the harassment, the Mormons retaliated. Rockwell joined up with the Danites, a quasi-military band of night riders formed to repay the terror tit for tat. But it seems Mormon religious leaders lost control of the Danites. On occasion the band spread terror of their own, going so far as to burn out villages, threaten a judge, rustle livestock, and plunder household goods. Although it can be verified that Rockwell rode with the Danites, how or whether he participated in their exploits is unclear. It seems likely, however, that his abilities as a tough and rowdy gunman—skills he later developed to a high art—were spawned on the Missouri frontier.

Forced out of Missouri with a threat of extermination issued by Governor Lilburn Boggs, the Saints settled in Illinois and established the city of Nauvoo, which soon grew to become that state's second-largest city.

But it was back in Missouri where Porter Rockwell made his first indelible mark on the history of the West.

Lilburn Boggs, an early Missouri settler and politician, had no use for the Mormons. From the moment they arrived in Jackson County, his home for the preceding five years, he resented their presence there. Like many old settlers, he disagreed with them in matters of the economy, politics, culture, and religion.

Lieutenant governor of the state during early Mormon difficulties, Boggs did nothing to protect the Saints. In fact, after a mob destroyed several homes and a printing office, the politician waded through the debris and warned the victims that more of the same was in store if they didn't quit the area.

Boggs served as governor during the more severe fighting of 1837 and 1838, and called up militia units on several occasions to punish the

Mormons for wrongdoings, real or imagined. Rather than tame the situation, his actions as chief politician of the state inflamed opposition to the Saints and inspired greater acts of terror and retaliation. Eventually, Boggs issued orders to the commander of the militia, saying, "The Mormons must be treated as enemies, and must be exterminated or driven from the State if necessary for the public peace."

While not exterminated, the Latter-day Saints were driven out of Missouri, leaving behind virtually all their earthly goods as recompense for supposed wrongs. The governor's "extermination order" became infamous in Mormon history and galled the Saints for years afterward.

It also served as impetus for the first great crime laid at the feet of Porter Rockwell.

Rockwell's in-laws remained in the Independence area through the years, and it was to there he returned with his wife in 1842, as she supposedly sought the comfort of family during pregnancy and confinement. Others assigned more nefarious motives for the visit.

Taking on the alias of Brown, Rockwell found work tending horses, including a valuable stallion, for an area stockman—no doubt honing his impressive skills with the animals. He left the job without notice and quit the area in early May of 1842, his move prompted by the shooting of Mormon archenemy Lilburn Boggs.

As the former governor sat reading the newspaper on the rainy evening of May 6, 1842, an assassin shot a heavy load of buckshot through a window. Four balls tore into Boggs's head and neck, causing severe damage. Several doctors declared he wouldn't last the night, and although he survived, newspapers throughout the region reported his death by violent hands.

The only evidence investigators uncovered was the assassin's pistol, left at the scene. The weapon was identified as stolen from a local store, and the merchant recalled its being examined in his shop by a man he knew as Brown, whose true identity was soon discovered. It was likewise discovered that Rockwell had left town the day after the shooting and was soon in the protective cocoon of Nauvoo, where repeated attempts to haul him back to Missouri for trial—along with Mormon leader Joseph Smith, accused of ordering Boggs killed—came to naught.

For decades Mormon gunfighter Orrin Porter Rockwell was infamous and feared on the western frontier. USED BY PERMISSION, UTAH HISTORICAL SOCIETY, ALL RIGHTS RESERVED

Rockwell eventually left Nauvoo and spent a few months on the lam in eastern states, but, unable to find a way to support himself, made his way back toward Nauvoo. But the trip went awry and he did not make it home for another nine months. As he walked off a riverboat in St. Louis to await transfer to an upriver steamer to Nauvoo, a pair of bounty hunters recognized Rockwell and took him into custody. He festered in the Independence jail while a determined sheriff, prosecutor, and judge explored every avenue to try to convict him for attempted murder. But, owing to lack of evidence, a grand jury refused to indict. Still, he stayed locked up without cause and survived attempts on his life until a sympathetic defense attorney forced the issue and got Rockwell released.

Making his way by stealth across Missouri to avoid enemies, he showed up on Joseph Smith's doorstep on Christmas Eve. Filthy, vermin-infested, unshaved and unshorn for months, Rockwell was at first mistaken for a drunken party crasher. But Joseph soon recognized his friend and, in his exuberance, pronounced a blessing that would follow Rockwell for life and become part of his mystique—Joseph prophesied that if Porter remained true to his faith and did not cut his hair or beard, neither bullet nor blade could harm him. Smith also numbered Rockwell among his bodyguards—and, some say, as an assassin—an assignment he held until the prophet's death and beyond, serving in the same capacity, and others, for the Mormon leader who followed, Brigham Young.

Of the many killings history—and myth—laid at Rockwell's feet, there is little disagreement about when, where, and why his first documented shooting occurred.

Although unrelated, the incident was linked by circumstance to the assassination by mob of Joseph Smith in 1844 in Illinois. Implicated in that mob was a local militia unit, the Carthage Greys, commanded by one Frank Worrell. With the Mormon leader out of the way, Worrell and others stepped up their attacks on Mormons, wishing to drive them out of Illinois as they had been driven out of Missouri. Standing in their way was the sheriff of Hancock County, Jacob Backenstos. Backenstos sympathized with the Mormons and their plight and attempted even-handed enforcement of the laws—actions that Worrell and others interpreted as pro-Mormon, making the sheriff unpopular and the target of threats.

One afternoon on the Warsaw Road, Worrell and two horseback companions spotted Backenstos driving in a buckboard and, with evil intent, set off in pursuit. The sheriff outran them to a roadside watering hole where several people were stopped, Rockwell among them. Backenstos hauled his team to a dusty halt and deputized Rockwell and a companion on the spot, ordering them to protect him from the pursuers.

Worrell soon topped a rise in the road ahead of his two companions, refusing Backenstos's order to halt. Instead, he raised his pistol, prompting Rockwell to draw a bead with his rifle and blast him out of the saddle. Worrell's mounted escorts did not pursue the fight, and when others in his party, traveling by wagon, arrived, they loaded up the body, turned tail, and drove away to Carthage.

Despite the presence of several disinterested witnesses who called the killing justified, Worrell's supporters dubbed it a murder, and accounts unfavorable to Rockwell down through the years record it as such.

No matter how one judges the death of Frank Worrell at Rockwell's hand, it would not be the last. Nor would most of those to follow be any less controversial. In fact, Worrell may not have been his first victim. There were persistent, if unproven, rumors around Nauvoo that Rockwell had killed fellow church member John Stephenson, and, at Joseph Smith's request (and, some said, with his assistance), drowned a woman who was spreading uncomplimentary stories about the prophet. In any event, the nickname "Destroying Angel" had already become firmly attached to Rockwell, deserved or no.

For long periods over the next several years, Rockwell was occupied with relocating the Mormons to the new Zion in the Great Basin of the West. Few men, if any, made the trip as often as Rockwell. He accompanied Brigham Young in the pioneer company that reached the shores of the Great Salt Lake in July of 1847, and made the trip several more times in both directions, as well as making his way westward from Utah to California, both on the northern and southern routes. He served at various times as scout, guide, and hunter. He hauled freight, herded cattle, carried the mail, and recovered lost livestock. He covered the trail summer and winter, in the saddle and in wagons, and occasionally endured extreme hardship. Through it all Rockwell earned a reputation as tough and reliable, fearless and capable.

And wherever he traveled, his reputation as a killer followed—or preceded—him, including his visits to the California goldfields.

The California gold rush is inextricably linked to Mormon history. Vast herds of gold seekers passed through Utah Territory, and profits from supplying them for the final leg of the journey across the deserts of the Great Basin may well have saved the tenuous Mormon existence in Salt Lake City and the spreading colonies. The discovery itself came at the hands of veterans of the Mormon Battalion, and Samuel Brannan, who settled in the San Francisco area after shepherding a shipload of Mormons around the horn in 1846, first publicized and soon profited from the resulting rush.

In one of the strange quirks of history, among those in California at the time with whom Brannan did business was Lilburn Boggs, former governor of Missouri and victim of Rockwell's supposed assassination attempt.

Brannan, as leader of the California Mormons, collected tithes and other offerings from the Saints. Once Young and the main body of the Mormons were established in the Salt Lake Valley, he sent a group to California in 1849 to convince Brannan to turn over the money. Rockwell, recently appointed US deputy marshal for Utah Territory, went along.

The visit was to be an extended one, so Rockwell made his way from Sutter's Fort to the goldfields and quickly realized he would find greater wealth in the bottom of a whiskey glass than a gold pan. He again adopted the alias of Brown—his own name being too infamous among the miners, many of whom came from Missouri and Illinois—and as insurance against discovery by Boggs. Now alcalde, an influential political office akin to mayor, at Sonoma, Boggs was a powerful man in the region and Rockwell feared his supposed victim would seek to have him killed.

Rockwell and a partner soon operated three enterprises in the Gold Country: a saloon, an inn, and a halfway house at various places along the American River. While his partner ran the places day to day, Rockwell spent most of his time leading pack trains laden with whiskey and supplies up the hill and gold dust down the hill. "Brown" always went well armed to protect himself and the goods, and proved his shooting skills in target contests on occasion. Brown's identity, however, was a poorly kept secret.

After nearly a year and a half in California, Rockwell returned to Salt Lake City, guiding a large group of eastbound travelers. Somewhere east of the Sierra, Indians made off with much of the party's livestock. Rockwell and a few others tracked the raiders and stole some horses in retaliation. The Indians continued to harass the travelers, and one dark night an unidentified Indian attempted to bluff his way past the guards. He did not fool Rockwell. He fired on the intruder, whose bullet-pierced body was discovered with the dawn.

Back in Salt Lake City, Rockwell was accused of many crimes, including a number of murders committed in his absence. Lurid tales of his exploits were common currency on the trail; many travelers feared him as much as any other hazard of the plains and mountains. Prominent writers and journalists of the day passing through Salt Lake City often included an interview with the notorious Rockwell on their itineraries.

Sir Richard Francis Burton visited the place in 1860 to write *City of the Saints*, wanting to chronicle a visit there as he had with other "holy cities" of the world. The traveler met Rockwell in Utah County, where he was herding cattle. "His tastes are apparently rural; his enemies declare his life would not be safe in the City of the Saints," Burton wrote. "An attempt had lately been made to assassinate him in one of the kanyons." Rockwell, he said, was about fifty years old at the time, and put away a good deal of whiskey during their visit without apparent effect as he regaled his audience with tales of the frontier. "When the drinking was finished we exchanged a cordial poignée de main [handshake] with Porter and our hospitable host, who appeared to be the crème de la crème of Utah County."

During an 1863 visit to Utah Territory, Fitz Hugh Ludlow interviewed Rockwell for an *Atlantic Monthly* story. He reported that Rockwell "had the reputation of having killed many men—forty, reports said; and there are not lacking those who suspect him of still more." He described the man and their meeting, saying his subject did not meet his expectations of "a destroying angel." Still, Ludlow reported a recent supposed murder by "the heaven-elected assassin of Mormonism" and said that although Rockwell had likely killed many more than the forty men attributed to him, he was "one of the pleasantest murderers I ever met."

Rockwell's displeasure with Ludlow's reporting was evident in 1865 when Albert Richardson of the *New York Tribune* visited Utah. Richardson wrote that Rockwell "confused me with Fitz Hugh Ludlow, who had passed through two years before and given an unflattering description of him for the *Atlantic Monthly*." The Mormon gunman was of the impression that Richardson had accused him in print of murdering 150 men. "He significantly remarked," Richardson reported, "that if I had said it he believed he would make it one hundred and fifty-one!" The confusion was cleared up and the reporter unharmed. But, he said, Rockwell assured him "he would kill any journalist who should publish such falsehoods about him."

Years later, in 1871, newspaperman George Albert Townsend, reporting for the *Cincinnati Commercial*, wrote, "I talked to Porter Rockwell, the alleged leader of the 'Danites,' a fat, curly-haired, good-natured chap, fond of a drink, a talk, and a wild venture. The United States authorities have several times used him to make arrests of lawless characters."

While not living up to expectations of a cold-blooded killer in appearance or demeanor, Rockwell still inspired curiosity among writers—and readers.

While no reliable body count of those killed by Rockwell can ever be known, there is no doubt he killed. Harold Schindler, whose *Orrin Porter Rockwell: Man of God, Son of Thunder* remains the only biography of the man that can be considered objective, records several shooting scrapes in which Rockwell's participation is known and documented by witnesses, participants, or reliable contemporary accounts.

Perhaps the most infamous of these is an incident, or series of incidents, that came down through history as the "Aiken Affair." Twenty years after the episode, when Brigham Young's death supposedly loosened the church's grip on Utah Territory, federal authorities brought charges against a number of Mormons for past misdeeds. An indictment for murder was issued against Rockwell for his role in the Aiken Affair, and he was arrested, bailed out, and awaiting trial when he died.

This particular incident started in 1857 when the Mormons, facing war with some two thousand US Army troops on the march toward Utah, grew increasingly suspicious—to the point of paranoia—of strangers. Brothers John and Tom Aiken and four companions—"Colonel" Eichard, John Chapman, Tuck Wright, and "Honesty" Jones—rode in from California. The men were believed to be gamblers set on skinning the coming soldiers, but Mormon leaders feared they were spies and arrested them. Rather than being locked up, the men were tucked away in a hotel and allowed to move about the city more or less at will.

A month or so later, the men were set free but ordered to either confine themselves to Salt Lake City or leave the Territory. Chapman and Jones chose to stay. Deputy Marshal Rockwell, with Sylvanus Collett and two other men, got the assignment to escort the Aiken brothers, Wright, and Eichard out of Utah, taking the southern route to California owing to the lateness of the season. The party overnighted in Nephi, some seventy-five miles south of Salt Lake City, then continued south, camping the next evening on the banks of the Sevier River.

Sometime during the night, according to the scant evidence available, Rockwell and the other escorts set upon the gamblers under the guise of an Indian attack. The men were bludgeoned, but Wright got the best of his attacker, and someone—Rockwell, it was said—shot him. Beaten and wounded, Wright managed to escape into the night. The other three were dumped into the river. But John Aiken, believed dead by his attackers, was of tougher stuff, and survived and made it ashore downstream. Separately, the wounded men made way back to Nephi. Also seen in town were Rockwell and Collett, with horses and other goods belonging to the Aiken party. Some later reported overhearing Rockwell and others talking about the need to finish the job of disposing of the men.

Aiken and Wright spent a few days recuperating, then asked for transportation back to Salt Lake City. Two young boys were assigned the task, and the group started north in a buggy. Not too many miles later, at a place called Willow Creek, the boys stopped to water the team, and someone, concealed in a shack, gunned down Aiken and Wright. The bodies were again dumped into water—this time weighted down with rocks and sunk into a network of spring-fed ponds a few miles away.

Contemporary reports of Rockwell's return to Salt Lake City say he had at least one horse and a mule that had belonged to the Aiken party, and that fancy hats and clothing, guns, and other items were given away to settlers along the way. There was even a report that "Honesty" Jones met up with Rockwell not far from the city and, recognizing items belonging to his erstwhile companions, barely escaped the encounter with his life.

"Honesty" wasn't the only person named Jones to run afoul of Rockwell. Early in 1858, a man named Henry Jones was accused of incestuous sexual relations with his mother. Multiple, but unconfirmed, reports claim Rockwell—on orders from church leaders—first castrated Jones, who then fled, and later killed both the man and his mother in a dugout shack at Payson, slitting their throats, then collapsing the cabin atop them.

Rockwell carved another notch in his pistol grip less than two years later. In January of 1860 a freighter named Martin Oats, employed by the government to haul goods to the troops at Camp Floyd, stopped off at Rockwell's roadside Hot Springs Brewery and Hotel. Rockwell broke up an altercation between the abrasive bullwhacker and his bartender, and sent the angry teamster back into the stormy winter evening to continue his journey. The story goes that Rockwell left soon afterward for his home in Lehi and overtook Oats on the road, where the man had apparently been lying in wait for him. Ignoring the gunman's warnings, the attacker would not let up. Rockwell drew his pistol and shot Oats dead, then rode on to Lehi and gave himself up to the sheriff there. The law deemed the killing justified.

Two Salt Lake City brothers, Kenneth and Alexander McRae, joined up with a few other young men in August of 1861 to try their hands as road agents. With the law—including the sheriff and Deputy US Marshal Porter Rockwell—hot on their tails for robbing a traveler, the brothers fled up Emigration Canyon east of the city. Stories differ as to what happened when the posse overtook them. One account claims the young men were taken into custody, disarmed, and murdered in cold blood with a shotgun. A local judge recorded the boys were arrested then shot while attempting to escape.

No one noted the trigger man, but legend assigned the killings to Rockwell.

History does record a shootout with outlaws in which Rockwell prevailed. A young tough named Lot Huntington, with numerous disreputable crimes to his credit, hit the road for points west to escape arrest for a series of misdeeds.

A band of rowdies, of which Huntington was one, attacked, beat (some say castrated), and nearly killed territorial governor John W. Dawson. The governor's term lasted all of three weeks, barely time enough to offend an entire territory, but he managed. He took office with a woman, not his wife and of questionable background, on his arm. Despite such full-time company, he was said to have propositioned a respected Mormon woman. That behavior—and other distasteful incidents—angered his constituents so much he opted to quit the Territory rather than face their wrath. While awaiting an eastbound stage at an out-of-the-way station on New Year's Eve in 1861, the aforementioned gang of thugs set upon him.

Many believed Dawson deserved what he got. Nevertheless, Huntington and others were charged and arrest warrants—which no one seemed eager to serve—were issued. A few weeks later, Huntington was accused of stealing money from an Overland Mail station, stealing a horse, and leaving town, making his capture and arrest a priority. Rockwell, famous for his abilities as a tracker and skill as a man hunter, took up the trail.

He caught up with the gang on a cold, predawn January morning at Faust Station, a stage and mail stop on the Overland Trail some fifty-five miles from Salt Lake City. Rockwell deployed the posse to surround the station. The station operator finally came out for morning chores, was accosted by Rockwell, and verified that Huntington and two companions were there and having breakfast. Rockwell sent the man back inside to inform the gang of his presence and convey a demand for surrender.

Instead of surrendering, Huntington drew his pistol and made for the stable, ignoring Rockwell's orders to stop. Huntington climbed aboard his stolen horse bareback and took aim at the lawman. (Other reports have Huntington afoot and hiding behind his horse, which shied as the outlaw opened a gate, exposing him to gunfire.) Rockwell opened fire in earnest and shot the bandit off his horse. Huntington's fall was broken by the corral fence, but it didn't matter. He dangled there, entangled in the fence rails, his wounds draining the lifeblood from him. The other two fugitives surrendered in a bid to avoid a similar fate at Rockwell's hand.

The longhaired gunman's name was associated with many other killings before and after the shooting of Lot Huntington, if only by gossip, rumor, and innuendo. For years any body that turned up between the Missouri River and the Sierra Nevada Mountains was as likely as not to be attributed to Rockwell.

Forever associated with killing—he was under indictment for murder at the time of his death—Rockwell pursued many exploits that seem to make him deserving of a richer legacy. He ran to ground and arrested many outlaws as a deputy US marshal. His uncanny ability as a tracker of man and animal was often successfully employed where others had failed. His repute with horses—as a rider, driver, breeder, and trainer— was widespread, and animals with his brand were sought after. Whether with lines or reins in hand, he could urge a horse to cover more miles in less time without ill effect than most, as chronicles of his travels attest. His advice and skill as a tracker and guide were employed by emigrants, freighters, armies, and others traveling in the West. His reliability as a messenger earned widespread trust when critical information had to be conveyed. He approached every job with unbridled tenacity, and every employer with unquestioning loyalty.

Still, it is as a gunfighter and killer that Rockwell was known in his time, as evidenced by these lines from an Old West campfire verse:

For Port is a devil in human shape . . .
. . . He's black, bitter death, and there's no escape. . . .
Somewhere a wife with her babes kneels to pray,
For she knows she's a widow and orphans are they.

Porter Rockwell died with his boots on at age sixty-five on June 9, 1878. After an evening at the theater and a few hours' drinking at a local saloon, he took to his bed in his office at the Colorado Stables. It was a troublesome night. He complained to the hostler of nausea and chills but resolved to get out of bed the next day. Old Port managed to sit up and pull on his boots before collapsing. While medical diagnoses of the day are vague and unreliable, it seems likely from doctors' reports that he died of a heart attack.

Such a mundane death did not satisfy the *Salt Lake Tribune*, which reported, "Thus the gallows was cheated of one of the fittest candidates that ever cut a throat or plundered a traveler."

Edward Fitzgerald Beale:
A Frontiersman for All Reasons

1846—California

Not many people nowadays know much about Edward Fitzgerald "Ned" Beale. But he was known—well known—in the latter half of the nineteenth century. Among his friends were frontiersmen Kit Carson and Buffalo Bill Cody, generals William Tecumseh Sherman and Ulysses S. Grant, and Emperor Franz Josef I of Austria-Hungary.

Five presidents of the United States put Beale to work, starting at age fourteen when Andrew Jackson appointed him to the Naval School at Philadelphia, forerunner of the US Naval Academy. Later, Millard Fillmore named Beale superintendent of Indian Affairs for California and Nevada; he surveyed and improved a wagon road from New Mexico to California under orders from James Buchanan; Abraham Lincoln appointed him surveyor general of California and Nevada; and he served as ambassador to Austria-Hungary in the administration of Ulysses S. Grant.

But that does not begin to tell the story of Ned Beale. During his years on the frontier, he left more tracks in more places than most men could even imagine.

Beale was born February 4, 1822, in Washington, DC, into a family firmly rooted in the US Navy. Emily Truxton, his mother, was the daughter of a commodore. George, his father, who died in 1835, was a naval officer decorated for valor during the War of 1812. The widow Beale reportedly took the teenage Beale to visit President Andrew Jackson, seeking an appointment to the Naval School based on the service the family had performed for the country. Jackson granted her wish. As a student Beale served as a midshipman on voyages to Russia, Brazil, and the West Indies; upon graduation in 1842 he sailed to Europe and South America.

Beginning in 1845, Beale served aboard the ship *Congress* under Captain Robert F. Stockton. Stockton soon sent Beale on a mysterious voyage aboard a Danish ship encountered at sea, reportedly on a clandestine visit to England to assess that country's intentions concerning the Oregon country. Beale reported to President James K. Polk in the nation's capital, gathered messages for his captain, sailed to Panama, crossed the isthmus by land, caught a ship to Peru, and resumed his duties aboard the *Congress* in 1846, now with the office of master.

Stockton sailed north to Monterey and Yerba Buena and, with John C. Fremont, claimed possession of California. With the Mexican-American War well underway, Stockton sailed south to Los Angeles and San Diego to occupy those ports. Beale and a small contingent of men were put ashore at San Diego to find and join forces with General Stephen W. Kearny and his troops, marching to the coast across the deserts of New Mexico, Arizona, and California.

Kearney's orders were to reach California and assume command of US forces there and see to setting up a government, which he had just accomplished in Santa Fe before setting out for California. But at Valverde in southern New Mexico he met scout Kit Carson, who was carrying word to Washington of the occupation of the ports and cities by naval forces and Fremont's troops and volunteers. With that news Kearny sent most of his troops north to deal with marauding Navajos and, with some one hundred soldiers and Carson as a guide, pushed hard toward the coast.

Beale and about twenty troops, along with a group of volunteers, met Kearney some forty miles inland. Although the Americans had taken control of California with relative ease, by now the Mexicans, the Californios, were offering resistance. Kearny, Carson, Beale, and the rest would meet that resistance at San Pasqual, twenty-five miles from San Diego.

The battle started badly the cold, wet morning of December 6, 1846, with Kearny's advance forces attacking prematurely owing to misunderstood commands. The Americans, with damp powder and swords, were no match for the Californios with their lances and reatas, or lariats. The Mexicans roped the Americans and dragged them from their horses, while their comrades attacked them on the ground. Kearny was wounded in hand-to-hand combat. Eighteen others were wounded and seventeen killed before artillery arrived at the scene and forced the Californios to retreat. Kearny and the troops attempted to carry on toward San Diego on December 7, but harassment by the Mexican lancers pinned them down atop a hill.

Not only was the fight a disaster for the Americans, they now found themselves stalled, surrounded, and under siege. Kit Carson, Ned Beale, and Indian guide Chemuctah volunteered to attempt to slip through the Mexican lines and hurry to San Diego for reinforcements from Stockton. The rescue party left after dark on December 8.

The night was so quiet while the men eased their way down the hill that they feared the slosh of the water in their canteens would alert the enemy, so they abandoned them. Beale and Carson also feared the noise of their boots on the rocky slope would alert the enemy, so they pulled them off and tucked them away. At times they were within inches of the roving Californio sentries, and Carson later said it was so tense that at one point he could hear Beale's heart pound. But they got through, only to realize they had lost their boots in the process. Beale and Carson would spend the next twenty-four hours or so barefoot, picking their way through rocks, thorns, and cactus. Chemuctah's moccasins were not much better suited to the terrain.

The men made their way through the desert with as much caution as they could muster, but Mexican lookouts continually blocked their progress. They decided to split up and take different routes, believing at least one would get through. As it happened, all three made it and Kearny's troops were rescued.

Beale was so worn out, hungry, and thirsty following the ordeal that Carson wondered if he would recover. The young naval officer spent the best part of the next few months in sick bay and even then did not regain all his strength before setting out on his next adventure.

Carson and Beale again joined forces for a trip to Washington, DC, to deliver dispatches from acting governor John C. Fremont apprising government and military leaders of affairs in California. The men set out on the Gila Trail to the Rio Grande, rode north to Santa Fe, and then took the Santa Fe Trail east to Missouri. Carson said Beale was so weak at times during the trek that he had to bodily lift him on and off his horse. Two months later they were in St. Louis, able to complete the journey using more modern modes of transportation, steamboats and railroads.

They arrived in the nation's capital in May. Carson was somewhat surprised to find himself a celebrity in the East, owing to his exploits with Fremont and other adventures on the frontier. For much of their stay in his hometown, Beale showed Carson around and helped the frontiersman cope with society and celebrity. The mountain man was concerned he would be shunned because of his prior marriage to an Indian woman, but Beale assured him that the standards of Eastern society did not extend to the frontier.

Beale returned to California, but not for long. Thomas Larkin, formerly consul to California when it was in Mexican hands and now an agent in Monterey for the US Navy, penned a June 1848 letter to the State Department, affirming the discovery of gold in California. He wrote:

> *I have to report one of the most astonishing excitements and state of affairs. There has been discovered a placer, a vast tract of land containing gold, in small particles. . . . It is now two or three weeks since the men employed in these washings have appeared in this town with their gold, to exchange for merchandise and provisions. I presume nearly twenty thousand dollars of this gold has been so exchanged.*

Beale saddled up and embarked on another trip across the continent, this time in disguise via Mexico, carrying Larkin's letter along with related information from the commander of the Pacific Naval Squadron and samples of gold to Washington, DC. His arrival in Washington in September drew the attention of showman P. T. Barnum, who wrote to Beale:

> *Mr. Harding of the* Philadelphia Enquirer *has just informed me that you have in your possession an eight-pound lump of California gold.*

As I am always anxious to procure novelties for public gratification I write this to say I should be glad to purchase the lump. If not that, I should like to procure it for exhibition for a few weeks. Your ob't servant, P. T. Barnum.

The gold Beale carried to Washington could be weighed in ounces, not pounds. Other than a small amount held out to make an engagement ring for his intended, Mary Edwards, the gold was in the hands of the government. He married Miss Edwards June 27, 1849—but not before Beale made two more horseback journeys across the continent. Two more would yet follow—for a total of seven trips from the far West, six of them within less than two years. Beale resigned from the Navy with the rank of lieutenant in 1851. His marriage produced two daughters and a son.

However, Beale was not finished with the West, or with government service. The adventurer Beale went back to California, this time to manage real estate and ranching interests for himself and Commodore Robert F. Stockton and William Henry Aspinwall—a merchant, trader, and owner of a fleet of clipper ships.

Beale was soon back in the government harness when, in 1853, President Millard Fillmore called him to Washington, DC, and named him superintendent of Indian Affairs, with jurisdiction over California and what is now Nevada. But there was a job to do on the way west. When Beale left the capital in May, he took with him a surveying party to determine a route for a transcontinental railroad through Colorado and Utah to Los Angeles. After serving as superintendent of Indian Affairs until 1856, Beale was appointed brigadier general in the California State Militia, in which office he continued working and negotiating treaties with Indians.

President James Buchanan and 1857 brought more adventure. This time, Beale's assignment was to survey and construct a wagon road from Fort Defiance in New Mexico across one thousand miles of arid deserts and mountains to the California border on the Colorado River beyond Kingman, Arizona. Beale wrote of the road in a report to the Secretary of War:

It is the shortest route from our western frontier by 300 miles, being nearly directly west. It is the most level: our wagons only double-teaming once in the entire distance, and that at a short hill, and over a surface heretofore unbroken by wheels or trail of any kind. It is well-watered: our greatest distance without water at any time being twenty miles. . . . It is temperate in climate, passing for the most part over an elevated region. . . . It is well-grassed: my command never having made a bad grass camp during the entire distance until near the Colorado. It crosses the great desert (which must be crossed by any road to California) at its narrowest point. . . . It is passable alike in winter and summer.

What would be known as the Beale Wagon Road proved a great success, followed for years by herds of cattle and sheep as well as freighters and emigrants. Later, automobile highways Route 66 and Interstate 40, as well as the Santa Fe Railway, followed, more or less, the road Beale surveyed and built. Construction of Beale's Wagon Road also played a role in one of the most unusual—if not downright bizarre—experiments ever indulged in by the US Army. The scheme, originally conceived in 1836 by Major George H. Crosman and later taken up by Secretary of War Jefferson Davis, involved using camels as pack animals. Beale was ordered to utilize camels on the road project, and brought in twenty-five dromedaries from Texas. He praised their performance in his report to the Secretary of War:

An important part in all of our operations has been acted by the camels. Without the aid of this noble and useful brute, many hardships which we have been spared would have fallen to our lot; and our admiration for them has increased day by day, as some new hardship endured patiently, more fully developed their entire adaptation and usefulness in the exploration of the wilderness. At times I have thought it impossible they could stand the test to which they have been put, but they seem to have risen equal to every trail and have come off every exploration with as much strength as before starting.

Few men were as adventurous on the Western frontier as US Navy officer Edward "Ned" Beale. NAVAL HISTORI-CAL CENTER

Despite Beale's praise, the government eventually abandoned the camel experiment for a variety of reasons. Beale's admiration for the beasts did not wane, however, and when the army sold off the camels later, he bought a few and kept them on his Tejon Ranch in California. But the Tejon Ranch would come later. During the Civil War Beale served, at President Abraham Lincoln's insistence despite his desire for a military commission, as surveyor general of California.

The 270,000-acre Tejon Ranch, near Bakersfield, came to be in 1865 and 1866 when Beale purchased Mexican land grants—Rancho El Tejon, Rancho de los Alamos y Agua Caliente, and Rancho Castac—to add to his 1855 acquisition of Rancho La Liebre. In addition to his camels, Beale raised beef cattle and crops. Beale retired to the ranch for a time after the war, and Tejon Ranch remained in the family until his son sold it in 1912.

In 1870 he purchased Decatur House, a Washington, DC, landmark, and lived there and at the ranch. His retirement was interrupted for a year in 1876 by President Ulysses Grant, when he appointed Beale minister to Austria-Hungary.

Beale died at his Washington home on April 22, 1893, drawing to a close an unparalleled life as a frontiersman.

The Free and Independent State of Deseret

1847—Great Basin

Since the United States of America formally organized with the Constitution in 1787, there has only been one formerly independent nation added to the Union—Texas, in 1845. (One could make an argument for California's Bear Flag Republic, but that political entity never came to fruition and was unrecognized, so it would be a weak argument.)

But that very nearly was not the case. The Great Basin, along with some territory falling outside its bounds, came within a war or two and some political wrangling of becoming the Free and Independent State of Deseret. When independence wasn't in the offing, there was a failed effort at statehood that would have resulted in a star on the flag for a state that dwarfed Texas in land area.

How it happened dates back to 1820 and the birth of the Mormon movement and what would become its main sect, the Church of Jesus Christ of Latter-day Saints. The founder of the new religion, Joseph Smith, was but fourteen years old when a heavenly vision, in answer to a prayerful inquiry about which church to join, informed the youth to join none of them but to stand by for the restoration of God's true religion, of which Smith would be the leader.

Several years later, Smith claimed that other heavenly messengers delivered to him golden plates, on which, he said, were written records of an ancient people who once lived on the American continent and were visited by Jesus Christ after his death and resurrection in Jerusalem. Smith turned the plates into what he considered a companion to the Bible, the *Book of Mormon*, first published in 1830. The book is named for

Mormon, said to be the primary compiler of the record in ancient times. Shortly after publishing this book, Smith officially organized the Church of Christ, with himself as prophet. His church would undergo a number of modifications in its name, but from the beginning, the people were known as "Mormons," after their holy book.

Converts joined the new religion in scores, then hundreds, then thousands. But greater in number for many years were the prophet's detractors. Many of his neighbors in upstate New York accused him of treasure seeking and fraud and other misdeeds, and Smith and his followers eventually left town, with many relocating to Kirtland, Ohio. Others were sent to the Missouri frontier in 1833 to establish the "New Jerusalem" in Jackson County and turn the rough-and-tumble town of Independence into the "City of Zion."

Within a year of arriving in Ohio, Smith and his right-hand man were tarred and feathered. There followed a year or two of relative peace, but money problems brought all kinds of trouble to the fledging church. An illegal bank, a spate of lawsuits to collect unpaid loans, and accusations of counterfeiting turned the community—including many of the prophet's friends and followers—against Smith.

Animosity toward the church was more pronounced in Missouri. And it was here that many of Smith's most controversial doctrines became evident. His vision for the church was, in many ways, in direct opposition to American values—cultural, economic, political, and religious—especially those on the frontier.

The majority in Missouri at the time supported the notion of slavery, even if most were too impoverished to participate in the practice. The Mormons, on the other hand, were mostly of New England Yankee stock and had little sympathy for slavery, even voicing abolitionist sentiments. And where Indians were but a nuisance to be pushed aside by most Americans, according to the Mormon holy book the natives were remnants of a wandering band of Israelites who migrated to the Americas back in Old Testament times. As such, they were among the chosen and crucial to the Mormon view of end times. Like many religious people at the time, the Mormons believed the end times and the second coming of Christ imminent—leading to the ultimate name for the sect: the Church of Jesus Christ of Latter Day (later Latter-day) Saints.

In a land of economic individualism, free-market capitalism, and the sacredness of private property, the Saints sought to establish a communal economy, with church ownership of all property and most wealth. Members would be assigned a "stewardship" over the amount of land and size of home and property required to sustain their families—but even then much of the work would be performed as a community. Greed and avarice were to have no place in the Mormon Zion. But most of the Saints were less than saintly in that regard, and despite repeated efforts to establish a communal society over the next several decades, none took root. Still, the pooling of funds to acquire property for the church often put them at an advantage over individuals in the real estate market, which offended other settlers in Missouri, both new and established.

In the realm of politics, one-man, one-vote was a basic tenet of the United States, and was certainly the goal, if not always the reality, in nineteenth-century America. The Mormons saw no sin in voting as a block, with their leaders' expressed choices among candidates almost always enjoying unanimous support on Mormon ballots. This attitude, coupled with the large number of Saints continually arriving in Missouri, spawned fears of a Mormon takeover.

Beyond that the Saints expressed little interest in politics. They believed they were to establish the New Jerusalem, or the Kingdom of God on Earth, in which politics, even government itself, had no place. Christ himself would rule, if not directly then through his mouthpiece, the prophet. All would be welcome in the earthly Kingdom of God, no matter their origins or beliefs, so long as they went along with theocratic rule and didn't make waves. While the Mormons looked forward with hope and faith to that day, and worked actively to bring it about, their Missouri neighbors wanted none of it.

On the religious front the Saints tended toward an arrogant belief in the superiority of their religion. The Mormon Church was the one and only true faith, a restoration of the church Jesus Christ established during his mortal sojourn, the truth of which was lost sometime after his chosen apostles left the mortal realm. So the Saints were dismissive of nonbelievers—"Gentiles," they called them—and those who cared not to convert were dismissed, often rudely.

These multilayered clashes resulted in no end of difficulties for the Mormons in Missouri. Beatings, burnings, and all manner of mob violence could—and did—arrive at any time. Finally, they were kicked out of Jackson County and eventually sent into exile in a sparsely populated region of northern Missouri where a county was established for them.

As they settled and started building communities there, their brethren from Ohio, including Joseph Smith, started arriving in numbers, having given up on their continued presence there as a lost, if not bankrupt, cause. Overseas converts, mostly from England, were also showing up in ever-larger numbers. More Mormons, of course, did not sit well with the citizens of Missouri, and by 1838 it was all but civil war in the state.

Vigilante groups on both sides rode at night, terrorizing settlers in the opposite camp with threats and violence and burnings and destruction. By day many of the same men marched in militia units, either under the auspices of the State of Missouri or the military arm of the Mormon Church. While they sometimes gave as good as they got, the Mormons could not withstand the power of the state and, in the end, got the worst of it. Their anger is expressed in an 1838 speech celebrating the Fourth of July, given by Joseph's right-hand man, Sidney Rigdon:

> *We take God and all the holy angels to witness this day, that we warn all men in the name of Jesus Christ, to come on us no more forever. For from this hour, we will bear it no more, our rights shall no more be trampled on with impunity. The man or the set of men, who attempts it, does it at the expense of their lives. And that mob that comes on us to disturb us; it shall be between us and them a war of extermination; for we will follow them till the last drop of their blood is spilled, or else they will have to exterminate us: for we will carry the seat of war to their own houses, and their own families, and one party or the other shall be utterly destroyed. Remember it then all MEN.*

More violence followed. Not to be outdone, Missouri governor Lilburn Boggs took a step unprecedented, and since unmatched, in the history of American government when on October 27, 1838, he issued a frightening order to his militia commander, which read, in part:

> *I have received by Amos Reese, Esq., of Ray county, and Wiley C. Williams, Esq., one of my aids, information of the most appalling character, which entirely changes the face of things, and places the Mormons in the attitude of an open and avowed defiance of the laws, and of having made war upon the people of this state. Your orders are, therefore, to hasten your operation with all possible speed. The Mormons must be treated as enemies, and must be exterminated or driven from the state if necessary for the public peace—their outrages are beyond all description.*

A score or so of arriving Mormon settlers, many of them women and children, were massacred by a Missouri mob—or militia—at a place called Haun's Mill. That incident, and a Missouri militia of overwhelming strength staring him down, took the wind out of the prophet's sails. He surrendered his army, was arrested for treason, and with several of his closest associates spent more than five months in jail. While they moldered in their basement dungeon, Brigham Young and other church leaders organized the removal of the Mormons, settling them across the Mississippi in Illinois, the only place, it seems, that would have them.

When Smith escaped jail (or was allowed to flee) and arrived in Illinois, he gave Commerce, the community around which his people had settled, the new name of Nauvoo and set out once again to build the "City of God." He negotiated with the state a liberal charter for the city, which gave the Mormons considerable control over the political and legal systems. There was little distinction between church leadership and civic government in the city, and control of the courts proved beneficial in disputes with non-Mormon neighbors. Nauvoo grew rapidly and was soon second in population in Illinois only to Chicago. It had its own army— the Nauvoo Legion—with some 2,500 men under arms, at a time the US Army's strength stood at 8,500.

As it had been in Missouri, and for essentially the same reasons, the citizens of Illinois soon tired of the Mormons and, again, persecuted the

Saints mercilessly. Smith also faced opposition from within the ranks. As clashes with neighbors increased in both number and severity, Smith announced his candidacy for president of the United States to, if nothing else, force the government to protect his people should he win election.

At the same time he searched for a new home for the Mormons. Having effectively given up on the United States, he considered several locations in the West, including Vancouver Island, Texas, and Mexico—including the Great Basin. A "Council of Fifty" (or, more formally, the Kingdom of God and His Laws with the Keys and Power thereof, and Judgment in the Hands of His Servants, Ahman Christ) was established to represent the interests of the coming theocracy. Most members were, of course, chosen from among Smith's most trusted followers and proven leaders.

As troubles multiplied Smith declared martial law in Nauvoo and ordered destroyed a newspaper and printing press established by former followers who questioned his leadership and prophetic call. Among other things, his detractors claimed Smith had introduced the practice for himself and his most reliable associates of taking multiple wives. He denied it, but it later proved to be true.

By the summer of 1844, neighboring non-Mormons were demanding the government of the state and county rein in Smith or they would lay waste to the Mormons and their city. The prophet surrendered himself under a promise of protection from the governor, and he and a few other leaders were jailed at Carthage, the county seat. But the governor's protection proved inadequate, and the upstairs room where the Saints were held was overrun. Following a brief gunfight, Joseph and his brother Hyrum were shot and killed on June 27, 1844.

Many thought the death of the prophet would be the death of his church. It was not to be. The persistent Mormons tried to make peace with their neighbors, but the local residents had had enough and continued to harass the Saints. Brigham Young, who assumed leadership of the church, eventually arranged an exodus out of Nauvoo.

Later, in justifying his state's inaction, Governor Thomas Ford said, "The Mormons openly denounced the government of the United States as utterly corrupt, and as being about to pass away and to be replaced by the government of God, to be administered by his servant Joseph."

If Illinois would not allow them to build their kingdom, Young and his thousands of followers would try again in the West, beyond the reach and control of the United States. Orson Pratt, a member of the church's Quorum of the Twelve Apostles—the governing body of the church, second in authority to the president and his counselors—said, "It is with the greatest joy that I forsake this republic; and all the saints have abundant reason to rejoice that they are counted worthy to be cast out as exiles from this wicked nation." Young said in 1845 that he did not "intend to winter in the United States." He did not quite make his self-appointed deadline to be shed of the nation. Instead, he spent months trying to organize a move, and the Saints spent the bitter winter of 1846–1847 scattered across Iowa, squatting—with quasi-permission—on Indian land, with the greatest concentration of refugees straddling the Missouri River at Kanesville in Iowa and Winter Quarters in Nebraska.

By spring Young had carefully planned in great detail what would be the greatest organized mass migration in American history. Leading a pioneer group of just over 140 men and a few women, he lit out for the West. A larger party of Saints would follow later that year, and more and more would follow in years to come—some seventy thousand before the transcontinental railroad was completed in Utah in 1869. Many of the migrating Mormons were converts from Great Britain, Scandinavia, and elsewhere in northern and western Europe.

Young's destination was the Salt Lake Valley in the Great Basin, a place he learned about from studying John C. Fremont's reports of his western explorations, and from other inquiries. The valley was then part of Mexico, and with war between the United States and Mexico imminent, Young may have already feared his intended homeland would soon be absorbed by the nation's greedy pursuit of "Manifest Destiny." Still, he pressed on, reaching the new Zion on July 24, 1847, and declaring it "the right place." Young said of his new home, "Give us ten years of peace and we will ask no odds of the United States."

A couple of days later, Young and a handful of followers hiked to the top of a hill at the north end of the valley for a panoramic view. While there the men hoisted a yellow bandana atop a walking stick in latter-day fulfillment of Isaiah's biblical prophecy that "He will lift up an ensign to the nations" and invite all to come to Zion. The place has been known since as Ensign Peak.

The Treaty of Guadalupe Hidalgo, signed February 2, 1848, ended the war with Mexico and the brief absence of the Mormons from the confines of the United States. Once again, they were Americans—and not necessarily happy about it. But the Mormons were not high on the list of problems the federal government was dealing with at the time, so little, if anything, was done to welcome the Saints back to the country they had fled. Brigham Young put the Council of Fifty to work to govern the place.

While sovereignty and independence were the hope, the fallback position was territorial status, and the council put the wheels in motion to petition Congress to create the Territory of Deseret. Others realized a territory would put control in the hands of the federal government, so the Mormons also pursued a request for statehood for Deseret. Boundaries were drawn, and elections were held in 1849 to validate the office holders church leaders had already appointed. Young was appointed, then elected, governor and also named by the council as king and president. The Council of Fifty also published the *Constitution of the State of Deseret*—all this before any action from Washington. The area claimed by the Mormons and defined in their constitution was enormous, encompassing most of the land the United States had just won from Mexico in the war:

> *WE THE PEOPLE, grateful to the supreme being for the blessings hitherto enjoyed, and feeling our dependence on Him for a continuation of those blessings, do ordain and establish a free and Independent Government, by the name of the STATE OF DESERET; including all the territory of the United States, within the following boundaries, to wit: Commencing at the 33°, North Latitude, where it crosses the 108°, Longitude, west of Greenwich; thence, running South and West, to the Northern boundary of Mexico, thence West to, and down the Main Channel of the Gila River, [or the northern line of Mexico] and on the Northern boundary of Lower California to the Pacific Ocean; thence along the Coast North Westerly to the 118°, 30' of west Longitude; Thence North to where said line intersects the dividing ridge of the Sierra Nevada Mountains; Thence North, along the Summit of*

the Sierra Nevada Mountains, to the dividing range of the Moun-
tains, that separate the Waters flowing into the Columbia River, from
the Waters running into the Great Basin; thence Easterly, along the
dividing range of Mountains that separate said waters flowing into
the Columbia river on the North from the waters flowing into the
Great Basin on the South, to the summit of the Wind River chain of
mountains; thence South East and South, by the dividing range of
Mountains that separate the waters flowing into the Gulf of Mexico,
from the waters flowing into the Gulf of California, to the place of
beginning....

The federal government, of course, all but ignored Mormon wishes and on September 9, 1850, created Utah Territory as part of the Compromise of 1850. While Utah was considerably smaller than Deseret, it still covered a lot of country, encompassing the entirety of present-day Utah, all of Nevada save the southern tip of the wedge, Colorado west of the Continental Divide, and southwestern Wyoming. Washington officials went along with Young's appointment as governor of the new territory, but several other offices were filled by federal appointees the Mormons had little use for, resulting in a revolving door of ineffective leadership and limited federal involvement. Instead, Young ruled the Territory with help from the Council of Fifty, but more and more that group proved unwieldy and he relied instead on the Quorum of the Twelve Apostles to implement his will.

The General Assembly of Deseret formally disbanded the Free and Independent State of Deseret in April 1851, but that was mostly for show. Young and the Mormon hierarchy continued to run the show. But it was not without opposition. Westbound emigrants who spent time in the Territory claimed abuse at the hands of Mormons. Military surveyors reported the people of Utah and their leaders were disloyal to the United States. Federal appointees complained they were ignored, insulted, and sometimes driven from office.

And in the middle of it all, polygamy, or plural marriage, came out of the shadows to be practiced openly, which only served to fan the flames of hatred so many Americans felt for the Mormons.

The feeling was returned, with the Saints in no mood for reconciliation. Unhappy with the power the federal government held over the Territory, Young said in 1856, "I say, as the Lord lives, we are bound to become a sovereign State in the Union, or an independent nation by ourselves, and let them drive us from this place if they can, they cannot do it."

Shortly after taking office in 1857, President James Buchanan decided to take action. He replaced Young as governor with a non-Mormon, Alfred Cumming. Fearing Young and his followers would resist the transition, Buchanan mounted the Utah Expedition to escort the new governor to Utah and install him in office—at gunpoint, if necessary. The expedition amounted to the largest assembly of troops in the nation at the time— the commander in chief ordered a force of 2,500 to march on Utah. The orders to General W. S. Harney, originally chosen to lead the expedition, included this:

> The community and, in part, the civil government of Utah Territory are in a state of substantial rebellion against the laws and authority of the United States. A new civil governor is about to be designated, and to be charged with the establishment and maintenance of law and order. Your able and energetic aid, with that of the troops to be placed under your command, is relied upon to insure the success of this mission.

Before the expedition was well underway, the army reassigned Harney and passed leadership on to General Albert Sidney Johnston.

Despite the secrecy surrounding the preparations, the Mormons knew the army was coming, and they extended every effort to prepare for and repel what they viewed as little more than an armed mob. Young intended to match blood with blood and resist the army at all costs:

> We are invaded by a hostile force, who are evidently assailing us to accomplish our overthrow and destruction. . . . We should not quietly stand still and see those fetters forging around us which are calculated to enslave us in subjection to an unlawful military despotism.

Paranoia and hysteria ran rampant among the Mormons. Men were pressed into militia service, and families prepared to abandon their homes and farms and businesses if necessary and readied themselves to relocate, either temporarily or permanently. One upshot of all the fear and upheaval and hatred was the September 11, 1857, murder of some 120 innocent California-bound pioneers at Mountain Meadows in the southwestern part of the Territory.

On the plains of what is now Wyoming, members of the Mormon militia, the Nauvoo Legion, met the expedition's supply trains and cattle herds. Mormon raiders burned wagons carrying tons of provisions for the troops marching behind, rustled a herd of cattle intended as beef for the soldiers, and established fortifications in Echo Canyon to turn back the army before it could reach the Salt Lake Valley. But the army did not try, opting instead to hunker down for a long, cold, hungry winter near the burned ruins of Fort Bridger.

As the soldiers shivered, secret negotiations between Young and Cumming defused the situation and an all-out shooting war was avoided—but barely. Young stepped aside, officially, and let Cumming (and his successors) pretend to govern the Territory. In reality, the Mormon leader was still in charge. In fact, from 1862 until 1870, he reorganized the State of Deseret in the form of a shadow government to ratify, in secret, the actions of the territorial legislature—just to ensure the laws were consistent with what the Saints considered the laws of the coming Kingdom of God.

Dissatisfied with the outcome of the expedition, General Johnston wrote in a letter that little had changed: "The theocracy exists, the obligations to which are in as full force now as before, the people are as much bound to go by Council now as before."

With secession of the southern states, formation of the Confederate States of America, and the Civil War, the army left Utah. But the war added to federal distrust of the Mormons. Utah Territory's location was a particular cause for concern, standing between the eastern states and the wealth of California and the silver mines in what would soon be Nevada, and maintaining communication was seen as essential to the war effort.

For his part Young maintained his distance from the conflict, favoring neither side. He was said to hope the warring nation would destroy itself, North and South, allowing the establishment of Zion and the long sought-after Kingdom of God. Among all the states and territories of the Union, only Utah failed to provide troops for the war, save a handful of volunteer ninety-day enlistments to protect mail routes through the territory.

That job, much to the dismay and dislike of the Mormons, was soon reassigned to the US Army, in the form of volunteer troops from California under command of Patrick Edward Connor. His soldiers wanted to fight the rebels, and the assignment to Utah Territory was an unwelcome disappointment. Connor wanted to use his troops to bring the disloyal Mormons into line. After visiting Salt Lake City ahead of the arrival of his army, he wrote:

> *I found them a community of traitors, murderers, fanatics, and whores. The people publicly rejoice at reverses to our arms, and thank God the American Government is gone, as they term it. . . . I intend to quietly intrench my position, and then say to the Saints of Utah, enough of your treason.*

Connor was thwarted in his intentions by his commander in chief. President Abraham Lincoln forbade any aggressive action against the Saints.

And so the California Volunteers were reduced to fighting Indians. But they made a job of it, perpetrating the deadliest massacre of Indians by the US Army in western history when they killed some 250 to 350 Shoshoni men, women, and children along the banks of the Bear River on January 29, 1863.

The Civil War also provided the impetus for the federal government to whittle away at Utah Territory. In 1861 it sliced off the eastern end and awarded it to Colorado. It cut off a large chunk of the western end to create Nevada, and gave that state two more slices in 1862 and 1866. In 1868 the northeastern corner of the territory was whittled out and awarded to Wyoming, finally creating borders that have held to the present.

Utah made repeated attempts at statehood through the years, but to no avail. The linking of the transcontinental railroad in 1869 ended the

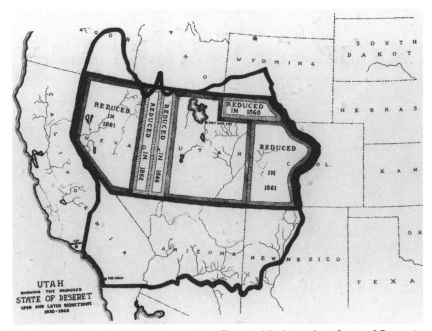

The US government whittled away at the Free and Independent State of Deseret until it became the state of Utah.

Territory's relative isolation from the rest of the nation. Cries for independence waned as the fight to maintain the practice of plural marriage waxed. Congress passed law after law outlawing it and forcing its demise. It was clear statehood would never be granted so long as Mormon men married multiple wives. The government, through legislative and court action, made it all but impossible for the church to survive unless it abandoned the practice. In 1890 Wilford Woodruff, then president of the church, issued a press release stating he would advise the members of the faith to abide by the law.

Six years later, on January 4, 1896, Utah became the forty-fifth star on the American flag. One of the first places in the West to be settled, "Deseret"—or what little was left of it—was nearly the last to be granted statehood.

Samuel Brannan: The Man Who Started the Gold Rush

1848—California

On January 24, 1848, Henry Bigler, a discharged Mormon Battalion member working on a crew building a mill for John Sutter in California, wrote in his diary, "This day some kind of mettle was found in the tail of the race that looks like goald."

James Marshall, ramrodding the crew, carried the "mettle" to Sutter's Fort, where he and his boss, Sutter, performed definitive tests to verify that what the workers had found in the mill race was, indeed, gold. Sutter and Marshall intended to keep the discovery secret, but that was not to be. By the time their tests were complete, other Battalion veterans had dished up more and more of the yellow metal at what would be one of the richest places in the coming gold rush, Mormon Island, as well as at several other sites. Still, for a time, reports of the strike were seen as rumor and speculation and did not spread far beyond the local area.

Until Sam Brannan let the cat out of the bag.

Before the year was out, men from Oregon, Mexico, Central America, and Hawaii were already arriving to strike it rich. Before the gold rush played out, more than three hundred thousand people would make their way to the goldfields, from the United States and several other countries. Yerba Buena, or San Francisco, was home to just two hundred people in 1846 before Brannan or the forty-niners arrived. By 1852 the city would host thirty-six thousand residents.

When Bigler wrote of the discovery in his diary, what is now California belonged to Mexico. However, US military forces fighting the Mexican-American War occupied and controlled the region, and within ten days of the find, on February 2, Mexico would cede the area to the United States when they signed the Treaty of Guadalupe Hidalgo.

A few weeks later, Sam Brannan would start the gold rush. Once he did, everything changed—including the history of America. And while the discovery of gold in California and its effects are well chronicled and familiar to most, the same cannot be said for the man who started the gold rush.

Brannan was born in Maine on March 2, 1819. At age fourteen he moved to Kirtland, Ohio, to join the Mormons—members of the Church of Jesus Christ of Latter-day Saints—gathering there. The church put him to work in its printing office, where he stayed for a few years before extending his experience working for printers throughout the region. In 1844 he went to New York City to edit and publish newspapers for the Mormon Church. He fell out with church leaders for a time in 1845, either owing to overzealousness in the emerging practice of taking multiple wives—in his case without benefit of marriage—or for backing the murdered prophet Joseph Smith's brother, William Smith, in his bid to assume leadership of the church. Brigham Young won that contest, but Brannan was soon welcomed back into the fold.

When Young and the Mormons were hounded out of their home at the time in Nauvoo, Illinois, and planning to seek refuge in the wide-open spaces out west, Brannan was authorized to gather as many New York Mormons as were willing and set sail for the west coast of the continent. The *Brooklyn*, with 238 Mormons aboard, got underway in February 1846 and rounded Cape Horn, apparently the first civilian craft to do so. Brannan saw to the spiritual well-being of the Saints on board, with a list of rules governing conduct, daily community prayer, and Sunday services.

The *Honolulu Friend* reported the ship's arrival there on July 1 and published information, provided by Brannan, about Mormon beliefs. During this visit Brannan also preached several public sermons. Of the leader the newspaper said,

He is a young man, about 27 years of age, a native of Saco, Maine, a printer by trade, he has resided for three years in the family of Joseph Smith, Jr., has been editor of a weekly newspaper in New York City called the New York Messenger, *and is intending to establish another paper on his arrival in California.*

On July 31, 1846, about six months after setting sail, the *Brooklyn* docked at Yerba Buena in San Francisco Bay. Intending to settle in Mexican territory, the refugees apparently expressed dismay to see the American flag flying there. Only three weeks earlier, with the Mexican-American War building up steam, the US Navy had seized the port. Despite the presence of armed forces from the nation they were fleeing, the Mormons disembarked, immediately tripling the population of the town that would become the city of San Francisco. Among the cargo was a printing press, with which Brannan published California's second and San Francisco's first newspaper, the *California Star*, with the first number issued August 15.

Brannan and his flock had no idea where Brigham Young and the thousands of other Saints leaving the United States were, so in 1847 he set out to find them. Crossing the Sierra Nevada, the deserts of the Great Basin, and the Wasatch Mountains, Brannan found Young and his "Pioneer Company" at the Green River in what is now Wyoming. Already a California booster, Brannan sang the praises of his adopted home and encouraged the Mormon leader to settle there. But Young had other ideas, intent on a building the Kingdom of God in the valley of the Great Salt Lake. Brannan went home, believing Young would see the error of his ways and follow him to California the next year.

Back home by fall, Brannan furthered his entrepreneurial interests by opening a store at Sutter's Fort at New Helvetia, which would become Sacramento. When he later heard rumors of the discovery of gold, he followed the gossip up the South Fork of the American River to Sutter's mill to see for himself. He filled a medicine bottle with gold and set out for San Francisco and, there, stood in the street, held the bottle aloft, and almost single-handedly started the California gold rush.

"Gold!" he yelled. "Gold! Gold from the American River!"

The fact that Brannan's general store at Sutter's Fort was the only mercantile of any significance between San Francisco and the goldfields may have played into his decision to publicize the big find, for he had stockpiled every pick and shovel and pan and other supply he could manage. He sold to the gold seekers at a handsome profit, reportedly pocketing $36,000 in just over two months. When the rush got underway full force in 1849, his store at Sutter's Fort was reportedly raking in as much as $5,000 a day and $150,000 a month. And by then it wasn't the only

The California gold rush made the man who started it, Samuel Brannan, California's first millionaire. COURTESY OF WILL BAGLEY

one—Brannan had opened other stores to mine the miners. The gold rush made Sam Brannan California's first millionaire.

Despite his earlier zeal, after arriving in California Brannan's religious activity waned. While still the leading Mormon in the region, he was slow to organize church congregations or otherwise see to the spiritual health of his people. His *California Star* newspaper, unlike his earlier publishing ventures, was expressly secular.

There seems to be one exception to his neglect of church duties—the collection of tithes and offerings from his fellow Saints, particularly those working the goldfields. While historians are not in agreement about his plans and purposes, there is no doubt that he collected money. There are contemporary reports that Brannan was collecting tithes for the church. Other accounts from the time call it a toll, or rent. Other evidence suggests Brannan collected a 30 percent cut from Mormon miners to secure titles to their claims—which he could not and did not do—and kept a third of it for his efforts. Then and now, many say Brannan wrongfully pocketed the money and used it for his own purposes.

Never mind the circumstances. Brannan's money gathering resulted in an oft-told tale that should be true, even if it isn't. According to the story, Brigham Young sent a delegation, including the notorious enforcer Porter Rockwell, to convince Brannan to turn over the tithing funds, as they were the Lord's money and belonged in church coffers. Brannan reportedly told the men he would gladly give up the money if they would produce a receipt signed by the Lord. When and where the story started is unknown. Some suggest Brannan himself spread it in later years for a laugh and to signify his departure from the Mormon Church.

What is certain is that in the spring of 1849, Young sent a group of Mormon leaders to California to, among other things, get money from Brannan for the church. The envoys delivered a letter from Young to Brannan that even specified the expected amount, and went on to "hint" at a further personal payment to Young himself.

I do not doubt that you have been blessed abundantly and now shall have it in your power to render most essential service. I shall expect ten thousand dollars, at least, your tithing . . . and if you have accumulated a million to tithe, so as to send $100,000.00, so much the better, and you may get two million next year. If you want to continue to prosper, do not forget the Lord's treasury, lest he forget you, and with the liberal, the Lord is liberal, and when you have settled with the treasury, I want you to remember that Bro. Brigham has long been destitute of a home, and suffered heavy losses and incurred great expenses in searching out a location and in planting the Church in this place, and he wants you to send him $20,000 (a present) in gold dust to help him with his labors. This is but a trifle where gold is so plentiful but it will do me much good at this time. . . . A hint to the wise is sufficient, so when this is accomplished you will have our united blessing. . . . But should you withhold when the Lord says give, your hope and pleasing prospects will be blasted in an hour you think not of, and no arm to save. But I am persuaded better things of Brother Brannan.

Brannan refused to part with any of his money, save, perhaps, giving $500 to one of the collectors, supposedly to gain his support. He did return some books to the church, but that seems to have ended his relationship with the Mormons for all practical purposes.

It was not, however, the end of Sam Brannan's influence in California. He sat on the first town council in San Francisco, established a school, developed real estate, dealt in international trade, was elected to the California state senate, opened banks, started a telegraph company, and organized and served with the San Francisco Committee of Vigilance. His reportedly violent activity as a vigilante, incidentally, was the reason given by the Mormon Church when he was officially cast out of its ranks in 1851.

Brannan also bought land and developed a resort he called Calistoga and lost a good deal of money building a railroad to reach it. A divorce in 1872 cost him half his fortune and doomed the rest of his empire, as his wife demanded her share in cash, which required selling off a lot of real estate. He built a brewery and may have drunk up the profits, for he developed a drinking problem that lasted for years.

Apparently having had his fill of San Francisco, Brannan relocated to San Diego and elsewhere in southern California and attempted to rebuild his fortune speculating in real estate. There are reports he was reduced to selling pencils on the street for a time. He died impoverished on May 5, 1889. The body of the man who started the gold rush lay unclaimed for about a year before being buried in a donated grave. His burial site was marked only by a stake for years until the installation of a headstone reading:

"SAM" BRANNAN

1819 1889

CALIFORNIA PIONEER OF '46

–DREAMER–LEADER–

AND

EMPIRE BUILDER

Before Civil Rights: The Chinese in America

1849—California

If you were living in southern China in the mid to late 1800s, you might well have noticed this handbill, or one like it, posted and distributed by agents and brokers in Hong Kong whose task it was to recruit workers for American jobs:

> *Americans are very rich people. They want the Chinaman to come and make him very welcome. There you will have great pay, large houses, and food and clothing of the finest description. You can write to your friends or send them money at any time and we will be responsible to the safe delivery. It is a nice country, without mandarins or soldiers. All alike; big man no larger than little man. There are a great many Chinamen there now, and it will not be a strange country. China god is there, and the agents of this house. Never fear, and you will be lucky.*

The lure was strong. The economy in China was in shambles. Opium wars, the loss of territory to foreign powers, disastrous floods, and widespread poverty made the opportunity to emigrate and grow rich irresistible for many. Thousands of young men answered the call, sometimes individually, sometimes in groups, and sometimes an entire village's young men were sent in attempts to save the community and secure its future with American riches.

Some were able to finance the journey themselves and others relied on relatives or the community, but recruiting agents paid the way for many. Once in America, they repaid the agents from their earnings.

Chinese emigration to America started as early as the 1820s, but the numbers were few until the California gold rush. During the 1850s some fifteen thousand came to Gam Saan, or "Gold Mountain." Construction of the Central Pacific railroad brought more, so that by the early 1880s there were three hundred thousand Chinese immigrants living in America, most in California. Most were working men. According to an 1850 report, there were 4,018 Chinese men and seven Chinese women in San Francisco; the ratio in California in 1852 was 1,685 men to every woman (women made up only 2 percent of the Chinese population in America); by 1890 the share of females was still less than 5 percent.

At the beginning of the gold rush, Chinese miners fared well. But as more whites arrived, Asians were victims of violence, ore was stolen, and Chinese miners were driven off their claims. As a result, Chinese miners congregated in camps, worked claims in groups, and reworked areas already mined and abandoned by others—often with rich results. And they stayed with it—while other gold seekers were likely to rush off to the next big strike, many Chinese miners kept working the California goldfields until, by 1870, one-third of the miners there were Chinese.

Officially sanctioned discrimination against Chinese miners started in 1852 when California lawmakers assessed a tax on foreign miners of three dollars a month. The tax was rescinded in 1870, but more severe inequities would come.

Many Chinese left mining to build the Central Pacific Railroad as it worked its way east to link up with the Union Pacific and form the transcontinental railroad. Hiring Chinese workers saved money on labor costs—as much as one-third—and they were in no position to negotiate for the safe working conditions white laborers demanded. In addition to hiring Chinese workers already in the area, the railroad recruited thousands more in China. As many as eleven thousand Chinese were on the Central Pacific payroll during the heyday of building the railroad.

The Burlingame Treaty of 1868 welcomed Chinese immigration. The agreement granted China "most favored nation" status and supposedly guaranteed the rights of Chinese workers in America:

Chinese subjects visiting or residing in the United States, shall enjoy the same privileges, immunities, and exemptions in respect to travel or residence, as may there be enjoyed by the citizens or subjects of the most favored nation.

But while the rights of the Chinese were protected by treaty, the reality of life in America for Chinese workers was much different. Laws forbade a Chinese person from testifying against a white person in court, restricted land ownership, criminalized marriage between whites and Chinese, and denied citizenship to Chinese immigrants.

In addition to such broad, far-reaching laws were numerous regulations controlling—or prohibiting—actions of everyday life and work among the Chinese. At various times over the years, laws were enacted that denied Chinese children admission to public schools in San Francisco, forbade the admission of Chinese people to hospitals, banned street salesmen peddling vegetables from carrying them with a pole, criminalized the setting off of firecrackers and ringing of gongs, required queues be cut off Chinese men when they were arrested, disallowed Chinese from commercial fishing or using nets to catch fish, and prohibited ironing clothes in all-night laundries.

Yick Wo fought one such law all the way to the United States Supreme Court—and won. San Francisco passed a law prohibiting the operation of a laundry business in a wooden building without a special permit. With the threat of fire, the idea seems reasonable enough on its face. It is worth noting that nearly all laundries were in wooden buildings at the time, and two-thirds of them were owned and operated by Chinese entrepreneurs. When non-Chinese launderers applied for the permits, all but one was granted. Chinese applications were all denied. Yick Wo continued working without a permit and was convicted of violating the ordinance. He appealed. The Supreme Court found in his favor in an 1886 ruling that says, in part:

The rights of the petitioners, as affected by the proceeding of which they complain, are not less because they are aliens and subjects of the Emperor of China.

The Fourteenth Amendment to the Constitution is not confined to the protection of citizens. It says: "Nor shall any State deprive any person of life, liberty, or property without due process of law; nor deny to any person within its jurisdiction the equal protection of the laws.". . .

The facts shown establish an administration directed so exclusively against a particular class of persons as to warrant and require the conclusion that, whatever may have been the intent of the ordinances as adopted, they are applied with a mind so unequal and oppressive as to amount to a practical denial by the State of equal protection.

Despite such official guarantees of rights as spelled out by the Supreme Court and the Burlingame Treaty, discrimination against the Chinese heated up during the 1870s, and racist violence was commonplace. White workers accused Chinese laborers of stealing their jobs and depressing wages, and agitated for government and public action against the Asians.

In 1878 a plea from the president and secretary of the Workingman's Party of California, Dennis Kearney and H. L. Knight, was published in newspapers in California and across the country. After complaining of government corruption, greed, the rule of "moneyed men" over working men, and other societal ills, the appeal takes aim at the Chinese.

To add to our misery and despair, a bloated aristocracy has sent to China—the greatest and oldest despotism in the world—for a cheap working slave. It rakes the slums of Asia to find the meanest slave on earth—the Chinese coolie—and imports him here to meet the free American in the Labor market, and still further widen the breach between the rich and the poor, still further to degrade white Labor.

These cheap slaves fill every place. Their dress is scant and cheap. Their food is rice from China. They hedge twenty in a room, ten by ten. They are whipped curs, abject in docility, mean, contemptible and obedient in all things. They have no wives, children or dependents. . . .

The father of a family is met by them at every turn. Would he get work for himself? Ah! A stout Chinaman does it cheaper. Will he get a place for his oldest boy? He can not. His girl? Why, the Chinaman is in her place too! Every door is closed. He can only go to crime or suicide,

This advertisement for a washing machine is indicative of public attitudes concerning Chinese immigrants in the late nineteenth century. LIBRARY OF CONGRESS

his wife and daughter to prostitution, and his boys to hoodlumism and the penitentiary. . . .

California must be all American or all Chinese. We are resolved that it shall be American, and are prepared to make it so. May we not rely upon your sympathy and assistance?

During the 1879 Constitutional Convention in California, page after page of articles and subsections and amendments concerning the Chinese presence in the state were proposed and discussed and implemented or discarded. Among these, perhaps the most telling and certainly the most succinct is this offering that still resides in the California State Archives:

Proposed Amendment to the Constitution
Resolved: "The Chinese must go"

Popular culture, too, shows evidence of racist and discriminatory attitudes about the Chinese in America. Popular writer Brett Harte wrote of a crooked card game involving two white men and a Chinese man called "Ah Sin" in a humorous—but nonetheless racist—1871 poem titled "The Heathen Chinee." The final stanza reads:

> Which is why I remark,
> And my language is plain,
> That for ways that are dark,
> And for tricks that are vain,
> The heathen Chinee is peculiar,—
> Which the same I am free to maintain.

It only got worse for Chinese immigrants in the 1880s. The 1882 Chinese Exclusion Act put the brakes on immigration. No more Chinese were allowed into the country, and those already here were denied citizenship. The act was the first time in American history the federal government limited—or eliminated—an ethnic group's admittance to the United States. The law, when passed, was to stand for a decade. It was extended another ten years in 1892 and in 1902 made permanent. This is how it begins:

Whereas in the opinion of the Government of the United States the coming of Chinese laborers to this country endangers the good order of certain localities within the territory thereof: Therefore,
    Be it enacted by the Senate and House of Representatives of the United States of America in Congress assembled, That from and after the expiration of ninety days next after the passage of this act, and

until the expiration of ten years next after the passage of this act, the coming of Chinese laborers to the United States be, and the same is hereby, suspended; and during such suspension it shall not be lawful for any Chinese laborer to come, or having so come after the expiration of said ninety days to remain within the United States.

Section 14 of the act reads:

That hereafter no State court or court of the United States shall admit Chinese to citizenship; and all laws in conflict with this act are hereby repealed.

Discriminatory laws against Chinese workers, who "endanger the good order of certain localities," continued until 1943, when the Chinese Exclusion Act was repealed in favor of the Magnuson Act. With its passage Chinese people living in the United States were allowed to gain citizenship. Chinese immigration also returned—at least for the 105 people who were allowed to enter the country each year.

Various discriminatory laws against the Chinese in numerous communities continued into the 1950s; they were not officially laid to rest until the civil rights movement of the 1960s and the Civil Rights Act of 1965. While such blatantly racist discrimination seems distasteful, and perhaps quaint, in our time, such practices grew from attitudes that were widespread in the nineteenth century. The great orator Thomas Hart Benton, US senator from Missouri and proponent of Manifest Destiny, said this about the Chinese (he also made contemptuous statements about other racial and ethnic groups) in an 1846 speech to Congress supporting the United States' claim to Oregon:

It would seem that the White race alone received the divine command to subdue and replenish the earth: for it is the only race that has obeyed it. . . .

The Mongolian, or Yellow race, is there, four hundred millions in number spreading almost to Europe; a race once the foremost of the human family in the arts of civilization, but torpid and stationary for thousands of years. It is a race far above the Ethiopian, or Black—above the Malay, or Brown, (if we admit five races)—and above the American Indian, or Red; it is a race far above these, but still far below the White, and, like all the rest, must receive an impression from the superior race whenever they come in contact.

Given the prevalence of such attitudes at the time, it is perhaps understandable—if not forgivable—that for more than a century Chinese immigrants didn't have "a Chinaman's chance" of taking their rightful place in American history.

Dear Sir: Corresponding via the Jackass Mail

1851–1860—California and the Great Basin

The year 1848 is, arguably, the most pivotal year of them all in the establishment of the American West. True, the 1803 Louisiana Purchase added some 827,000 square miles to the United States and led to the acquisition of the Oregon country, which added yet more.

But 1848 brought the end of Mexican War and the Treaty of Guadalupe Hidalgo, which added 525,000 square miles to the nation, including what are now the states of California, New Mexico, Arizona, Nevada, Utah, and parts of Wyoming and Colorado. That year also saw the discovery of gold in California, which did more to populate the West than any and all other events put together. Within a year the few thousand settlers in Oregon and California and the Mormon pioneers in Utah were joined by tens of thousands of Americans in or on their way to California to seek fortunes in the goldfields.

When they got there they were, for all practical purposes, cut off from the settled parts of America, even though government post offices were opened in California even before the calendar turned on the year 1848. Writing home meant your letter boarded a steamship on the coast and made its way to Panama to be carried overland across the fifty-mile isthmus to the Caribbean shore to await a steamship to New York for distribution through the postal system.

Estimated time of arrival: three months—give or take.

The reply, at best, took just as long. So, father or brother, uncle or son, cousin or grandfather in the goldfields may well hear nothing of family, friends, births, deaths, weddings, or other news of interest for half a year or more. And that's just on a personal level. Governments and businesses faced essentially the same obstacles to communication, with larger-scale consequences.

It was, of course, an untenable situation.

And so Congress authorized, in 1850, four mail routes to open and maintain more regular, more timely communication with the West Coast of the now continental nation as well as the newly acquired lands along the way.

Since mail service from the east to Salt Lake City was well established, a route extending from there to California was the obvious choice to lead the way. George Chorpenning declared himself the man for the job.

Born in Somerset, Pennsylvania, in 1820, Chorpenning joined the wave of California-bound gold hunters in 1850. As for so many of his kind, riches—even a living—proved elusive, and the contract to carry mail looked enticing. He partnered with a man named Absalom Woodward and signed an agreement to move the mail between Sacramento and Salt Lake City, in both directions, once a month for a year in return for payment of $14,000. The initial route crossed the Sierra to Mormon Station, now Genoa, then struck out for and followed the Humboldt River across what is now northern Nevada, angled northeasterly across northern Utah until east of the Great Salt Lake, then south to Salt Lake City. In good weather the trip, just over nine hundred miles, took about sixteen days to accomplish.

Chorpenning loaded mules—hence the name "Jackass Mail," by which his service was known—and set out from Sacramento on May 3, 1851, on the inaugural trip and made it across the mountains and deserts to Salt Lake City as planned. His partner's luck wasn't as good. On his first trip Woodward strayed from the rest of his party, and Indians nearly captured him. He was also attacked by Indians on the return trip in August, but managed to escape again. Woodward set out from California to Utah on the November run but this time did not arrive. His remains were found the following spring, but the mail was gone.

Other carriers suffered similar hazards. Indians claimed the lives of two in September 1851. On an October trip the mailmen managed to escape an attack by Indians, but did so at the expense of the mail, which they left behind in the fracas.

Despite the dangers and difficulties and the loss of his partner, Chorpenning opted to keep at it. Then winter hit.

Snow depths in the Sierra Nevada have been recorded in excess of seventy feet, and accumulations of twenty feet and more are not uncommon. Travel in such conditions is obviously difficult, and often impossible. There are reports that Chorpenning and his men built giant wooden mallets to pound down the snow by hand to firm up a trail so the mules of the Jackass Mail wouldn't bog down in the deep snow. High-country landmarks tend to disappear under the snow, as well, concealing even the most familiar routes. Severe storms, frigid winds, and freezing temperatures further complicate travel.

The December 1851 and January 1852 mule trains had to turn back. Chorpenning sent the mail farther north to try Feather River Canyon and Beckwourth Pass. The mail got through, but winter conditions and the detour more than tripled the length of the trip to some two months, which was more than either men or mules could tolerate on a regular basis. In fact, some of the mules did not survive and ended up providing fodder for the hungry mail carriers.

Chorpenning tried another route—this time, by sea. He sent the mail by ship from San Francisco to San Pedro in southern California, whence it went muleback up the Old Spanish Trail and on to an extended trail built by Mormons from southern Utah to Salt Lake City.

The accumulated difficulties were added to by complaints from folks in California about slow and inconsistent mail delivery. Chorpenning lost the contract briefly, but a trip to see the postmaster general in Washington, DC, won it back and, over time, extended the contract, extended the routes, increased his pay, and added stagecoaches and passenger service on some routes.

His final contract was inked in 1858, the terms of which required Chorpenning to carry mail between Placerville, California, and Salt Lake City, Utah, with arrivals and departures every two weeks and, later, weekly. Late in 1858 Chorpenning switched to a new, more direct route across the Great Basin from the eastern slope of the Sierra Nevada at Carson City to the western slope of the Wasatch Mountains at Salt Lake City. The trail was pioneered, in part, by Captain E. G. Beckwith, who led a US Army mapping expedition in 1854, and by Mormon explorer Howard Egan.

Egan, along with a few other Mormons, left Salt Lake City muleback one day in 1855 and followed Beckwith's general route across the Great Basin to the Humboldt River at Lassen Meadows, near today's Lovelock, Nevada, then followed the well-traveled California Trail over the Sierra to Sacramento. Egan made the trip in just ten days. Later, in 1859, Captain James Simpson of the US Army Corps of Topographical Engineers would survey much of the same trail and reroute other portions. Simpson's route led the way for the Overland Stage and Pony Express through much of Utah Territory—which included most of Nevada at the time. Still, Beckwith, Egan, and Chorpenning deserve some measure of credit for blazing the trail that hastened travel across the deserts and mountains of the Great Basin.

The new trail served Chorpenning well for most of the year, and he built a string of stations along the way that long outlasted the Jackass Mail. Still, even with the new route, winter in the Sierra Nevada continued to pose a challenge.

Now comes another character in this tale: John "Snowshoe" Thompson.

A Norwegian immigrant born April, 30, 1827, in Tinn, Telemark County, Jon Torsteinson-Rue came to America at age ten and lived at times in Illinois, Missouri, Iowa, and Wisconsin. Like Chorpenning and countless other young men in those days, Jon got bitten by the gold bug and hit the trail—following a herd of milk cows—for California in 1851. He dug gold for a time and pocketed enough money to go into ranching. Somewhere along the way, Jon Torsteinson-Rue simplified and Americanized his name to become John Thompson.

But when remembered at all in the history of the West, he is known as Snowshoe Thompson.

Sometime during the winter of 1855, in the midst of the Jackass Mail's difficulties crossing the snowbound Sierra, Thompson saw a newspaper ad placed by the postmaster in Placerville, calling for someone to pack the mail over the mountains to Carson Valley. Thompson took up the challenge.

Vague memories from his childhood included the snowshoes he used as a boy in Norway. Snowshoes is a misnomer nowadays, but in Thompson's time, the boards he strapped to his feet were known by that term. And calling them boards accurately describes his skis, as well as understates the case. Thompson's skis, which he made himself from sturdy oak, were reportedly ten feet long and some four inches wide and weighed twenty-five pounds. He also crafted a ski pole of sorts, a lengthy rod held horizontally in both hands that served more to provide balance when speeding down the slopes than anything else. And speed he did—in certain places he reportedly exceeded sixty miles an hour, and he was sometimes airborne for as much as one hundred feet.

And that with a pack on his back containing mail weighing sixty, eighty, or even a hundred pounds. Thompson made the trip over the mountains from Placerville to Carson Valley in three days and made it back in just two, as the western slope of the Sierra was tougher to climb going eastward, but offered more opportunities to ski with gravity when westbound. He seldom stopped for any length of time, carried little food and no gun, and never lost his way.

For twenty years Thompson skied the Sierra with a mailbag on his back. Besides mail he carried all manner of items, from books and newspapers to medicine and clothing. Thompson is said to have carried the first ore samples from the Comstock Lode to assayers in California, and the type and newsprint that gave Virginia City's *Territorial Enterprise* its start.

In 1858 Chorpenning hired Thompson to pack mail over the mountains when winter conditions made it impossible for his mules or coaches to navigate the Sierra.

Chorpenning's four-year contract, signed in 1858, didn't last beyond 1860. Behind the change was a new postmaster general, who believed the post office ought to pay its own way. He slashed service on the highly subsidized western routes, including those operated by Chorpenning, in half. Service suffered, as did those who provided the service. Reduction of the contract, along with late payments from the government, forced Chorpenning into bankruptcy. For more than twenty-five years, Chorpenning fought with the government to recoup his losses. In 1870 Congress

The Pony Express came after the Jackass Mail in an attempt to speed up mail
service, but it was soon replaced with the telegraph. LIBRARY OF CONGRESS

agreed to reevaluate the situation and determined they owed Chorpenning nearly $500,000, but the next Congress repealed that resolution and
reinvestigated Chorpenning's claims. The mess ended up in the lap of the
Supreme Court, which in 1876 determined that, for a variety of reasons
mired in legal gobbledygook, Chorpenning would get nothing.

Back in 1860, when Chorpenning's contract was cancelled, William
Russell, of the Russell, Majors and Waddell conglomerate, took over
and formed the Central Overland California and Pikes Peak Express
Company. The contract stretched the company's stagecoach and express
lines, which already reached Salt Lake City, on to California. When
Russell established the short-lived but romantic Pony Express to hasten mail from St. Joseph, Missouri, to Sacramento, California, many
of Chorpenning's way stations across the Great Basin served as home
stations for the Pony Express's ambitious network, which at its peak
included some 190 home and swing stations, more than four hundred
horses, and eighty riders.

The Pony Express lasted only about a year and a half and was a financial disaster. The transcontinental telegraph, which followed Chorpenning's route across much of the Great Basin, linked up in Salt Lake City
on October 18, 1861. Two days later the Pony Express shut down.

Of the four mail routes to California originally authorized in 1850, only Chorpenning's Jackass Mail on the central route and the Butterfield Route—from St. Louis, Missouri, and Memphis, Tennessee, through present-day Oklahoma and Texas to San Antonio, El Paso, Tucson, Yuma, Los Angeles, and San Francisco—were of much note. With the completion of the transcontinental railroad in 1869, all the mail routes to California authorized in 1850 were disbanded.

After losing the Jackass Mail, George Chorpenning returned to the eastern states, where he organized military regiments for Civil War service and served as a major and colonel in the Union army. He died in New York City on April 3, 1894. An obituary in the hometown newspaper of his youth, the Somerset, Pennsylvania, *Herald*, said, "He was the first man to carry the United States mails across the continent."

Ships of the Southwest Desert: Camels Join the Army

1856—Texas

Had you been at the wharf in Indianola, Texas, on May 13, 1856, you would have witnessed a curious sight. On that day the US Army unloaded thirty-three camels, along with one Turk and six Arab handlers. The camels had been aboard the naval ship *Supply* since sailing from the Mediterranean port of Smyrna on February 15, 1856, and according to reports were so overjoyed—or frightened—at once again setting foot on dry land that they went berserk. Handlers were all but helpless as the dromedaries jerked and kicked, lunged and bucked, reared and wrestled at halters and lead ropes, some of which broke.

The camels were the first shipment—there would be a second—to arrive in the United States as part of an army test of the animal's ability to pack supplies and pursue hostile Indians in the deserts of the Southwest.

It was an idea that had cropped up from time to time in military and political discussions. As early as 1836, US Army Major George H. Crosman floated the idea of using camels in Florida in attempts to track down Indians, believing the camels' endurance would give the soldiers a distinct advantage. Crosman made little headway outside of putting an idea in circulation that later aroused the interest of Major Henry C. Wayne, who studied the notion in detail and pursued it tirelessly.

Jefferson Davis, US senator from Mississippi and chairman of the Senate Committee on Military Affairs, joined the effort but made little headway in Congress. Before abandoning the Union to become president of the secessionist Confederate States of America, Davis served as secretary of war under President Franklin Pierce beginning in 1853 and, with the influence of that office, gained traction for the idea. The camel's appeal to Crosman, Wayne, Davis, and other supporters is understandable given the animal's qualities and the situation facing the nation.

Much of the land lately gained in the Mexican-American War through the Treaty of Guadalupe Hidalgo was arid desert, rugged and rocky, and thinly populated by Indian tribes with no more interest in their current landlords than they had in the previous. Bringing the tribes to heel was a concern to the secretary of war, and the notion of employing camels as pack animals in the attempt to subdue the territory appealed to him. He lobbied Congress at length, employing such logic in his appeals as, "On the older continents, in regions reaching from the torrid to the frozen zones, embracing arid plains and precipitous mountains covered with snow, camels are used with the best results." The 1853 campaign for funding proved fruitless, but Davis kept at it, trying again in late 1854.

I again invite attention to the advantages to be anticipated from the use of camels and dromedaries for military purposes, and, for reasons set forth in my last annual report, recommend that appropriation be made to introduce a number of the several varieties of this animal to test their adaptation to our country.

After the usual wrangling and deal-making between the House of Representatives and Senate, Congress appropriated $30,000 in 1855 for use by "the War Department in the purchase of camels and the importation of dromedaries, to be employed for military purposes."

As soon as possible, Davis dispatched the US Navy ship *Supply*, under command of Lieutenant David D. Porter, with Wayne aboard, to the Mediterranean and various Levantine cities to determine the best course of action, acquire camels, learn the finer points of their use and care, and bring them home. They boarded their first camels at Tunis, primarily to learn how to load camels onto the ship and how to accommodate them during the long voyage to America. Three camels came as a gift from the local leader. Two were later sold out of fear of spreading disease, but the third would be with the ship for the next nine months and then disembark in Texas in fine fettle. The ship made other stops in Constantinople, Alexandria, and Smyrna.

Wayne and Porter compared the qualities of Bactrian and Arabian camels—usually called dromedaries, but there was a distinction based on use in those days. The one-humped dromedary, they learned, typically carried loads in the neighborhood of six hundred pounds, and hauled the burden some twenty-five to thirty miles a day. The two-humped Bactrian camel, larger and stronger, carried more than twice as much weight, but was slower and more difficult to load given the double humps. The two breeds can be crossed, resulting, as with the mule, in nonbreeding offspring called a booghdee, the male of which was a Tuilu and the female a Maya. The booghdee gets size and strength from the Bactrian father and the single hump from the Arab mother.

When the *Supply* set sail from Smyrna, it carried thirty-three camels, comprising thirty single-humped dromedaries, one calf, and two Bactrian males for breeding purposes. The thirty-third camel, a Tuilu, proved a challenge. The male booghdee was enormous, standing seven feet five, measuring nine feet nine inches around and ten feet long, and weighing in at a ton. A hole had to be cut in the deck—which was the roof of the camels' quarters—for the Tuilu's huge hump. The cost of the camels ranged from around $100 to $400, with $250 as the average price.

Porter took the well-being of his live cargo seriously, establishing rigorous rules for their care and feeding. Stalls were mucked out every day. Each camel's daily ration consisted of ten pounds of hay and a gallon each of oats and water. The animals were curried and brushed and their feet inspected daily.

The voyage was a rough one, with high seas and storms so severe the camels spent a good deal of the time on their knees, as their caretakers feared the buffeting of the ship might cause injury if they were allowed to stand. Camels died and calves were born en route, but the *Supply* reached the Texas coast on May 13, 1856, with thirty-four live and healthy camels—one more than it started with.

With some two-thirds of the appropriation unspent, the *Supply* charted a course for a return voyage to the Levantine ports within a month, with $10,000 to purchase more camels. That shipment would yield forty-one animals, which arrived the following February. Also on that voyage was a camel handler named Hadgi Ali, called "Hi Jolly," who would become a legendary resident of the Southwest owing to his work with camels and other endeavors until he died in 1902.

The camels soon lined out for Camp Verde, near San Antonio, which would be headquarters for the army's experiment. Wherever the animals went, fascinated crowds gathered to witness demonstrations of all kinds, from watching the camels simply kneel and stand to more involved displays. One story claims some of the camels got haircuts in Victoria, Texas, and a woman there knit a pair of camel hair socks that were presented to President Franklin Pierce. Another story has Wayne burdening a kneeling camel with more than 1,200 pounds in front of a skeptical audience. But the camel, on command, easily got to its feet and walked away with the load.

Not all the camels' activities were in fun, however, as Secretary Davis indicated in his 1856 annual report to Congress:

> *The capacity of the camel for traveling over steep acclivities and on muddy roads was tested with the most satisfactory result. Instead of making the detour rendered necessary by the location of the road to avoid a rugged mountain impracticable for wagons, the camels followed a trail which passed directly over it and, a heavy rain occurring while they were at the depot to which they had been sent for supplies, the road was rendered so muddy that it was considered impassable for loaded wagons. The train of camels were nevertheless loaded with an average of 323 pounds each and returned to their encampment, a distance of 60 miles, in two days, suffering, as it is reported, no interruption or unusual fatigue from the mud over which they passed or the torrents of rain which fell upon them. These tests fully realize the anticipations entertained of their usefulness in the transportation of military supplies. The experiment of introducing them into the climate of the United States has been confined to the southern frontier of Texas. Thus far the result is as favorable as the most sanguine could have hoped.*

The experiment suffered a setback when President James Buchanan took office March 4, 1857. Under his administration John B. Floyd was named secretary of war, replacing the enthusiastic Jefferson Davis. Major Henry C. Wayne, who saw to the details of the scheme, was transferred from Texas to Washington, DC, to serve in the office of the quartermaster general.

But the experiment did not die, as Floyd took up the torch and promoted expansion of the program. Later that year, industrious navy lieutenant Edward Fitzgerald Beale was sent to survey and open a wagon road from Fort Defiance in New Mexico to the border between Arizona and California on the Colorado River. Beale was issued twenty-five of the Texas camels for use in building the road. The job was a success, and so were the camels. Beale reported, "An important part in all of our operations has been acted by the camels. Without the aid of this noble and useful brute, many hardships which we have been spared would have fallen to our lot."

After finishing the road, Beale, as enthusiastic a supporter as the camels ever had, continued to test their capabilities—including their ability to withstand cold. After a January 1858 visit to the high country at the southern end of the Sierra Nevada, his journal reports:

> *The camels . . . I had placed in camp within a few hundred yards of the summit of the Sierra Nevada, and to this date they had lived in two or three feet of snow, fattening and thriving wonderfully all the while. Lately, in a terrible snowstorm, the wagon, carrying provisions to the camp, could proceed no further. The camels were immediately sent to the rescue, and brought the load through the snow and ice to camp, though the six strong mules of the team were unable to extricate the empty wagon.*

In June 1860 US Army lieutenant William H. Echols of the Topographical Engineers subjected camels to a test as hot and dry as his naval counterpart's trial had been cold and wet. Echols described his extended reconnaissance of the Big Bend Country in his journal, which he later submitted as a report to Congress. It begins:

*I left San Antonio on the 11th instant with orders to resume the recon-
naissance commenced last year of that portion of northwestern Texas lying
between the San Antonio or El Paso road, the Rio Grande and Pecos rivers, with twenty camels and twenty five pack mules, with an escort under
the command of Lieutenant Holman, first infantry, of twenty infantry
men, reinforced by eleven from Camp Hudson on my arrival at that post.*

The journey lasted more than sixty days, and Echols's almost daily
entries recorded time and distance, weather, road conditions, topography,
availability of grass for grazing, presence of water, wildlife, Indian activity, injuries, mishaps, and virtually everything else that happened on the
expedition in mind-numbing detail. Some of the information he recorded
told about the camels—their performance, health, difficulties, and recom-
mendations for future consideration.

June 30
*Whilst ascending to the Mesa two camels fell and bursted two of the
kegs and injured several others, wasting about forty gallons of our
most appreciated loading. The animals I believe are not injured. One
of them lost its foothold, fell, and pulled the others from the trail by the
rope attaching the train. Others might have suffered the same fate but
for the timely assistance of Lieutenant Holman, who cut the lead line.
During the ascent they had to resort to their feat of walking on their
knees, which they do when the inclination of the trail is very great and
heavily laden, to throw the center of gravity equally over the four legs,
or on a slipping trail when their feet slip from under them.*

July 1
*Our mules will not fare well no forage and a very limited supply of
water. The camels have performed most admirably to-day. No such
march as this could be made with any security without them.*

July 2
*This is the fourth day since the camels drank, which was at the Pecos,
brackish water, the same that we have, not only brackish, but when*

the bung is taken from a barrel a stench proceeds; it contains so much filth and impurity, and being barreled so long. The camels display quite a thirst.

July 4

Thus, and most joyfully, too, have we celebrated this memorable day; if it ever would have been, now, never will it escape having its anniversary remembered; the camp resounds with "hurrah for the 4th." The animals exhibited a remarkable knowledge of approaching water some time before reaching it, particularly the camels, which made a remarkable change in their speed ten miles from it. They had to be held back to keep them with the mules that before had been leading them. . . . After marching four miles, we encountered one of the highest, roughest, and most difficult descents we have met, which required a long while to overcome. One of the camels fell, notwithstanding great caution was taken with them, but not hurt.

July 10

Camels doing finely, no indication of having undergone any severities.

July 25

The camels are getting on pretty well. We have only sixteen mules in the command, for riding purposes only; one or two of them are very slow.

July 30

The camels were without water three days; the mules also, except a very limited supply last night; both are beginning to show exhaustion; the mules are lame and halt; the camels have several sore feet; their soles have actually been abraded off to the quick by the sharp cragged rocks, and others have very sore backs, indeed; holes in the humps are large enough to thrust in both fists; these sores do not injure them so much, being in the fleshy part of the hump, so long as they can be kept from the bones. I would recommend to any one using the camels over rough country, in case of tender feet, to shoe them with a piece of *(circular) raw hide, gather around the leg by a slipping cord; this will be found an absolute necessity in some instances.*

August 2
Now the condition of the animals is even worse, nearly every mule barefooted and lame, or exhausted, several of the camels almost unable to march at all from tender feet. We have water in our barrels, but to attempt the trip would be at the expense of several, both mules and camels. We will have to go to Fort Stockton to leave those that cannot go and have the mules shod.

As the Echols report shows, the camels experienced serious difficulties on the trip—but it appears they fared considerably better than the mules and, perhaps, better than the men. With proven performance on the Beale and Echols expeditions and other uses, and the support of influential leaders in the military and government, the camel experiment seemed a success, with use of the beasts of burden destined for widespread use by the military in the West.

But it was not to be.

There were detractors. Most, it seems, were opposed to the camels owing to their exotic nature and unfamiliarity with their ways. The army's muleskinners and packers disliked the camels and, as soldiers and civilian contractors can be, were loud and long in their complaints. The camels also frightened mules and horses until they grew accustomed to their presence. The camels could, and did, cause chaos in many of the towns and camps they passed through. It is likely this difficulty would have been overcome with time and familiarity. The spreading railway network also limited the practicality of livestock transport, whether by camels, mules, horses, or oxen.

The barrier that could not be overcome was the Civil War, which proved an understandable distraction for military and government leaders for years to come, as well as a sink for any and all resources, both human and monetary. Most of the camels, headquartered at Camp Verde, with others at Fort Bliss and Fort Yuma, came under Confederate control following Texas's secession from the Union. The rebels abandoned many of the forts around the Southwest and, for the most part, ignored the camels. Some were sold at auction to private buyers; others simply wandered away.

After the war the government gathered some of the wandering charges and sold them at auction. Among the buyers was Edward Beale, who kept camels at Tejon Ranch. Other private buyers used the camels for packing, exhibited them in circuses, or simply kept them as curiosities.

As for those that were turned out or not recaptured, camels were seen wandering the West for many years. Some did not stray far from towns and overland trails, showing up at inopportune times and stampeding cattle, frightening mules, upsetting freight wagons, and causing other mischief. Some were shot and killed by angry freighters.

Camel sightings were reported in remote southwestern deserts for decades, and wandering dromedaries became the stuff of legend. One, the "Red Ghost," was said to carry the bones of a dead rider on its back and was accused of stomping a woman to death. Prospectors claimed camel sightings near Death Valley in 1891, and that same year camels wandered out of the desert near Harrisburg, Arizona, and stampeded a herd of cattle. Rail passengers reported seeing camels in the Arizona desert in the 1890s, and one was struck and killed by a train in 1901.

Just when the last of the army camels—or their descendants—was spotted in the wild cannot be determined with any degree of accuracy. Some say it was in 1901 along the Mexican border, others claim a sighting near Wickenburg, Arizona, in 1913, and there's a report of camels stampeding horses in the California desert in 1929.

The camel experiment is memorialized at the grave of "Hi Jolly," the most famous of their handlers, in Quartzite, Arizona. The grave marker is a pyramid topped by the silhouette of a single-humped dromedary. A plaque briefly describes the use of camels by the US Army and offers this fitting conclusion: "Officially, the camel experiment was a failure, but both Lt. Beale and Major Wayne were enthusiastic in praise of the animals. A fair trial might have resulted in complete success."

American Royalty: Emperor Norton I

1859—San Francisco

From the beginning America has been governed, not ruled. Our country was settled and founded largely from a distaste for royalty and monarchy and aristocracy and the like. And so our leaders have been presidents and governors, mayors and legislators rather than kings and queens, princes and lords, dukes and dictators.

Except, that is, for one brief period in our history, from 1859 through 1880, when our nation was ruled by Norton I, Emperor of the United States and Protector of Mexico.

Or so he thought.

The circumstances of the birth of Joshua Abraham Norton are sketchy. Most accounts say he was born in England, while a few suggest Scotland or perhaps South Africa. He was probably born in 1818, though it may have been 1811 or 1814 or 1819. His parents were John and Sarah Norton, although the emperor is said to have claimed on one occasion that those parents were mere stand-ins, and that he was actually of the Bourbon line, descended from the kings who ruled France for nearly two centuries. And there were claims he was the son of Napoleon III.

It is fairly certain that, whatever his origins, Joshua Norton was raised in South Africa. Along with tens of thousands of other men from every corner of the world, he arrived in San Francisco in 1849. But rather than seek wealth in the goldfields, he set up shop as a merchant and dealt in real estate in the city, parlaying a $40,000 inheritance into a $250,000 fortune.

All went well until, in 1852, he gambled on rice. Prices skyrocketed owing to a Chinese embargo, so Norton purchased an entire shipload of the grain bound from Peru, hoping to profit from scarcity. Unfortunately, several other shiploads of Peruvian rice got there first, and Norton's gamble not only failed to pay off, it wrecked his finances. The loss, and the back-and-forth lawsuits that followed, bankrupted him in 1856.

Norton disappeared for a time, but by 1859 he had resurfaced. He announced his presence with a flourish on the pages of the *San Francisco Bulletin's* September 19 issue:

At the peremptory request and desire of a large majority of the citizens of these United States, I, Joshua Norton, formerly of Algoa Bay, Cape of Good Hope, and now for the last 9 years and 10 months past of S. F., Cal., declare and proclaim myself Emperor of these U. S.; and in virtue of the authority thereby in me vested, do hereby order and direct the representatives of the different States of the Union to assemble in Musical Hall, of this city, on the 1st day of Feb. next, then and there to make such alterations in the existing laws of the Union as may ameliorate the evils under which the country is laboring, and thereby cause confidence to exist, both at home and abroad, in our stability and integrity.

—NORTON I, Emperor of the United States

Norton's self-appointment as sovereign of the nation elicited all manner of response, from befuddlement to disbelief to hilarity. But the man seemed sincere and meant to solve the nation's many problems—or at least pretend to. The next step in the campaign was to do away with Congress, which body, it seems, was corrupt and subject to undue influence. The order abolishing the Congress appeared October 12, again in the *San Francisco Bulletin*:

It is represented to us that the universal suffrage, as now existing throughout the Union, is abused; that fraud and corruption prevent a fair and proper expression of the public voice; that open violation of the laws are constantly occurring, caused by mobs, parties, factions and undue influence of political sects; that the citizen has not that protection of person and property which he is entitled to by paying his pro rata of the expense of government—in consequence of which, WE do hereby abolish congress, and it is therefore abolished; and We order and desire the representatives of all parties interested to appear at the Musical Hall of this city on the first of February next, and then and there take the most effective steps to remedy the evil complained of.

When, in January 1860, the Senate and House of Representatives convened despite Norton's proclamation, he issued orders for the army to put them out:

WHEREAS, a body of men calling themselves the National Congress are now in session in Washington City, in violation of our Imperial edict of the 12th of October last, declaring the said Congress abolished;

WHEREAS, it is necessary for the repose of our Empire that the said decree should be strictly complied with;

NOW, THEREFORE, we do hereby Order and Direct Major-General Scott, the Commander-in-Chief of our Armies, immediately upon receipt of this, our Decree, to proceed with a suitable force and clear the Halls of Congress.

General Scott was otherwise engaged and, like Congress, ignored the emperor's call. Congress was not the sole recipient of Norton's wrath. A few weeks earlier, in December, he had turned out Henry A. Wise, governor of Virginia:

DISAPPROVING of the act of Gov. Wise of Virginia in hanging Gen. [abolitionist John] Brown at Charlestown, Va., on 2nd December;

AND CONSIDERING that the said Brown was insane and that he ought to have been sent to the Insane Asylum for capturing the State of Virginia with seventeen men;

NOW KNOW ALL MEN that I do hereby discharge him, Henry A. Wise, from said office, and appoint John C. Breckinridge, of Kentucky, to said office of Governor of our province of Virginia.

Breckinridge, like Scott, was otherwise engaged at the time, serving as vice president to James Buchanan.

When disbanding Congress and firing a governor didn't do the trick in solving the nation's problems, the emperor made what may well have been his most audacious move:

WHEREAS, it is necessary for our Peace, Prosperity and Happiness, as also to the National Advancement of the people of the United States, that they should dissolve the Republican form of government and establish in its stead an Absolute Monarchy;

NOW, THEREFORE, WE, Norton I, by the Grace of God Emperor of the Thirty-three states and the multitude of Territories of the United States of America, do hereby dissolve the Republic of the United States, and it is hereby dissolved;

And all laws made from and after this date, either by the National Congress or any State Legislature, shall be null and of no effect.

All Governors, and all other persons in authority, shall maintain order by enforcing the heretofore existing laws and regulations until the necessary alterations can be effected.

Given under our hand and seal, at Headquarters, San Francisco, this 26th day of July, 1860.

America was otherwise engaged and this decree, too, went unheeded.

The emperor's attentions weren't always confined to his adopted homeland. When France invaded Mexico in 1863, Norton appended his title and was thereafter known as Norton I, Emperor of the United States and Protector of Mexico. Not surprisingly, he affected conditions in Mexico even less than those in the United States.

Norton did, however, attract the attention of some world leaders. Dom Pedro II, the real and actual emperor of Brazil, visited San Francisco in 1876 and asked to meet his counterpart, which he did, reportedly visiting with Norton for more than an hour in a suite at the Palace Hotel.

While Norton attempted to spread his influence far and wide and issued far-reaching proclamations and decrees, his interests were not solely on the national and international scale—the well-being of his adopted

Norton I, Emperor of the United
States and Protector of Mexico,
ruled America from San Francisco.
WIKIMEDIA COMMONS

city was an important plank in his political platform. He was a constant presence on the streets of San Francisco and involved in the city's social, educational, and civic endeavors in many ways. While ridiculed by some, he was revered by many. And while his aspirations may have been extravagant, his circumstances were humble. He resided for many years in a shabby six-by-ten-foot room at the Eureka Lodging House, surrounded by tacked-up pictures of other royalty, well-worn clothing hanging from nails, and a collection of headgear and walking sticks.

His street attire was often a fancy—if threadbare—blue uniform festooned with gold braid and epaulettes acquired from army stores at the Presidio. He wore a variety of hats, including an elegant beaver top hat decorated with a plume or peacock feather. When his apparel became too shabby, his constituents in San Francisco saw to it that he was reoutfitted in clothing more befitting his rank. An umbrella or walking stick was usually in his hand, and admirers far and wide sent fancy walking sticks—one said to be a gift from the city of Portland in Oregon as an inducement to lure him there.

Norton's travels and inspection tours around the city took him to construction sites and public works, where he offered encouragement and advice to workers. He engaged in lengthy conversations, philosophical discussions, and well-reasoned debates on public policy whenever an opportunity presented itself, and he freely mixed with his subjects in city parks, on the streets, and at public gatherings. Afternoon might find him reading at the library, and he spent many an evening in the audience at lectures, debates, speeches, and sermons. Theaters and music halls were said to reserve a seat for the emperor on opening nights.

Businesses supported the frugal emperor with small handouts he collected as a "tax," and when he didn't take advantage of the free lunch counters at saloons, restaurants would stand him to a meal. Many San Francisco businesses proudly displayed plaques reading, "By Appointment to his Imperial Majesty, Emperor Norton I of the United States" or similar sentiments as a lure to attract customers. His own currency, issued in a variety of small denominations, was widely accepted.

Not everyone loved the emperor, however, if their actions are any indication. Certain newspapers published fake decrees and proclamations that they falsely and knowingly attributed to Norton. In Norton's possession was a stack of telegrams and correspondence supposedly from other heads of state and famous people, but these, too, were hoaxes. And on one occasion in 1867, a rookie San Francisco police officer, apparently finding Norton a nuisance, arrested him for vagrancy and attempted to have him committed as a lunatic. The vagrancy charge did not hold, however, as the emperor had money in his pocket amounting to nearly five dollars, as well as the key to his room at the Eureka Lodging House. As for the charge of lunacy, the chief of police thought better of it and released the prisoner—but not before upsetting the citizenry and the press. The *Evening Bulletin* reported:

> *In what can only be described as the most dastardly of errors, Joshua A. Norton was arrested today. He is being held on the ludicrous charge of "Lunacy." Known and loved by all true San Franciscans as Emperor Norton, this kindly Monarch of Montgomery Street is less a lunatic than those who have engineered these trumped up charges. As they will learn, His Majesty's loyal subjects are fully apprised of this outrage. Perhaps a return to the methods of the Vigilance Committees is in order.*
>
> *This newspaper urges all right-thinking citizens to be in attendance tomorrow at the public hearing to be held before the Commissioner of Lunacy, Wingate Jones. The blot on the record of San Francisco must be removed.*

According to some reports, the "kindly Monarch" pardoned the young policeman, and thereafter it was the practice of San Francisco police officers to salute the emperor when they encountered him on the streets of the city.

If there is a lasting monument to Emperor Norton and his influence, it is, perhaps, the San Francisco–Oakland Bay Bridge. On at least two occasions, and perhaps three—the provenance of the first decree is said to be suspect—he ordered construction of such a bridge:

WHEREAS, it is our pleasure to acquiesce in all means of civilization and population:

NOW, THEREFORE, we, Norton I, Dei Gratia Emperor of the United States and Protector of Mexico, do order and direct first, that Oakland shall be the coast termination of the Central Pacific Railroad; secondly, that a suspension bridge be constructed from the improvements lately ordered by our royal decree at Oakland Point to Yerba Buena, from thence to the mountain range of Sacilleto, and from thence to the Farallones, to be of sufficient strength and size for a railroad; and thirdly, the Central Pacific Railroad Company are charged with the carrying out of this work, for purposes that will hereafter appear. Whereof fail not under pain of death.

Given under our hand this 18th day of August, A.D. 1869.

Norton issued a similar order in March 1872:

The following is decreed and ordered to be carried into execution as soon as convenient:

I. That a suspension bridge be built from Oakland Point to Goat Island [also called Yerba Buena Island], and then to Telegraph Hill; provided such bridge can be built without injury to the navigable waters of the Bay of San Francisco.

II. That the Central Pacific Railroad Company be granted franchises to lay down tracks and run cars from Telegraph Hill and along the city front to Mission Bay.

III. That all deeds by the Washington Government since the establishment of our Empire are hereby decreed null and void unless our Imperial signature is first obtained thereto.

And again, later that year:

WHEREAS, we issued our decree ordering the citizens of San Fran-
cisco and Oakland to appropriate funds for the survey of a suspension
bridge from Oakland Point via Goat Island; also for a tunnel; and
to ascertain which is the best project; and whereas the said citizens
have hitherto neglected to notice our said decree; and whereas we are
determined our authority shall be fully respected; now, therefore, we
do hereby command the arrest by the army of both the Boards of City
Fathers if they persist in neglecting our decrees.
    Given under our royal hand and seal at San Francisco, this 17th
day of September, 1872.

The San Francisco–Oakland Bay Bridge, built much as Norton
ordered it, opened to automobile traffic in 1933 and today carries nearly
a quarter of a million cars a day across one of the longest spans of any
bridge in the United States.

The emperor's reign ended on January 8, 1880, when he collapsed on
California Street and died. *The San Francisco Chronicle* covered his death
with a lengthy story under the headline "Le Roi Est Mort," French for
"The King is Dead." In the days to come, newspapers across the nation
reported his death.

Thousands—perhaps as many as ten thousand—reportedly viewed
Norton as he lay in state at the morgue. Thousands created a funeral cor-
tege two miles long, witnessed by some thirty thousand mourners lining
the streets, on the way to the cemetery when he was laid to rest on January
10. Some attributed a solar eclipse on January 11 to the emperor's passing.

While the curiosity who was Norton I, Emperor of the United States
and Protector of Mexico, is largely forgotten elsewhere, his memory is
still honored in various ways in the city where he reigned. Be warned, by
the way, how you refer to said city, for the emperor decreed in 1872:

Whoever after due and proper warning shall be heard to utter the
abominable word "Frisco," which has no linguistic or other warrant,
shall be deemed guilty of a High Misdemeanor, and shall pay into the
Imperial Treasury as penalty the sum of twenty-five dollars.

Root Hog or Die: The Pig War

1859—San Juan Island

Americans called it Oregon. The British called it Columbia. Spain once claimed it. So did Russia. The rights of the various groups of native people who had occupied the area for thousands of years weren't considered.

By the time the 1800s rolled around, it was down to Great Britain and the United States. A joint occupation treaty between the two nations, signed in 1818, put the dispute on hold until a final agreement could be reached, but that proved unworkable in later years as more people—mostly American settlers aiming to fulfill their nation's "Manifest Destiny"—arrived.

Hudson's Bay Company, the British fur-trading conglomerate, was the dominant presence in the area, particularly north of the Columbia River, but it was there to build a business, not a nation. The American settlers who trickled in, then flooded the country as the Oregon Trail gained popularity in 1840s, stayed mostly south of the Columbia River, settling along the valley named for a tributary river, the Willamette.

Still, the United States wanted it all. All the way to "Fifty-four forty or fight."

Negotiations culminated in 1846 with the Treaty of Oregon, establishing the enduring border between the western United States and Canada—with one exception.

According to the treaty, everything north of the forty-ninth parallel went to Britain and everything south of the line was labeled US territory. Once the agreed-upon line of latitude reached the sea, the border took a dip southward to give Great Britain Vancouver Island. The treaty defines the boundary as continuing "westward along the said forty-ninth parallel of north latitude to the middle of the channel which separates the continent from Vancouver's Island; and thence southerly through the middle of said channel, and of [Juan de] Fuca's Straits to the Pacific Ocean."

The problem is, there's a group of islands lying in "the middle of said channel," most notably San Juan Island. Despite the landmass of the isle, some fifty-five square miles, not to mention the numerous other islands large and small in the archipelago, it was overlooked by the negotiators. Inaccurate maps may be to blame. Fatigue may be the culprit. But, for whatever reason, the Treaty of Oregon fails to note there are two straits, not one—Haro Strait, nearest Vancouver Island and west of San Juan, and Rosario Strait, east of San Juan and nearer the mainland.

All of which created a situation ripe for dispute. And that would arrive in 1859, triggered by a pig.

The British, as you might imagine, favored a Haro Strait interpretation of the treaty, placing San Juan Island firmly in their camp. James Douglas, chief factor for Hudson's Bay Company and governor of the Colony of Vancouver Island, was among those who thought the British got the short end of the stick with the Treaty of Oregon and was determined to keep as much territory in the Empire's hands as possible. And so, in 1851 he arranged for Hudson's Bay Company to set up a salmon-processing facility on San Juan Island. Then in 1853 he sent Charles Griffin to established Belle Vue Farm there to raise crops and livestock.

Including pigs.

The Americans, of course, held that Rosario Strait defined the international border and that San Juan Island was theirs. Officials from Washington Territory made repeated attempts to collect customs fees and taxes for the livestock imported onto the island. The British refused to recognize American authority, let alone pay.

All it took for the simmering situation to boil over was to throw a few American settlers into the pot. By 1859 some twenty of them had taken up residence on the island, among them Lyman Cutlar, who staked out a claim near Belle Vue Farm. Just as the British refused to recognize the authority of Washington Territory, American settlers rebuffed British demands that they abandon the island.

Remains of the English camp on San Juan Island, where a rooting pig brought America and England to the brink of war. LIBRARY OF CONGRESS

Rather than leave, Cutlar planted a garden. To Griffin's hogs the garden plot looked like a dinner plate. The would-be farmer tired of driving pigs out of his potato patch, and in a fit of pique on June 15, he shot and killed a burrowing boar. Cutlar hightailed it to Belle Vue and reported the shooting to Griffin, who was less than pleased. They argued. Legend has it that when Cutlar told Griffin he should have kept his pig out of the potatoes, Griffin told Cutlar he should have kept his potatoes out of the pig.

In any event, the pig paid the price for ravaging the garden. Cutlar offered to pay the price for the pig, offering his neighbor ten dollars in recompense. Griffin demanded one hundred. Cutlar refused. Griffin threatened to have him arrested. Cutlar may have been threatened by Hudson's Bay officials, but no legal action was taken.

Still, the incident upset all involved. During a Fourth of July celebration a few weeks later, American settlers erected a tall flagpole and raised the Stars and Stripes on a hill above Belle Vue Farm. As the story goes, General William S. Harney, military head of the Department of Oregon for the US Army, happened by aboard a ship a few days later, saw the flag flying, and stopped by to see what was happening. Being as ill-disposed toward the British as James Douglas was toward the Americans, Harney ordered troops to the island to protect the settlers.

The troops were led by Captain George Pickett, who would later, as a Confederate general, lead his troops to slaughter at Gettysburg. Fortunately, no such disaster awaited Pickett on San Juan Island.

But it might have. The arrival of Pickett and his sixty-six infantry troops on July 27 prompted the British to respond with three warships under command of Captain Geoffrey Hornby. Hornby ordered the Americans to withdraw. Pickett refused. Both sides called in reinforcements. By the end of August, there were 461 American soldiers on the field, aiming fourteen cannons at the British warships, with their seventy guns and more than two thousand men.

Pickett kept his powder dry and Hornby kept his calm. Neither commander ordered an attack, choosing, instead, to hold firm and await orders from higher authority.

Those authorities, thank goodness, were shocked that a single pig could bring two nations to the brink of war. Commander of British naval forces in the Pacific, Rear Admiral Robert L. Baynes, told Governor Douglas he would not attack the American army to settle "a squabble about a pig." The commanding general of the US Army, Winfield Scott, hurried out from Washington to settle the situation and promptly dressed down Harney for adding fuel to the fire.

Scott and Douglas withdrew most of their respective troops and agreed to joint military occupation with a small contingent of American troops on one end of the island and their British counterparts on the opposite end. The troops stayed for the next twelve years. Fortunately, those years were peaceful, with the Brits and the Yanks joining together for entertainment, sporting events, and other activities.

Little else happened, as the Americans were distracted by the Civil War. With that disagreement settled, attention once again turned to San Juan Island. High-level squabbling between the two nations settled nothing, so the dispute was sent to Kaiser Wilhelm of Germany for arbitration. It took a year for his committee to rule. Finally, in October 1872, he found for the Americans and declared an imaginary line through the swells of Rosario Strait as the international boundary.

When all was said and done, the British pig whose rooting around in an American garden caused the whole kerfuffle was the only casualty of the Pig War.

Randolph B. Marcy: Tour Guide for the Westward Emigration

1859—Emigrant Trails

There is, to some extent in the popular imagination, the notion that west-bound pioneers set out into an untracked wilderness. Yet, owing to their competence, self-sufficiency, and independence, they found their way.

That was true, perhaps, of some, early on. But for most the trail west was a communal effort. While the landscape along the emigrant roads was strange and forbidding and largely unpopulated, with the progression of time, it became far from a wilderness. Along the main routes the trail was well-traveled and clear, often marked with signs, and occasionally wagon tracks, even deep ruts, clearly showed the way. As long as you paid attention and stayed with the popular routes, it would have been difficult to get lost.

Outfitting for the trail was another matter, particularly in the early years. The Mormons engaged in the largest organized exodus in American history and had it down to a science—mostly. Lists of supplies, down to the pound, were provided and expected to be adhered to. Advice on conveyances and draft animals was clearly spelled out. The Saints even developed a financing program to help the poverty stricken make the trip, with the expectation they would pay it back when settled in their Zion, replenishing the "Perpetual Emigrating Fund" for the benefit of other needy pioneers.

There were lapses, of course. The biggest single disaster on the trails saw more than two hundred Mormon pioneers perish from cold and hunger when stranded on the high plains by early winter storms. Those unfortunate souls were walking west, pushing and pulling handcarts as part of a failed financial experiment. The handcarts and the few accompanying supply wagons carried scant provisions, barely enough to maintain the health of the travelers when the trek proved uneventful. But there was no margin for error, so any delay or difficulty carried the potential for disaster, as evidenced by the deaths of so many members of the Martin and Willey handcart companies of 1856.

Few travelers outside the Mormon migration enjoyed the benefit of the ever-improving planning and outfitting guidance passed along by church leaders, accumulated from the experience of thousands of Saints who had made the trip in previous companies.

The year before the Mormons struck out from the banks of the Missouri in 1847, the Donner-Reed party suffered the results of poor planning, bad trail advice, ineffective leadership, and inclement weather—the outcome being starvation and cannibalism. It is worth noting that many other pioneers who traveled with the Donner and Reed parties disagreed with their decision to follow a cutoff promoted by Lansford Hastings, and instead stayed with the proven trail. Those emigrants made it to California, well ahead of the Donner-Reed company, and with relatively little difficulty along the way.

The forty-niners were something else altogether. The thousands of gold seekers racing one another up the trail ranged from drivers of overstuffed wagon trains to ill-equipped Argonauts pushing wheelbarrows or carrying only rucksacks. Many travelers, eager to make good time and anxious that someone else might get there first and hoard all the gold, went out of their way to impede fellow travelers. While cooperation and assistance along the trails was certainly the norm during most years, those qualities often fell by the wayside during the gold rush.

But back to ordinary emigrants on a routine trip west. Those people often needed help, and the quality of advice available at jumping-off points where wagon trains assembled was often poor, even when well-intentioned.

Stepping into the picture in 1859 to fill the void was Captain Randolph B. Marcy of the US Army. Experienced from long service in the

US Army officer and author Randolph B. Marcy helped thousands of travelers find their way west. LIBRARY OF CONGRESS

West and a competent writer, Marcy set out, with the encouragement and cooperation of the War Department, to create a guide to assist emigrants. The result was *The Prairie Traveler*, labeled "The Best-Selling Handbook for America's Pioneers." The cover promised that the book included "Routes, First Aid, Recommended Clothing, Shelter, Provisions, Wagon Maintenance and the Selection and Care of Horses, Information Concerning the Habits of Indians." The book offered all that and more.

The tour guide and author, Marcy, was born in April 1812 in Greenwich, Massachusetts, and became a career army officer upon graduation from West Point in 1832. He served in the Black Hawk War and the Mexican War, then spent years in the West exploring, mapping, aiding emigrants, and locating sites for military forts. During the 1857 Utah War, he led a heroic winter march from the area near Fort Bridger, then in Utah, now in Wyoming, when the army was stranded and short of provisions owing to the destruction of supply trains by Mormon raiders. Marcy and a few dozen soldiers set out for Fort Massachusetts in Colorado's San Luis Valley (then part of New Mexico), crossing mountains and deserts through cold and storms. More than six hundred miles later he returned with hundreds of cavalry mounts and mules as well as other supplies to aid the troops huddled in winter camp.

Shortly after the Utah Expedition, Marcy was assigned to the State Department in Washington, DC, and given the duty to prepare the guidebook for emigrants.

In the book's preface Marcy says experience taught him "what great disadvantages the 'voyageur' labors under for want of timely information into those minor details of prairie-craft, which, however apparently unimportant in the abstract, are sure, upon the plains, to turn the balance of success for or against an enterprise."

He claims to "have waited several years, with the confident expectation that some one more competent than myself would assume the task" of preparing such a handbook for travelers. "But it seems no one has taken sufficient interest in the subject. . . . Our frontier-men, although brave in council and action, and possessing an intelligence that quickens in the face of danger, are apt to feel shy of the pen."

And so Marcy took up the challenge. "The main object at which I have aimed in the following pages has been to explain and illustrate, as clearly and succinctly as possible, the best methods of performing the duties devolving upon the prairie traveler, so as to meet their contingencies under all circumstances."

Throughout the book's 252 pages (plus another 34 pages of "Itineraries"), Marcy offers advice in fascinating detail:

> *Wheels made of bois-d'arc, or Osage orange-wood, are best for the plains as they shrink but little, and seldom want repair. . . .*
>
> *Bacon should be packed in strong sacks of a hundred pounds to each; or, in very hot climates, put in boxes and surrounded with bran, which in a great measure prevents the fat from melting away. . . .*
>
> *Desiccated or dried vegetables are almost equal to the fresh, and are put up in such compact and portable form as to be easily transported over the plains. . . .*
>
> *The allowance of provisions for each grown person, to make the journey from the Missouri River to California, should suffice for 110 days. The following is deemed requisite, viz.: 150 lbs. of flour, or its equivalent in hard bread; 25 lbs. of bacon or pork, and enough fresh beef to be driven on the hoof to make up the meat component of the ration; 15 lbs. of coffee, and 25 lbs. of sugar; also a quantity of saleratus or yeast powders for making bread, and salt and pepper. . . .*

Cotton or linen fabrics do not sufficiently protect the body against the direct rays of the sun at midday, nor against rains or sudden changes of temperature. Wool, being a non-conductor, is the best material for this mode of locomotion, and should always be adopted for the plains. . . .

Green or blue glasses, inclosed in a wire net-work, are an effectual protection to the eyes; but, in absence of these, the skin around the eyes and upon the nose should be blackened with wet powder or charcoal, which will afford great relief. . . .

The bedding for each person should consist of two blankets, a comforter, and a pillow, and a gutta percha or painted canvas cloth to spread beneath the bed upon the ground, and to contain it when rolled up for transportation. . . .

Mules are very keenly sensitive to danger, and, in passing along over the prairies, they will often detect the proximity of strangers long before they are discovered by their riders. . . . Dogs are sometimes good sentinels, but they often sleep sound, and are not easily awakened on the approach of an enemy. . . .

Camp kettles, tin vessels, and other articles that will rattle and are likely to frighten animals, should be firmly lashed to the packs. . . . .

After horses' backs become chafed and sore, it is very difficult to heal them, particularly when they are continued at work. . . . A piece of bacon rind tied upon the collar over the wound is . . . an excellent remedy. . . .

Another source of very many sad and fatal accidents resulting from the most stupid and culpable carelessness is in persons standing before the muzzles of guns and attempting to pull them out of wagons, or to draw them through a fence or brush in the same position. . . .

It is not a difficult matter to distinguish the tracks of American horses from those of Indian horses, as the latter are never shod; moreover, they are much smaller. . . .

The Comanches, Sioux, and other prairie tribes make their attacks upon the open prairies. Trusting to their wonderful skill in equitation and horsemanship, they ride around their enemies with their bodies thrown upon the opposite side of the horse, and discharge their arrows

The Best-Selling Handbook for America's Pioneers

THE PRAIRIE TRAVELER

RANDOLPH B. MARCY
Captain, U.S. Army

INCLUDES
Routes · First Aid
Recommended Clothing, Shelter, Provisions
Wagon Maintenance and the Selection and Care of Horses
Information Concerning the Habits of Indians

A bestseller in its day, *The Prairie Traveler* offered advice on everything from foodstuffs to first aid.

in rapid succession while at full speed; they will not, however, often venture near an enemy who occupies a defensive position. . . .

When the buffalo are discovered, and the hunter intends to give chase, he should first dismount, arrange his saddle-blanket and saddle, buckle the girth tight, and make every thing about his horse furniture snug and secure. . . .

When the deer is reposing he generally turns his head from the wind, in which position he can see an enemy approaching from that direction, and his nose will apprise him of the presence of danger from the opposite side. The best method of hunting deer, therefore, is across the wind. . . .

The book concludes with a "List of Itineraries, Showing the distances between camping-places, the character of the roads, and the facilities for obtaining wood, water, and grass on the principal routes between the Mississippi River and the Pacific Ocean."

Marcy's *The Prairie Traveler* was an instant bestseller upon its release and remained so through the turn of the century. The author, promoted to major, bided his time in tedious assignments until the Civil War. He served as chief of staff to General George B. McClellan, who was married to Marcy's daughter, and later was an inspector-general and a brigadier general. He retired from military service in 1881 and died in West Orange, New Jersey, on November 22, 1887.

While *The Prairie Traveler* was not unique—there were numerous guidebooks published over the years of varying quality and usefulness—his is, perhaps, the best of the lot. Marcy's guidebook made journeying to the West easier for thousands of emigrants and may well have saved the lives of many. He wrote, in the preface, that he was "satisfied that a good Prairie Manual will be for the young traveler an addition to his equipment of inappreciable value." And so it was.

The Comstock Lode:
A Silver-Lined Mountain

1859—Utah Territory

Along the eastern slope of Mount Davidson the skin of the earth grows thin and the skeleton pokes through. In one particular place, known as the Kendall Cut, the rocky outcrop led to the discovery of a mountain filled with silver and a good deal of gold. Over the next twenty years and then some, miners mucked out somewhere between $300 million and $400 million in precious metal—nearly seven tons of silver and about eight million ounces of gold.

But it didn't come easy. And it didn't come cheap. And, with so much financial finagling going on above and below ground, estimates of how much money went into how many pockets are just that—estimates.

Like the more famous 1848 gold strike in California, the first ore in the Comstock region was unearthed by Mormons. On the way to the goldfields in the spring of 1850, a party of Saints pitched camp along the Carson River to wait for the snowbound passes over the Sierra to clear. They found color in their pans in a place later called Gold Canyon, but abandoned the find to pursue bigger riches across the Sierra.

But a couple of years later more prospectors started turning the earth in Gold Canyon, following the ore upstream to where the towns of Gold Hill and Silver City would later be built. More gold was discovered in neighboring Six Mile Canyon, but no miner in either canyon thought to work farther uphill to locate the veins that shed the placer gold. Still, there was enough metal in the area that by 1857, hundreds of miners were at work.

Among them were the Grosh brothers, Ethan and Hosea, who brought with them considerable experience mining in California along with formal training in mineralogy. They, with a partner named Richard Bucke, may well have discovered what would become the heart of the Comstock Lode and may have been the only miners in the area capable of recognizing the silver ore for what it was.

When an infection resulting from an errant strike with a pick took Hosea's life, Ethan and Bucke stored most of their samples and documentation in a cabin under the watchful eyes of one Henry Comstock, and then set out across the Sierra to obtain an assay to set a value on their find and record claims. They never made it. Lost and wandering in the mountains, both men suffered severe frostbite; by the time they found help it was too late to save their legs, and, in the case of Ethan Grosh, his life. According to sources, Bucke survived but never returned to exploit the discovery.

That left Comstock the caretaker, who laid claim to the late brothers' property. He pried open the trunk to find the ore samples but apparently paid little attention to the paperwork so never learned where the rock originated, and he was unable to locate the site through his own prospecting.

Four other miners, James "Ol' Virginny" Finney, John Bishop, Jack Yount, and Aleck Henderson, staked a claim at Gold Hill to a vein of ore intermingled with the blue-tinged rocks the Grosh brothers recognized as silver ore. Comstock thought this might be the source of the Grosh samples and filed a claim nearby.

If, in fact, the Grosh brothers were the discoverers of the Comstock Lode, Finney and his cohorts are credited by many as rediscovering it. Another story—one of those that ought to be true even if it isn't—credits Finney with naming the town that would become famous along with the Comstock Lode. "Ol' Virginny" (so named for his home state) reportedly was on a toot one night and dropped a bottle of whiskey. As he watched the dry desert dirt soak up the spilled pop skull, it is said that rather than mourn the hooch a total loss, he declared the event a christening of the growing miners' camp and named it Virginia Town.

But Finney had no idea what his town would become, or the land beneath it. Nor did anyone else.

Now comes 1859 and with it yet another discovery of the Comstock Lode—this time by Patrick McLaughlin and Peter O'Riley. This pair's attempts to wash gold in a cradle did yield results, but the work was hampered by sticky, heavy, dark blue-gray mud that filled the riffles in the cradle. It turned out to be silver ore worth some $2,000 a ton.

Again Henry Comstock enters the picture—this time to claim that the ore was discovered on ground on which he owned grazing rights. Somehow, Comstock managed to finagle his way into an interest on the mining claim that would lead to the biggest silver mining boom America had ever seen in a place that would bear his name: the Comstock Lode.

But there was little, if any, financial benefit associated with the naming rights. Comstock later sold his mining interests for around $11,000, opened a store with his newfound wealth until it was gone, then went off prospecting in Idaho and Montana, where he blew his brains out in 1870. Despite his name being attached to a rich mining boom, Comstock the man is little remembered. He was said to be a lazy and stupid loudmouth, nicknamed "Pancake," as he preferred griddle cakes to baked bread because they were easier to make.

His namesake would fare better. The rush to the Comstock Lode emptied out much of California's gold country as miners hustled across the Sierra in search of the next big chance. Mount Davidson was soon overrun with people with accents of many kinds, including English, Welsh, Irish, Italian, German, Canadian, Spanish, and Chinese. By 1862 Virginia City and environs was home to four thousand people, and it grew to twenty-five thousand residents by 1874 and thirty thousand by 1876. "Ol' Virginny Town" was among the largest and most important cities in the West, boasting somewhere between 100 and 150 saloons, three churches, an opera house, opium dens, Shakespeare plays, dogfights, twenty music halls, a booming red-light district, numerous restaurants, and several hotels, including a six-story wonder that housed the only elevator west of Chicago.

The Comstock strike created more than Virginia City—the entire state of Nevada owes its existence to the silver mining boom. In 1861 everyone with a dog in the fight ganged up on Utah Territory. Many people in the Comstock region cared little for the Mormons and wanted independence from the Saints. The federal government, too, was at odds with Utah. Despite having sent an army to the territory in 1857 to oust Brigham Young from the governor's office, then filling most government posts with outsiders, federal officials found that Young still ran things in the territory and would continue to do so. The loyalty of the Mormons to the United States was also suspect, and becoming a larger concern in light of a looming civil war.

The riches being mined from the mountains also gleamed bright in the eyes of Washington, DC, as the government saw in the Comstock a cash register to help finance the war that seemed sure to come.

And so Nevada Territory was born in 1861. But the newly created territory bore little resemblance to the state of Nevada on today's maps. While most of the northern and western borders are the same, the eastern and southern borders made significant moves over the years—all in Nevada's favor and most at the expense of Utah.

When drawn in 1861, the eastern border of Nevada Territory ran north and south along a line just west of where the town of Elko would later sprout astride the newly laid Central Pacific Railroad tracks in 1868. In 1862 the border shifted eastward another degree of longitude and would have barely excluded the town of Wells, had it existed.

But creating Nevada Territory was not enough. The desire for silver led the government on October 31, 1864, to grant statehood to the mostly empty territory—virtually all the population was centered in and around the Comstock region—and, in the process, to slice another degree of longitude off Utah Territory and add it to Nevada's eastern border, a demarcation that still holds today. Each of those bites cost Utah and gained Nevada more than eighteen thousand square miles. "Battle Born" became the state's motto, paying homage to the bloody and expensive Civil War so crucial in its formation, with the nickname "the Silver State" recognizing the Comstock mines that made the place relevant on the national map.

The final addition to Nevada's boundaries came in 1867, this time at the expense of Arizona Territory, creating the wedge at the southern end of the state where Las Vegas would grow from a sleepy Mormon way station to the state's most populous city; it would eventually reap riches from gambling that dwarf the wealth of the Comstock.

But that's another story.

Despite the rapid growth and economic importance of Virginia City, the community that clung to the slope of Mount Davidson led a tenuous existence in a harsh environment. The city, and everything else for hundreds of miles in every direction save west, lay in the lee of the Sierra Nevada. The hungry peaks and western slopes of that range slurped up most of the moisture the clouds carried, creating a vast desert that filled the Great Basin and beyond. One of the most lyrical descriptions of the region came from the pen of young Samuel Clemens, who described it in an 1861 letter to his mother:

> *The country is fabulously rich in gold, silver, copper, lead, coal, iron, quicksilver, marble, granite, chalk, plaster of Paris, (gypsum,) thieves, murderers, desperadoes, ladies, children, lawyers, Christians, Indians, Chinamen, Spaniards, gamblers, sharpers, cuyotès (pronounced ki-yo-ties), poets, preachers, and jackass rabbits. . . . It never rains here, and the dew never falls. No flowers grow here, and no green thing gladdens the eye. The birds that fly over the land carry their provisions with them. Only the crow and the raven tarry with us. Our city lies in the midst of a desert of the purest—most unadulterated, and uncompromising sand—in which infernal soil nothing but the fag-end of vegetable creation, "sage-brush," ventures to grow.*

Clemens came to Nevada in company with his brother Orion, appointed secretary of the new Nevada Territory as a reward for campaigning in Missouri for Abraham Lincoln in the 1860 election. Sam was to serve as his assistant but soon found the work boring and bereft of opportunities to put pen to paper. So, in 1862, after a failed bout at prospecting, he took the fifteen-or-so mile journey uphill to Virginia City and signed on as a reporter for the *Territorial Enterprise*. Soon, he would take to signing his work for the newspaper with the pen name Mark Twain, a nom de plume he would keep and make world-famous in the years to come.

Among the young reporter's colleagues at the newspaper was another writer who would make a name for himself in the heyday of the Comstock Lode and go on to earn fame—William Wright, better remembered as

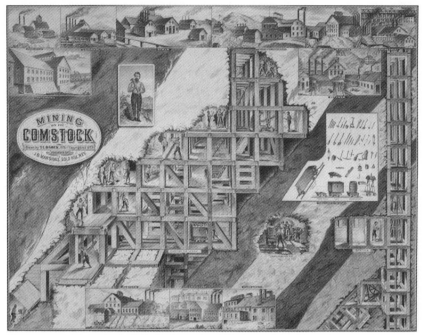

The square-set method of timbering mines illustrated in this poster was invented in Comstock mines and adopted worldwide. LIBRARY OF CONGRESS

Dan DeQuille. Unlike Clemens, Wright stayed at the *Territorial Enterprise* for more than three decades, and his reports from the area were reprinted widely across the country. He also wrote several books recounting the history of the Comstock Lode as well as other historical works about the region.

While all this was going on upstairs, downstairs at the Comstock Lode miners were developing methods of extracting ore that would change underground mining. The parallel veins of the lode that outcropped at the Kendall Cut lay at a steeper angle than the slope of Mount Davidson. So, as the veins burrowed further eastward away from the outcrop they also burrowed deeper. As a parade of mine shafts marched down the slope, each had to dig ever deeper to reach the lode. Later shafts in Comstock history intersected the lode at 3,200 feet below the surface, with the deepest intersection reported at 3,300 feet. With the depth came a pair of related problems: heat and water. Underground streams and reservoirs of water often flooded the mines, and as the mines grew deeper the water got hotter, making working conditions miserable, and sometimes deadly, for miners.

Like the ore, the water had to be brought to the surface, and the pumps and steam engines to lift the water were among the most advanced and innovative in the world. A Prussian-born engineer from San Francisco, Adolph Sutro, came up with a plan to drain the Comstock Lode by boring a tunnel, twelve feet high and sixteen feet wide, through some four miles of mountain, much of it solid rock. Sutro's tunnel started at the level of the Carson River near the town of Dayton and reached the mines 1,560 feet below ground near Virginia City. Lateral tunnels would extend two miles north and south from the main bore to reach other mines.

Shovels started turning in October 1869, and the blasting and boring and digging continued in the main tunnel until 1878. By that time Comstock mines were already some 1,500 feet deeper than the tunnel. Still, the drain served its purpose, removing, according to reports, millions of gallons of water from the mines every day. The Sutro Tunnel also provided ventilation and an alternative route for hauling out ore.

Sutro sold his interest in his borehole shortly after its completion and returned to San Francisco, where he acquired a good deal of real estate, served as mayor, and died in 1898.

Among the most far-reaching developments related to the Comstock Lode is the "square set," a method of timbering underground mines to prevent cave-ins. The rich silver ore in the Comstock often occurred in large pockets of earth so soft it could be excavated with a shovel. The traditional method of underground timbering involved the use of stulls, or props, or with two inward-angled vertical posts joined at the top by a horizontal cap. This worked well in drifts and adits, tunnel-like paths to and through veins of ore, and in small open areas. But mining large pockets of ore, or stoping, leaves large, open spaces that, in heavy ground and certain rock formations, are inherently unstable and subject to dangerous collapses and cave-ins.

Philip Deidesheimer, a mining engineer and superintendent of the Comstock's Ophir Mine, solved the problem around 1880 with a new method of timbering, the square set. Six-foot-long timber supports, cut square and with a square stub of smaller dimension milled into the ends, were assembled into cube-shaped latticeworks that could, in theory, reach any distance in any direction to shore up the soft earth. For additional support the lattice might be filled with waste rock below the working level as it rose, or when the stope was mined out and abandoned. Deidesheimer's square-set timbering was adapted throughout the mining industry.

Though effective, the use of square sets vastly increased the need for timber. The arid desert area around the Comstock was bereft of forests of any kind, and the nearest supply was over the Sierra summit in the Lake Tahoe Basin. Once cut and hauled to the top of the range, logs were dropped into a V-shaped flume and flushed to the valley below with the aid of water. Once at the bottom, however, there was still an uphill climb to reach the Comstock.

Isolated as it was, transportation proved an ongoing problem for Virginia City and the Comstock region. Long trains of large freight wagons pulled by teams of horses or mules hauled in everything out of California and over the Sierra. Machinery and equipment, timber and lumber, food and drink, furniture and fixtures, miners and merchants, opera stars and audiences all made the trip up and down the Sierra to the slopes of Mount Davidson at one time or another.

The length of the trip via horsepower of the four-footed variety lessened considerably in 1868 when the eastbound Central Pacific Railroad reached the Truckee Meadows, where the city of Reno would grow, some twenty to twenty-five miles to the north. But the journey became even easier in 1869 with the opening of the Virginia and Truckee Railroad from the Comstock to Carson City. Then, freight could be hauled by wagon from the Central Pacific Railroad to Carson City and loaded onto the cars of "the crookedest railroad on earth" for the trip to Virginia City. Outbound minerals and money made the same journey in reverse.

The origin of "the crookedest railroad on earth" nickname is the subject of some dispute. Some claim it is the result of all the underhanded financial wheeling and dealing involved in the railway's construction and operation. But most hold it arises from the turns the rails make in their sudden drop in elevation, descending some 1,600 feet during the short trip from Virginia City to Carson City. The sharp curves on this route—many exceeding the railroad standard of fourteen degrees—amount to seventeen full circles when added together. The sixteen-mile route required twenty-one miles of twisting rails to negotiate those curves. Six tunnels and the huge Crown Point trestle added to the wonder of the railroad.

Despite its necessity, the railroad was a long time coming. Since 1861, charter after charter had been granted to build a railroad connecting the Comstock with the coming Central Pacific. But all those ambitious plans came and went without laying track until William Sharon, local representative of the Bank of California, incorporated the Virginia and Truckee Railroad Company in 1867.

By then bank officials had, by hook and crook, acquired control of most of the mining operations on the Comstock. Control of transportation would, they believed, reduce costs, increase profits, and strengthen their stranglehold on the Comstock economy. Over the next year Sharon haggled and wrangled with other interests over the route of the rails and eventual connecting point to the Central Pacific.

Construction on the railroad linking Carson City and Virginia City started in February 1869, with the first rails laid in September. By December trains were making it to Gold Hill, just a mile or two shy of Virginia City, and the first passengers detrained at that boomtown in January 1870. Later that year, falling prices for silver and decreased production in the mines dented the Bank of California's fortunes, but construction on the railroad continued, eventually reaching north from Carson City through Washoe Valley to the Central Pacific rails at Reno on the Truckee River in August 1872.

Construction costs for the railroad approached $2 million, and with economic conditions at the time, the Bank of California may have been questioning its investment.

Then came the Big Bonanza.

John Mackay was one nut the Bank of California had been unable to crack in its quest to own it all. With his partners Mackay controlled the Consolidated Virginia and California Mine. In May of 1873 the biggest ore body in Comstock history was discovered in its depths. It produced hundreds of millions of dollars' worth of silver in less than a decade, and adjacent mines proved as rich. Mackay's "Bonanza Group" mined half the silver in America between the discovery and 1882, totaling more than $400 million in value and reported profits of $1 million a month.

Although the Bank of California had been unable to acquire Mackay's holdings when times were hard, they profited, through their railroad, during the Bonanza years. The Virginia and Truckee Railroad reportedly made $400,000 every month carrying freight and passengers in and out of the Comstock. Peak traffic amounted to forty trains a day and forty thousand tons of freight a month.

John Mackay's importance is still evident in what remains of Virginia City in the looming Mackay Mansion, now a museum. The building went up in 1860 as the offices for the Gould and Curry Mining Company and residence for its superintendent—George Hearst. The Comstock Lode was the source of the Hearst fortune, which George accumulated from $400 in borrowed seed money. The Hearst empire grew to become America's largest privately held mining company and newspaper and magazine publishing conglomerate, among other interests.

When most of Virginia City burned in 1875—along with the house Mackay lived in at the time—he bought Hearst's Gould and Curry building and used it for his business as well as his home.

Not all Comstock mine owners and investors fared as well as Mackay. In the early years a significant portion of the wealth dug from the mines financed little more than litigation as claims and counterclaims disputed ownership of the ore bodies. That expense, along with the high cost of equipment and manpower necessary to extract the ore, led most of the early prospectors and miners to sell out—often for what seemed a small fortune but proved, as discoveries grew, to be a pittance—to large firms with financial backing. Even then, most of those companies failed to earn a significant return on investment. Some reports claim that only fourteen of the more than one hundred companies mining in the Comstock Lode paid off in a big way; others say only six paid out more to investors than they took in, and the rest paid nothing at all. Skimming of profits, manipulation of stock, insider contracts for goods and services, and cooking the books all contributed to the wealth of some at the expense of others.

Once the Big Bonanza discovery was mostly mined out by the late 1870s, the Comstock, Virginia City, and all of Nevada dwindled. Mining continued in fits and starts well into the twentieth century, but not enough to even cast a shadow on the region's former glory. The Comstock, formerly home to as many as thirty thousand people, had fewer than four thousand residents in 1900. The state lost about one-third of its residents.

Today, the one-time source of so much wealth and innovation is a tourist attraction where the nine hundred or so residents of Virginia City entertain some two million guests with museums, mine tours, souvenirs, and short train rides on a remaining segment of the Virginia and Truckee Railroad tracks.

Samuel Clemens—Mark Twain—wrote about the Comstock in *Roughing It* through different eyes than those that informed his earlier letter to his mother. When all is said and done, much of what he said still holds true of the silver-lined mountain and its environs:

The "city" of Virginia roosted royally midway up the steep side of Mount Davidson, seven thousand two hundred feet above the level of the sea, and in the clear Nevada atmosphere was visible from a distance of fifty miles! . . . From Virginny's airy situation one could look over a vast, far-reaching panorama of mountains and deserts; and whether the day was bright or overcast, whether the sun was rising or setting, or flaming in the zenith, or whether night and moon held sway, the spectacle was always impressive and beautiful. . . . Look from your window where you would, there was fascination in the picture. At rare intervals—but very rare—there were clouds in our skies, and then the setting sun would gild and flush and glorify this mighty expanse of scenery with a bewildering pomp of color that held the eye like a spell and moved the spirit like music.

Barney Ford: From Runaway Slave to Wealthy Businessman

1860—Colorado

For many in nineteenth-century (and earlier, for that matter) America, the western frontier represented hope. Some who went west never realized their dreams, but many others did. Count Barney Ford in the latter category. Despite being disadvantaged in more ways than we can imagine today, he found riches and respect in the West—both of which had been denied him in the more settled regions of America.

Barney—the only name he had for the first twenty-seven years of his life—was born a slave in Virginia on January 22, 1822, to an enslaved mother and her white owner. He grew up in South Carolina and was later sold into Georgia. Like most in his station, Barney worked at whatever tasks his masters set before him, including working in the goldfields in Georgia. Sometime in the late 1840s, Barney's owner hired him out to work as a waiter and cook on a Mississippi River steamboat. It proved a bad bargain for the slave owner, as his property jumped ship in Quincy, Illinois, and made his way to Chicago via the Underground Railroad.

Along the way he met Henry O. Wagoner, an escaped slave who would remain a lifelong friend and associate. Wagoner's sister (or, according to some reports, sister-in-law), Julia Lyoni, and Barney married in 1849. In addition to a wife, Barney took on a middle and last name: Lancelot Ford, borrowed from a steam locomotive that caught his fancy. The ambitious Ford, who had already taught himself to read and write, learned barbering in Chicago but dreamed of better things for himself and his bride.

In 1851, like hundreds of thousands of other young American men, Ford decided to try his luck mining for gold in California and he and Julia booked passage aboard a ship bound for the West Coast. But when the ship docked at Greytown in the Miskito Kingdom, which is now part of Nicaragua, the couple decided to try their luck in the hotel and restaurant business. They built the United States Hotel and successfully offered home-cooked American meals and comfortable lodgings to travelers until 1854, when a US Navy warship, the *Cyane*, in a questionable action, bombarded and burned the city, including the Fords' hotel.

It was back to Chicago for Barney and Julia, where they used their savings from Greytown to build a livery stable that doubled as a station on the Underground Railroad. In 1860 the lure of gold at Pike's Peak once again called Barney to the West. Leaving Julia and a baby behind to join him later, Ford made his way to Leavenworth, Kansas, but stalled there temporarily when refused a ticket on westbound stagecoaches because he was black. But a job as cook on a wagon train soon turned up and he was on his way.

Ford located a claim in the Gregory Gulch mining area but lost it to white claim jumpers. He relocated to the newly discovered mining area at Breckenridge, high in the Colorado Rockies, and staked a claim there in French Gulch. Laws at the time would not allow Ford to file the claim, so he trusted a lawyer to file in his name in exchange for a share of the profits.

Working the claim into the fall, Ford took the gold dust he panned out and buried it under the floor of his cabin. When he ran short of cash, he took some of the treasure to town to exchange for coins, with the unfortunate result of letting word out that his claim was paying off. A few weeks later, the sheriff showed up with an eviction notice based on a complaint filed by the lawyer he had entrusted with the claim. During the night, mounted mobbers rode into the gulch to run Ford off. He escaped with little more than the clothes he wore and a portion of the buried gold dust. He fled in the dark and cold up a hill known today as Barney Ford Hill— but for more than a century was it shown on maps with a different, derogatory name indicative of the cruder sensibilities of the time: Nigger Hill.

And so it was off to Denver for Ford, where he found work as a hotel bellboy. Ford opened a barber shop at first opportunity and it proved a success, but fire destroyed it—and much of the city—in 1863. With borrowed money he built People's Restaurant, a barber shop, and a small hotel. He returned to Chicago in 1865 to bring Julia and their son, Lewis Napoleon—the first of three children, with Sadie and Frances to come later—to Colorado.

When Colorado petitioned for statehood following the Civil War, Ford, by then a respected businessman, lobbied against the application, since the proposed constitution did not extend voting rights to black males. Colorado did not gain statehood—with voting rights for blacks included in its constitution—until 1876.

With his longtime friend Henry Wagoner, Ford implemented numerous initiatives to improve life for Colorado's black citizens, including founding adult-education classes and fighting racial segregation in public schools. Ford and Wagoner also started the Colored Republican Club.

The two former slaves fought an uphill battle for civil rights in the city at the foot of the Rocky Mountains, but they did achieve some success in the political arena. Ford gained a seat on the Arapahoe County Republication Central Committee and won the Republican nomination for a seat in the territorial legislature in 1873 but lost in the general election. He was the first black man to run for public office in Colorado. He achieved another first for blacks when called to serve on a grand jury. And Wagoner was the state's first black law enforcement officer, serving as deputy sheriff in Arapahoe County.

But it was in business that Ford made his biggest mark. He parlayed his success and experiences in the restaurant and hotel business into the Inter-Ocean Hotel, opened in 1874 in downtown Denver, a high-class palatial establishment billed as "the Popular and Only First-Class European Hotel in the City." A year later he opened a second Inter-Ocean Hotel, this time in Cheyenne, Wyoming, at the behest of the chamber of commerce. Advertisements billed the establishment as "the largest and Finest Hotel between Omaha and San Francisco."

The Cheyenne hotel stretched Ford's finances to the breaking point, and he sold out his interests there and in Denver. Ford found himself back in Breckenridge. In an attempt to rebuild his fortune, he opened Ford's Chop House in 1879 as well as a boarding house and barber shop.

He used surplus income to grubstake miners and invested in a mine in French Gulch. Later, he sold his interest in the mine at a considerable profit.

The Fords became the wealthiest family in Breckenridge and retired to Denver in 1890. Julia died of pneumonia in 1899, and a stroke took Barney in 1902. The *Denver Post* recounted his life and contributions as one of Colorado's pioneers on December 31, 1903:

> *One of Denver's prominent citizens in the early days was a colored man, Barney Ford, who made and lost half a dozen fortunes and finally retired from business with a competence. . . . Barney Ford was the most noted caterer and restaurateur in the Rocky Mountain region, respected by everyone and patronized by the best people.*

Ford's accomplishments in frontier Colorado are a credit to any man, and even more noteworthy for a runaway slave.

Battle of Glorieta Pass:
The Gettysburg of the West

1862—New Mexico Territory

The two Civil War battlefields known as Gettysburg could not be more unlike.

The one in the East, in Pennsylvania, is a fertile, blood-soaked valley spread between two gentle wrinkles—Seminary Ridge, where Confederate forces assembled, and Cemetery Ridge, which the Union army defended. The most prominent physical features, a couple of rocky knolls hooked to the end of Cemetery Ridge, Big and Little Roundtop, would go unnoticed at the site of the other Gettysburg. There, evergreen forests and brushy valleys, high mesas and mountains, sheer cliffs and narrow gorges would swallow the Roundtops whole in the rugged expanses of the West.

The landscape dictated a different kind of fighting at Glorieta Pass, the Gettysburg of the West, as well. Canyons and cliffs and outcrops and trees and brush prevented the kinds of mass charges common at Gettysburg. Nor would the numbers of soldiers present support such tactics. At Gettysburg, for example, George Pickett's infamous charge alone involved some 12,500 Confederate troops—ten times the total Confederate strength at Glorieta Pass.

Still, just as the battle at Gettysburg proved a turning point in the Civil War back east and took the wind out of Confederate sails, the same is true of the battle at Glorieta Pass and the Civil War out west.

Like the war itself, the Battle of Glorieta Pass resulted from an unimaginable amount of hubris on the part of Southerners concerning their ability to wage war against the might of the Union. It all started in the West with the rebel government's rash notion—with a good deal of local support—to divide New Mexico Territory and add part of it to the secessionist nation.

At the time, New Mexico Territory of the United States of America consisted of all of present-day New Mexico and Arizona, as well as a wedge of southern Nevada. The Confederates ran an east-west line along the thirty-fourth parallel and claimed everything south of that line, roughly half of the Territory, as their own. Lieutenant Colonel John R. Baylor gathered up a band of secessionist soldiers in Texas, crossed over into New Mexico, and on July, 23, 1861, captured Mesilla—near Las Cruces—and declared it the capital of the Confederate Territory of Arizona and named himself governor.

Then came this, dated February 14, 1862: "I, Jefferson Davis, President of the Confederate States of America, do issue this, my proclamation, declaring said 'Act to organize the Territory of Arizona' to be in full force and operation, and that I have proceeded to appoint the officers therein provided to be appointed in and for said Territory."

General Henry Hopkins Sibley, commander of a brigade of volunteer cavalry in west Texas, had bigger dreams. He hatched a plan to march through the seized territory, conquer the rest of New Mexico, and capture supplies along the way, including weapons from the armory at Fort Union near the confluence of the Cimarron and Mountain branches of the Santa Fe Trail. Then, with volunteer soldiers recruited along the way, he would proceed northward to take over Colorado and its rich mines, head west through Utah, then Nevada, adding those places to his spoils, and carry on to California and take over the seaports there. His success would enrich the Confederacy and likely force European powers to recognize the fledgling nation and bring the war to an end.

The Confederate government signed off on his plan and bestowed the rank of brigadier general on the expedition's inventor.

For a time it looked like it might work. Sibley's Texans hastened to Fort Craig on the Rio Grande, near the village of Valverde. Colonel Edward Canby, commander of the Department of New Mexico, first refused to engage with his friend Sibley's forces, preferring the relative safety of the fort. An industrious Union officer did attempt to drive off the invading Confederates with an attack of exploding mules. But the mules, being mules, refused to pack their suicide bombs into the rebel lines and only managed, at the cost of two of their number, to stampede Confederate cattle and horses—a small victory, but an important one, as it put a big dent in already scant supplies.

Come the morning of February 21, 1862, the Confederates chose to ignore Fort Craig, since it chose to ignore them, and simply bypass it. But when they reached the ford across the Rio Grande at Valverde, Union troops were on hand to refuse their crossing.

An intense daylong battle ensued, with the soldiers fighting cold and snow as well as each other. Union forces had the best of it most of the day, but eventually caved under Confederate pressure and hobbled back to Fort Craig. The rebels captured six cannons and uncontested access to the road to the territorial capital, Santa Fe. But so many mounts were lost that one Confederate cavalry regiment was unhorsed and marched as infantry for the remainder of the campaign.

Neither commander earned his keep during the fight. Sibley was said to be so drunk that he turned command over to Colonel Tom Green, while Canby's abysmal battlefield tactics were blamed for the loss.

But the battle was over, and Sibley's troops took to the road. Along the way to the capital city, the invading force paused long enough to capture Socorro and Albuquerque. On March 13 the rebels unfurled the Stars and Bars above the Palace of Governors in Santa Fe, and New Mexico Territory was in Confederate hands.

It was, however, a hollow victory. Rebel troops were so short of supplies that their only recourse was to push up the old Santa Fe Trail another hundred miles or so to Fort Union, where a wealth of provisions and armaments were stored in warehouses and armories built by Sibley himself during his service in the US Army.

In order to reach Fort Union, the Confederate army would have to negotiate Glorieta Pass. The southern extreme of the Sangre de Cristo Mountains forms one boundary of the pass, Glorieta Mesa looms as the opposite barrier. The pass wanders some eight miles, with narrow

The arsenal at Fort Union was to supply arms for the Confederate army's expedition to conquer the West. LIBRARY OF CONGRESS

openings at either end and a valley, about a quarter of a mile wide, in between. Johnson's Ranch lay just outside the pass's western entrance, the narrow and rugged Apache Canyon. Within the pass was Pigeon's Ranch, and Kozlowski's Ranch lay outside the eastern end of the pass. The Santa Fe Trail and Glorieta Creek flowed along the narrow valley.

The US Army, despite its impotence thus far in stopping the invaders, was determined to make Glorieta Pass the end of the road for Confederate intruders. Aware of the approaching threat, the commander at Fort Leavenworth in Kansas ordered Colorado's acting governor, Lewis Weld, to mobilize a regiment of Colorado Volunteers under Colonel John P. Slough and hasten the 950 troops south to reinforce the 800 soldiers at Fort Union. The Volunteers battled weather and terrain to make the four-hundred-mile march in just two weeks.

They did not linger long at Fort Union, however. Volunteer and US Cavalry troops lit out on the Santa Fe Trail for Kozlowski's Ranch, arriving on March 25 to find rebel scouts already within the confines of the pass. Major John Chivington, who would later earn infamy as "the butcher of Sand Creek," led Union scouts into the pass and captured their Confederate counterparts.

Both armies continued moving into Glorieta Pass, the Confederates from a bivouac at Johnson's Ranch, Union troops from Kozlowski's Ranch. They met in Apache Canyon the afternoon of March 26.

The Confederates deployed two howitzers and opened fired on advancing Union forces. But the Colorado troops sent soldiers up the steep sides of the canyon to flank the enemy, forcing the rebels to fall back and dig in at a narrower part of the gorge. Along the way they demolished a sixteen-foot-long wooden bridge that spanned an arroyo cut by Apache Creek.

Again, Union soldiers scrambled up the sides of the canyon to catch the Confederate troops in a crossfire, with other troops applying pressure from the front. And again, the Texas solders fell back, prompting a charge by the Union cavalry. The mounted solders raced their horses down the Santa Fe Trail, leaping across the gorge and ripping into the rebels. While suffering severe casualties and seeing many of their troops captured, the Confederates managed to save their cannon and hang on until dark before falling back to Johnson's Ranch, minus some 130—or perhaps as many as 220—of their number killed or captured. Union soldiers spent the night at Pigeon's Ranch then fell back to Kozlowski's Ranch. Their losses on the day were fewer than thirty.

Come the morning, a truce was called to allow the dead to be buried. The day of respite also allowed the arrival of reinforcements. And so, on the morning of March 28, each side in the conflict had just shy of thirteen hundred soldiers to throw into the fight.

Confederate officers, led by Colonel William R. Scurry (Sibley was in Albuquerque, supposedly in his cups), pushed their entire number through Apache Canyon and toward Pigeon's Ranch, save a small force at Johnson's Ranch to guard supplies and animals. Colonel Slough, on the other hand, opted to divide his force, sending some four hundred and more men up Glorieta Mesa to ride beyond Apache Canyon and around the Confederates and attack from the rear. Chivington led that expedition, but it was New Mexico natives Lieutenant Colonel Manuel

Chaves and scout Anastasio Duran who knew the territory. Their mission failed in that the Confederates had pushed into Glorieta Pass well beyond Apache Canyon, putting them out of reach.

But, for those flanking forces, all was not lost.

As Chivington's soldiers topped the mesa, the Confederates established a line less than a mile from Pigeon's Ranch where they deployed nearly all their thirteen hundred troops, outnumbering Slough's remaining eight hundred soldiers. Slough, however, enjoyed an advantage in armament, aiming two twelve-pounder, two six-pounder, and four mountain howitzers at the Texans' one six-pounder and two mountain howitzers. The battlefield was broken and irregular, strewn with rocks and brush and trees, eliminating any possible use of mounted troops. Fighting would be afoot and fierce.

The battle started in late morning, and by early afternoon the rebels' superior numbers had the Union army in retreat, first falling back to Pigeon's Ranch, and a couple of hours later, to a position about a mile east of there. Played-out soldiers on both sides kept up the fight until late afternoon, when the bluecoats called it a day and retired to Kozlowski's Ranch, leaving the field and the victory to the rebels.

Their celebration, however, was short lived.

The troops atop Glorieta Mesa, unable to carry out their orders, discovered the Confederate supplies down below at Johnson's Ranch. Chavez and other officers eventually convinced Chivington to launch an attack, and Duran led the troops over the edge, clambering their way down cliffs and canyon walls and steep slopes. The surprised rebel guard gave up without much of a fight, and the Union troops set fire to some eighty wagons loaded with nearly all the Confederate army's supplies and killed off most of the herd of five hundred mules and horses.

So, despite Confederate victory in the fighting at Glorieta Pass, the loss of provisions, ammunition, and other stores turned the engagement into a bitter defeat. It is said the rebels were so impoverished they even had to borrow Union shovels to dig graves for their dead.

And so it was back to Santa Fe for the Confederates, where they lowered the Stars and Bars and limped back to Texas, never again to threaten New Mexico Territory or the West.

As is often the case in battle, precise casualty figures are difficult to come by. Each side brought, more or less, thirteen hundred troops to the fight. Depending on who you ask, the Union army lost thirty-one, or thirty-two, or thirty-eight, or fifty-one killed; fifty, or sixty-four, or seventy-five, or seventy-eight wounded; and fifteen, or twenty, or thirty, or thirty-five captured or missing. The Confederate army left behind thirty-six, or forty-eight, or sixty killed; sixty, or eighty, wounded; and twenty-five, or ninety-two, or ninety-three captured or missing.

Numbers at Gettysburg, Pennsylvania, if no more precise, are certainly larger. The Union army brought almost 94,000 soldiers to that fight, the Confederate army near 72,000. Each side left behind more than 23,000 casualties, either killed, wounded, captured, or missing.

Despite the disparity in numbers, the Gettysburg of the West, the Battle of Glorieta Pass, was every bit as pivotal in turning the tide in its theater of war as was the other Gettysburg.

Massacre at Bear River:
First, Worst, Forgotten

1863—Washington Territory

Dawn had yet to lighten the horizon when US Army cavalry troops led by Major Edward F. McGarry and under the command of Colonel Patrick Edward Connor rode over the edge of steep bluffs to slip and slide their way some two hundred feet down to the banks of the Bear River. Across the stream and a half mile of snow-covered river bottom lay a Shoshoni winter camp they intended to surround and destroy.

Darkness was only one obstacle in their path. Cold was another, with temperatures well below zero throughout the expedition. The cavalry had already lost about one-third of its strength to the chill—more than seventy soldiers felled by frostbite had been left behind days earlier. Ice blocks and slush streaming in the swift current complicated the crossing of the Bear River. But determined troops whipped and spurred reluctant mounts into the cold stream. All drenched their feet and legs, thereafter burdened by icy boots. A few were doused head to toe, falling off plunging horses and emerging from the stream looking—and likely feeling—something like human icicles.

The troops, Californians who volunteered to fight in the Civil War, found themselves instead stationed in Salt Lake City. There, rather than fighting rebels, they were to protect the telegraph line, mail service, and overland trails to keep California from becoming isolated from the Union. The army was also ordered to keep the Utah Mormons—whose loyalty to the United States was suspect—from fomenting a rebellion of their own, and to discipline hostile Indians as necessary.

And so the troops found themselves splashing across the icy Bear River on January 29, 1863.

Since western migration had begun in earnest twenty years earlier, most of the main trails passed through the homelands of the Shoshoni Indians. This network of related tribes occupied a broad swath of land from, roughly, South Pass on the east to the mountains and deserts of central and northern Nevada on the west, and from the Salmon River and Snake River plain on the north to the Salt Lake Valley and adjacent Wasatch mountain valleys on the south.

The Shoshoni had occupied the region for thousands of years, living in seminomadic family-based bands of a size local resources could support. These bands were loosely organized into larger groups on a regional scale for trade and defense, as well as with the larger Shoshoni nation. Culturally, the Shoshoni varied from a horseback Plains Indian way of life in the eastern bands to a tenuous desert existence, much like their Paiute neighbors, in the west. Buffalo, elk, deer, bighorn sheep, rabbits, fish, fowl, berries, seeds, pine nuts, roots, and tubers served as food at various times and places depending on season.

All that changed when emigrants rolled through Shoshoni homelands and Mormon settlers colonized the rich valleys the Indians had relied on for centuries. Game animals were killed off or scared away, streams and lakes fished out, native plants grazed off by cattle or plowed under, and seasonal migration patterns and village sites broken up by settlements and busy trails.

Along with the travelers and settlers came disease, killing off helpless Indians by the thousands. Other Shoshoni died at the hands of whites, gunned down in disputes over theft of property, with many killed for the crimes of a few. Some were abused, even killed, for sport.

Survival required response. Generally peaceful people, the Shoshoni tried to accommodate emigrants and settlers. While most saw the value of white goods and trade, others became increasingly belligerent as more of their homelands were lost and more of their people killed by emigrants, whether by weapons or sickness. Mormon settlers attempted to coexist, and did for a time, but cultural differences between Indians and whites were too great. As elsewhere on the continent, native people were pushed aside or exterminated in a relentless quest for land and wealth. More and more, the Shoshoni were pushed out of rich lands and into marginal areas where survival proved impossible.

Some raided wagon trains—and, later, settlements—in response, making off with food and livestock. Others begged and badgered for food. All of which the whites resented, which led to increased tension and bloodshed.

The Northwestern Shoshoni, who lived in the Cache Valley, Malad Valley, Bear River Valley, and adjacent areas, bore the brunt of the ongoing conflict and were very nearly wiped out of existence that January morning.

As they often did in winter, the Northwestern Shoshoni were living in a village in the Bear River bottoms, somewhat sheltered from winter by surrounding high bluffs. They bathed in nearby hot springs. Horse herds grazed rich pastures. Children played on the hillsides. Hunters rode out in every direction to search for game. Mormon settlers in Franklin and other Cache Valley settlements shared meager supplies of grain.

About seventy-five lodges made up the Shoshoni encampment, tucked into a brushy ravine cut by Beaver Creek between the bluffs and the Bear River. Shelters varied from hide- and canvas-covered tipis to wickiups built from brush. The village site was just across Utah Territory's northern border (the location of which was uncertain) in what was then Washington Territory but, before the year was out, would be Idaho Territory.

In the weeks leading up to the encounter with the soldiers, the Northwestern Shoshoni hosted other bands in a Warm Dance, a festival to hasten winter's end and encourage the arrival of spring. Thousands gathered for food, dancing, storytelling, games, and contests. During the celebration a group of young men riding through the countryside came upon a small party of Montana miners, lost and slogging through the snow in search of the road to Salt Lake City.

The Indians robbed the travelers, making off with supplies and livestock. Intervention by a local Mormon leader led to the return of most of the stolen goods, but the angry young men eventually opened fire on the white men, killing one. Report of the incident in Salt Lake City resulted in arrest warrants for Shoshoni chiefs—who were not involved in the affair, but named in the documents simply because their names were known.

Colonel Connor of the California Volunteers saw the murder as an excuse to punish the Indians and relieve the boredom of winter quarters for his troops, so he planned an expedition. The territorial marshal sought Connor's assistance in arresting the chiefs; though the army commander invited the lawman along, he informed him the warrants weren't needed, as he did not intend to take any prisoners.

Meanwhile, many Warm Dance visitors to the Shoshoni camp anticipated trouble after the shooting and left for home. The Northwestern Shoshoni stayed, assuming if trouble did come it would amount to a negotiation, and perhaps the surrender of the guilty parties—if they could be located. Otherwise, it was life as usual—until, that is, tribal elder Tin Dup had a dream in which he saw blue-coated horse soldiers attacking the camp and killing his people. His warning prompted others to leave. There were, perhaps, some four hundred to five hundred Shoshoni left in the camp on Beaver Creek the morning the soldiers came.

If there is anything at all heroic in the army's involvement in the affair, it is the cavalry march to Bear River. Connor led his troops out of Camp Douglas on the east bench above Salt Lake City after dark to maintain secrecy and surprise. The force, guided by notorious Mormon scout, frontiersman, and gunfighter Porter Rockwell, rode into the face of a howling north wind so frigid that blowing snow froze feet into stirrups; beards and mustaches iced over, making breathing difficult; and canteens froze solid—including those containing contraband liquor. But the cavalry rode on in the subzero gale, covering a remarkable sixty-eight miles before stopping near the town of Box Elder in a concealed camp at the mouth of a Wasatch Mountain canyon that led to Cache Valley.

Here is where more than seventy soldiers, frozen so severely they were unable to continue, were left behind. When darkness again fell, the others bucked deep snow in Sardine Canyon through the night to arrive the next day in the southern end of Cache Valley, where they would rendezvous with other soldiers and then move on to the northern end of the valley to attack the Shoshoni.

The soldiers they would meet were infantry troops, sent north by Connor a few days earlier as decoys. Under the guise of escorting a wagon train of grain back from Cache Valley, those soldiers, too, braved fierce winter weather, including a severe snow storm, as they marched with wagonloads of supplies and ammunition. So, while everyone—including the Shoshoni—was aware that the army was on the way to Cache Valley, few knew the size or nature of the force, or that its real mission was to attack and destroy the Indians.

After a brief rest near the Mormon village of Mendon, the forces moved northward through Cache Valley, with, again, the infantry plodding along ahead of the cavalry. The plan was to meet up at nightfall in Franklin, the northernmost settlement in the valley and the nearest to the Shoshoni camp on Bear River.

A few Shoshoni were visiting Franklin that afternoon, collecting a ration of grain from Mormon stores, and so were among the first to witness the arrival of the soldiers. They rode out in a hurry for camp, some twelve miles away, leaving part of their grain allotment behind. There is no doubt the Shoshoni were aware of the army's presence in the neighborhood—knowledge that allowed the village to prepare for attack.

Connor organized his troops in Franklin and prepared for the final night march on the Shoshoni. Again, his intent was to give the infantry and supply wagons a head start, with the cavalry troops catching up before dawn within striking distance of the village. The commander encouraged haste—fearing the Shoshoni would escape—but conditions conspired against speed.

Franklin residents were reluctant to aid the troops, and it took time and a significant amount of strong-arming on Rockwell's part to convince his Mormon brethren to provide a guide for the final leg of the journey. A pair of brothers finally agreed, and the infantry and supply wagons set out.

Until then the wagons had traveled on roads—snow covered and deeply drifted, but roads just the same. Now, they would travel cross-country. Cache Valley residents had long since learned to pull the wheels off their wagons in winter and replace them with runners—but the army's wagon masters either weren't given, or chose to ignore, advice to convert their conveyances to sleighs. So, the wagons soon bogged down in deep snow, with soldiers and teams fighting for every inch of headway.

The bloodiest massacre of Indians by the US Army in the Old West was led by Colonel Patrick Edward Connor.

Riding out as scheduled, Connor and the cavalry soon overtook the infantry and wagons, upsetting the plan to rendezvous near the village. The frustrated colonel stayed to sort out the situation with the wagons, sending Major McGarry ahead with the cavalry and orders to surround the Shoshoni encampment to prevent their escape, and then await the arrival of the rest of the troops.

And so McGarry, and some 150 mounted troops, slid down the bluffs to the banks of the Bear River in the dark before dawn.

With no doubt about the presence of troops, Shoshoni leaders debated late into the night about a course of action. Bear Hunter, ranking chief in the camp, listened as some chiefs encouraged a fight while others, including Sagwitch, recommended they wait and see—assuming the whites, as usual, would bluster and bully, take a few prisoners, and ride away. In the end they loaded the few guns they had, strung their bows, and settled in to await the morning.

A restless Sagwitch woke up in the early hours and wandered around the camp. Something—he was unsure just what—drew his attention to bluffs across the river, where a mist or cloud of churned snow, or perhaps steam from the sweat or breath of hard-working horses, signaled activity. The chief roused the village, and defensive preparations started in earnest.

The difficulty the cavalry encountered in the river crossing delayed the soldiers until dawn, so the Shoshoni witnessed the size and strength of their attackers. Indian fighters spread out along the edge of the ravine, concealed in willows as they faced the snowy plain over which the soldiers would come.

McGarry soon realized, given the terrain and the size of his force, that he could not follow Connor's order to surround the village. As the major, always primed for a fight, considered his options, activity at the village stirred his ire and prompted a hasty, perhaps unwise, decision.

Reports of exactly how it happened vary, but apparently a Shoshoni warrior rode onto the plain in battle regalia, waving a war lance decorated with scalps of emigrants and settlers. From their concealed positions, other Shoshoni taunted the soldiers with insults and war cries. However it happened, the Indians stirred McGarry's fighting blood. He immediately designated a quarter of his troops as horse holders, formed the rest into a battle line, and launched a frontal assault on the entrenched warriors.

Waiting patiently until the advancing soldiers were within deadly rifle range, the Shoshoni laid down a barrage that dropped several of the enemy. Of the fourteen army deaths that day, and the seventy-some wounds, most were likely inflicted during those opening stages of the fight. No matter the bravery or tenacity of the soldiers, they were no match for the concealed Indians protecting their homes and families. Shoshoni riflemen held the cavalry troops at bay, preventing them from reaching the village, let alone overrunning it, as McGarry had planned.

Meanwhile, Colonel Connor gave up on getting the supply wagons—and the howitzers concealed within—to the Shoshoni village. With infantry troops carrying as much ammunition as possible, they force-marched toward the fight.

From the top of the bluffs, the commander realized the difficulty McGarry and the troops faced. As soon as possible, he got the infantry to the riverbank and used the cavalry mounts to ferry them across the stream. McGarry's troops withdrew, and Connor sent the major on a flanking move up the opposite bluffs and across the upper reaches of Beaver Creek ravine. Other troops maintained pressure on the Shoshoni front while still others crossed the ravine's mouth near the river to flank the opposite end of the village.

The Shoshoni fought hard and held the troops off for a time, but soon exhausted their scarce supply of ammunition. Enfilading fire from the flanking attacks, combined with increased pressure at the front, soon drove the Indian fighters into the village to defend it as best they could with bows and arrows, lances, war clubs, and tomahawks. The soldiers pressed the attack, surrounding the camp. As they attacked from all sides, the Shoshoni had no avenue of escape and scores were cut down as they tried to climb the bluffs, swim the river, or cross the plain.

At some point discipline among the soldiers broke down, and what started as a battle became wholesale slaughter. In close quarters, with pistols as their primary weapons, troopers waded through the village, gunning down any Indian they encountered—including old men, women, and children. Women were raped and then killed. Others were cruelly tortured. Infants and small children were slung headfirst onto rocks, the frozen ground, or any hard surface at hand. Wounded and helpless Shoshoni were dispatched with a bullet to the head, or the blow of an ax.

Body counts in such situations are always uncertain, but within a few hours of the soldiers' arrival, somewhere between 250 and 350 Shoshoni were dead, left as carrion on the massacre field or floating away in the icy river.

Some did manage to escape—perhaps as many as 160. Among the survivors was Sagwitch, who, wounded, escaped on horseback with the help of others. But survival was tenuous, as the soldiers burned and scattered what food supplies they did not take, burned every lodge standing, and commandeered the horse herd.

Those who escaped eventually made their way, cold and hungry, to other bands in the area. Sagwitch eventually reassembled many of the survivors and, as a result, the Northwestern Shoshoni remain as a people.

As for the soldiers, although they were victorious against the Shoshoni, their survival that day was by no means certain. Temperatures remained below zero and the effects of the cold were crippling. Lodgepoles and firewood from the Indian camp fed fires to ward off the chill, but suffering—particularly among the wounded—was severe. While the army huddled around the meager warmth of campfires through the night, Porter Rockwell arranged for sleighs, teams, and teamsters in Franklin. Come morning, plunder, supplies, the wounded, and soldiers unable to ride their own or Shoshoni horses were loaded in sleighs and carried to Franklin. Dead soldiers were loaded into supply wagons for burial at Camp Douglas back in Salt Lake City.

The soldiers, dead and alive, received a hero's welcome. Connor, promoted to brigadier general in recognition of the accomplishment, said this to his troops: "Continuing with unflinching courage for over four hours you completely cut him to pieces, captured his property and arms, destroyed his stronghold, and burned his lodges."

Historian Hubert Howe Bancroft had a different view when he wrote in 1889, "Had the savages committed this deed, it would pass into history as a butchery or massacre."

But the massacre at Bear River did not pass into history at all. Celebrated by the army for a time, it seems to have disappeared into the lengthy chronicles of the Civil War era. Settlers in the area—many revolted by the cruelty of the soldiers—gave it short shrift in local history, perhaps believing it best forgotten. Historians, almost to a man, overlooked it in their accounts of the West, and those who did mention it often reported it inaccurately.

For a century, the little notice the massacre did receive referred to it as a "battle," implying some measure of equality between the combatants. Perhaps that is a defensible view of the fight's early going. But once the Shoshoni ammunition ran out, once the soldiers ignored cries for surrender and continued killing, once the soldiers resorted to rape, torture, and infanticide, claims of it being a battle become absurd. And while there remain a few holdouts for that point of view, all official accounts—including those of the army—now recognize it as a massacre.

Getting to that point was, in itself, a battle. But determined efforts by historians, particularly scholar Brigham Madsen and Shoshoni historian Mae Parry, along with members of the communities near the massacre site, eventually won the day. Still, questions remain as to why the single biggest massacre of Indians in the entire history of the West is, for the most part, unknown. Efforts to protect the site, to recognize it as a National Historic Site, have stalled out for nearly two decades despite the National Park Service's recognition of its worthiness. The designation has been blocked largely for political reasons, but some progress has been made and hope for future protection remains.

One might still ask, however, about history losing the massacre in the first place. While only conjecture is possible, some reasons seem obvious. One, of course, is the Civil War. Reports of the massacre may have been diluted and overwhelmed in a steady stream of news of bloodshed.

Another is location. Isolated as it was, in a remote corner of the West, it may have drawn little interest. Also related to location is that no one voiced a strong claim to that particular piece of real estate, then or later. While the Cache Valley is culturally and geographically tied to Utah, the massacre occurred just over the border, so it need not be included in histories of the state or territory.

Add to that the fact that Mormon settlers of the day had no desire to publicize violence in their midst, reeling as they were from incidents such as the Mountain Meadows Massacre, continuing claims that disguised Mormons were often responsible for depredations blamed on Indians, and suspicions about Mormon disloyalty to the Union.

On top of that, the Mormons came west to escape a history of disagreement and persecution in the States, and the people tended toward isolationism with little interest in communicating with anyone outside the fold.

Related to its obscurity is the lack of outrage about the incident—at least on a widespread, well-publicized basis—among the Mormons. Most of the common reasons for forgetting the massacre at Bear River ought to apply, as well, to the later Sand Creek Massacre. But that atrocity, owing largely to an infuriated public in Colorado, led to courts-martial, hearings, and investigations, making it much better known then and now. None of that happened in Utah. And much of the reason can be laid at the feet of an apathetic, or even approving, public.

Still, the massacre at Bear River deserves our notice if for no other reason than it remains the first, and worst, massacre of Indians by military forces in the entire history of the American West.

Adobe Walls: Ruins of a Way of Life

1864 and 1874—Texas

On the fringe of the Llano Estacado, near the Canadian River in the Texas Panhandle, stood, in 1864, the crumbling ruins of a fort, or trading post, built some two decades earlier by William Bent of the fur-trading Bent family. The family had been instrumental in westward expansion and trade from early days, with far-flung enterprises stretching from Missouri to beyond the edges of the frontier, including several outposts and forts to supply and trade with Indians, trappers, and Mexicans. But the fort near the Canadian was long since abandoned, and the adobe walls of the structures built by Bent were tumbling down.

Comanche, Kiowa, and Arapaho were among the wide-ranging native tribes frequenting the region and had, for years, fought settlement of their homelands by emigrants from the United States. Ever-growing freight trains along the Santa Fe Trail to the north were also troublesome to the Indians, as the traders represented further encroachment on their lands and way of life. With the full fury of the Civil War commanding the attention of the army in the 1860s, the tribes took the opportunity to increase raids on settlers, travelers, and commerce on the Texas plains and as far north as Kansas and into New Mexico.

Brigadier General James Henry Carleton, senior commander of army troops in the Southwest, determined to punish the Indians and assigned the task to Christopher "Kit" Carson, legendary mountain man, scout, Indian fighter, and recent nemesis of the Navajo. Carson, at the head of some three hundred volunteer troops and a large contingent of Ute and Apache scouts, left Fort Bascom in New Mexico in early November

1864 and followed the course of the Canadian River into the panhandle of Texas. With the plains tribes settling in for winter, army officials believed they would have better luck finding and destroying them. Carleton's orders to Carson did not include negotiation—he told Carson, "You know I don't believe much in smoking with the Indians. They must be made to fear us or we can have no lasting peace."

The first target to present itself was a Kiowa village, and the troopers tore into it with a vengeance. As the soldiers destroyed the village, the Indians scattered, taking refuge in nearby Comanche encampments and alerting their allies to the army's presence. Carson continued along the river to take up a defensive position near Adobe Walls, the ruins of Bent's fort, in the vicinity of several large Indian encampments. A pair of twelve-pounder mountain howitzers, dragged through the rough terrain all the way from the New Mexican fort, were deployed on high ground near the walls, and Carson and his soldiers watched nervously as warriors by the hundreds, more than a thousand, gathered.

The howitzers would prove instrumental in the fight. Sensing imminent attack by overwhelming numbers, Carson ordered his gunners to "throw a few shells into that crowd over thar." The long-range bombardment did little physical damage. But the Indians, seasoned fighters, spread their forces so as not to present convenient targets and approached the soldiers with greater caution. Rather than launch an immediate attack, the Indians awaited reinforcements, and by the next day they faced Carson's force some three thousand strong—outnumbering the soldiers by a factor of ten.

Although the Comanches outnumbered the soldiers, they were outgunned. Some had rifles, but most of the Indians fought with bow and arrow. Their skill with either weapon, however, was considerable, and their ability to fight from horseback remarkable. The mounted warriors attacked the dug-in troopers repeatedly for hours, launching sorties from different angles. But each assault was repulsed by the superior firepower of the soldiers, with cannon fire proving instrumental in holding off the relentless attacks.

Carson knew his advantage would last only as long as his ammunition, so late in the afternoon he ordered his forces to abandon Adobe

Walls and retreat upriver. The Comanche and Kiowa fighters pursued the soldiers, shooting down into the river bottoms from surrounding bluffs and setting fires to hinder the army's retreat. Bitter fighting continued until dark, when the Indians abandoned the fight, considering the day's battle a good showing against the army.

By some measures the Indians got the worst of the fight. Although no reliable body count exists, numerous Indians—perhaps as many as sixty dead and upward of one hundred wounded—were torn to pieces by cannon fire and shot down by rifles. By contrast the army, outnumbered ten to one, suffered only a half dozen dead and another two dozen wounded at Adobe Walls and in the vicious fighting during its withdrawal.

Still, the Indians held the field, and while the army claimed a win in official accounts, Carson later said, "The Indians whipped me in this fight." The soldiers, in fact, were fortunate to escape with their lives.

But seldom, if ever again, would the tribes of the Southern Plains force American troops to retreat from a fight. And, taking a longer view, the first battle at Adobe Walls would prove to be the beginning of the end of the free-roaming way of life for the Comanches and Kiowa, as the pressure of white encroachment would relentlessly force them off their homelands.

A decade later, Adobe Walls became the site of another battle, this time between Indians of the Southern Plains and whites in the buffalo trade.

Buffalo hunters had been traveling increasingly farther afield from the Kansas plains in search of their quarry and by 1874 were well established in the area near Adobe Walls, with a few hundred hunters at work. Wanting to capitalize on the activity, a small group of entrepreneurs set up shop near the ruins, taking hides in trade for food, clothing, powder, lead, cartridges, guns, and other supplies. With the nearest competition some 150 miles away at Dodge City, it seemed a safe bet.

A trading post, food establishment (with a female cook—the only white woman in the vicinity), stable, and hide yard went up in the spring, built picket-fence style from cottonwood logs chinked with clay. A less ambitious trading establishment soon opened for business, this one a sod-walled saloon, followed by a log blacksmith shop.

Business was brisk, and the settlement at Adobe Walls a going concern. Stacks of buffalo hides were abundant, with as many as one thousand a day taken in trade. Sales at the store were steady, and the cook, Mrs. Olds, is said to have served her fare on fine imported stoneware.

When the sun set on June 26, 1874, twenty-nine people inhabited Adobe Walls. In addition to Mrs. Olds was a mixture of buffalo hunters, skinners, drivers, cooks, bartenders, smithies, and shopkeepers. Bat Masterson was there, as was Billy Dixon, whose reputation would be established during the coming fight.

Sometime during the wee hours of the morning—two o'clock is the time usually given—the ridgepole in the sod saloon cracked. The report, as loud as a rifle shot, awakened most everyone, and they set to work to repair the damage and save the roof from collapsing on the tonsil varnish parlor. The mishap would prove providential.

The Indians, meanwhile, had been dealing with misfortunes of their own for years. With the Civil War settled, white settlers were pouring into their homelands at unprecedented rates. Buffalo hunters were wiping out the herds, threatening the very existence of the tribes as well as destroying their own hide trade.

Several tribes joined in the spring of 1874 for a sun dance and discussions on how to respond to the growing threat the whites represented. Several Comanche, Kiowa, Cheyenne, and Arapaho bands opted to follow the lead of Quanah Parker, a Quahadi Comanche chief born to white captive Cynthia Ann Parker and Peta Nocona, a leader of the Nokoni band.

Also instrumental in the Indian alliance was a Comanche medicine man named Isa-tai (usually translated to English as Coyote Dung). He claimed to have learned in visions that the Indians would be victorious, and even concocted a magic war paint that would make the warriors and their horses impervious to bullets fired by the whites. The Indians opted to test their medicine at Adobe Walls. Estimates vary as to their number the day they attacked the settlement, ranging from two hundred to seven hundred mounted fighters. By any count the allied fighters who assembled on the plains vastly outnumbered those gathered at Adobe Walls.

Intending to catch their victims asleep, Quanah Parker and his warriors thundered out of the sunrise. But, owing to the broken roof beam, most of the residents and visitors were wide awake when Billy Dixon spied the attackers and sounded the alarm, saving the lives of most of the Adobe Walls inhabitants. Two brothers, Isaac and Jacob Sheidler, were killed in the wagon where they had slept. Another man, Billy Tyler, was shot and killed before he could reach cover in the buildings. The only other death among the whites during the fight was the husband of Mrs. Olds—she accidentally shot him through the head when passing him a reloaded rifle.

Famous frontiersman Christopher "Kit" Carson led army forces in the first Battle of Adobe Walls, in 1864. LIBRARY OF CONGRESS

The Indian attack very nearly succeeded, and the rest of the fighters at Adobe Walls were lucky to survive the onslaught. Only the protection of log and sod walls spared the hunters and others in the settlement as the determined warriors swarmed around. Those in the buildings reported that Indians thrust the barrels of their guns between the logs in the walls to fire. Bullets and arrows peppered walls and doorways. Indian combatants tried to pound down doors with rifle butts and force them open by backing their horses into them. But it was all for naught, as the hunters effectively repelled the close-range attack with the superior firepower of their revolvers.

And the Indians learned, soon enough, that despite their overwhelming numbers Isa-tai's medicine could not protect them from the rapid fire of the handguns. Killed and wounded warriors fell in large numbers. Although the actual number of Indians killed can never be known, as the warriors carried their dead and wounded from the field, at least a dozen bodies,

Comanche leader Quanah Parker led Indian forces in the second Battle of Adobe Walls, in 1874. LIBRARY OF CONGRESS

perhaps as many as fifteen by some accounts, fell too close to the buildings to be recovered. Sensing the futility of their tactics—which may well have been successful had the whites been sleeping as expected—the Comanches and their allies withdrew.

For the rest of the day the attackers attempted various forays against the defenders of Adobe Walls. But the "Big Fifty" Sharps buffalo guns and marksmanship of the buffalo hunters now came into play, effectively keeping the Indians from drawing close enough to mount a meaningful attack.

The next morning found the fight still at a stalemate—the Indians settling in for a siege, the whites comfortable among vast stores of guns, ammunition, food, and other necessaries.

The next day, Billy Dixon and others watched a small group of Indians ride out onto a bluff in the distance, apparently to study the situation and plan their next move. Dixon, known for his marksmanship, accepted a challenge to shoot one of the remote warriors. Taking in hand a borrowed Sharps "Big Fifty," he drew aim and fired, knocking a mounted warrior from his horse.

Disheartened by this further demonstration of the ineffectiveness of Isa-tai's magical protection, the Indians quit the fight altogether and left the area.

Dixon's long-range shot soon became the stuff of legend. Some reports say that a team of US Army surveyors measured the distance a couple of weeks later and reported it at 1,538 yards, nearly nine-tenths of a mile. Dixon himself told his wife (who recorded it in his biography) that the distance was about 1,200 yards. In later editions she changed the figure to match the army's number. Archaeologists who researched the Adobe Walls battle site measured it at 1,028 yards.

No matter the exact distance, it was a remarkable shot with the powder and rifles of the day, and modern-day marksmen cannot easily match it. Besides, the shot effectively ended the fight, and, for that reason alone, it is futile to dispute its importance in the history of the American West.

Despite the Indians' withdrawal, the battle at Adobe Walls put fear into the merchants, and within weeks they pulled up stakes and abandoned what they couldn't haul back to Dodge City in their wagons. The "defeated" Indians put the torch to the buildings.

Any satisfaction or sense of victory the Southern Plains tribes may have felt with the destruction of the Adobe Walls trading post was short lived. The battle at Adobe Walls inspired action by the US Army and the resulting Red River War.

Army forces converged on the tribes scattered across the Southern Plains from every direction—from Fort Dodge (Kansas) in the north, Fort Concho (West Texas) to the south, Fort Griffin (Texas) to the southwest, Fort Sill (Oklahoma) to the east, and Fort Union (New Mexico) to the west. The converging columns fought as many as twenty battles with the Indians, bouncing the encircled Indians back and forth like so many billiard balls.

The noose drew to a close in Palo Duro Canyon, which is in the Texas Panhandle, approximately eighty miles southwest of Adobe Walls. There, on September 26, 1874, troops under the command of Colonel Ranald S. Mackenzie overran a large Indian village, destroyed winter stores, burned lodges, and slaughtered a thousand horses. Although some Indians escaped and evaded capture through the winter, they were all on reservations by summer with the surrender of Quanah Parker and his Quahadi Comanches at Fort Sill.

Billy Dixon, of the remarkable long shot, further aided the Indians' demise when he signed on as an army scout for the Red River War. Pinned down in a buffalo wallow with another civilian scout and four cavalry troopers, Dixon and the others held off a large band of Kiowa and Comanche attackers. One soldier died and all the men were wounded, but a fierce storm drove the disheartened Indians from the field. The survivors were each awarded the Medal of Honor, with Dixon and his fellow scout, Amos Chapman, among only a handful of civilians ever given the honor.

Dixon returned to Adobe Walls in 1880 to take up a homestead in the area. He became postmaster when a post office opened for business on his ranch and was the first sheriff of Hutchinson County.

It can be said that Adobe Walls proved the downfall of the free-roaming way of life of the Southern Plains tribes. The first battle convinced them of the strength and tenacity of the white soldiers; the futility of the second battle there likely wounded the spirit of the people so severely they would never recover, let alone find the ability to mount another offensive.

Like the crumbling ruins of William Bent's original fort and the ashes of the buffalo hunters' trading post, their way of life decayed, trampled into dust by the feet of white settlers and soldiers.

The End of the Civil War:
Battle at the End of Texas

1865—Texas

Texas is big. If you don't think so, ask a Texan. Outsized in both geography and history, the biggest state in the lower forty-eight ends in Brownsville. Or, it begins there, depending on your point of view. The city barely hangs onto the tag-end of Texas where the state, Mexico, the Rio Grande, and the Gulf of Mexico crowd together and shoulder one another for position. Beginnings and endings seem to define Brownsville.

For example, the Mexican-American War started there. And the Civil War ended there. Relations between Texas and Mexico had been tenuous even before the birth of the Republic of Texas in 1836. Among many things, they disagreed about the border: Mexico held it was the Nueces River; Texas—and the United States, once the nation admitted Texas as a state—claimed the Rio Grande as the boundary. The "Nueces Strip" represented a difference of some 150 miles, an insurmountable distance when it came to diplomacy. In an attempt to stabilize the situation and, most likely, intimidate Mexico, the United States sent troops to the mouth of the Rio Grande with orders to build a fort.

On April 25, 1846, some two thousand (reports of the actual number vary) Mexican cavalry troops attacked seventy (or eighty or some similar number) US Army dragoons patrolling the disputed area about twenty miles from the fort, upstream along the Rio Grande. The Mexicans killed sixteen Americans and took the rest hostage. This border incident, called "the Thornton Affair" after Captain Seth B. Thornton, the army captain who commanded the captured troops, provided an excuse for President James K. Polk—who, with "Manifest Destiny" aspirations, had designs on Mexican lands all the way to the Pacific Ocean—to ask Congress to declare war. He did, and they did, on May 13, 1846.

The Mexican-American War lasted one year, nine months, one week, and one day. And when the conflict, which started near Brownsville, ended with the signing of the Treaty of Guadalupe Hidalgo, the absence of Texas from Mexico's portfolio was reinforced and Mexico found itself without the territory that, today, encompasses California, Nevada, Utah, and Arizona, and sizeable slices of New Mexico, Colorado, and Wyoming.

Now, Brownsville's role in the end of another war.

Every student who paid attention in American History class will likely inform you the Civil War (or the War of Northern Aggression, War for Southern Independence, War of the Rebellion, or War Between the States, as you prefer) ended April 9, 1865, when Confederate general Robert E. Lee surrendered to Union general Ulysses S. Grant in the village of Appomattox Court House in Virginia.

That was certainly the beginning of the end. But it was not the end. When Lee surrendered the Army of Northern Virginia, his capitulation did not affect other Confederate armies amounting to some 175,000 soldiers. Among the at-large rebel forces were those in the Trans-Mississippi Department under the command of General Edmund Kirby Smith, who vowed to fight on even after learning that Lee had thrown in the towel.

Among the enemy forces facing Smith were about 1,100 Union soldiers (it may have been as many as 1,900) manning a make-believe blockade on Brazos Island at the mouth of the Rio Grande near Brownsville. Earlier, US soldiers numbering more than 6,000 had held Brownville, but in July of 1864 most decamped to fight back east, and those left behind, an insufficient force to occupy the city, relocated to Brazos Island and set up their ineffective blockade.

While the Union troops could, in theory, halt traffic on the Rio Grande to Brownsville, they lacked the authority to hinder trade at the Mexican port of Bagdad, on the opposite bank of the river near Matamoros. And so it was that Confederate cotton made its way to Brownsville, across the river to Matamoros, then to Bagdad, and off to market. Bagdad and Brownsville were also home to all manner of inbound smuggling the Federals were helpless to stop.

The opposing forces had, for a time, honored an informal truce and had even held negotiations for surrender of the Confederate forces early in 1865, once it became clear that the rebel cause was lost. However, a Confederate commander up the line pulled the plug on the talks. Then the Union commander was replaced by Colonel Theodore H. Barrett, who had yet to win his spurs in combat and seemed determined to do so.

In May Confederate soldiers at Brownsville learned of Lee's surrender, and some packed up and went home. Also in the air were reports that the rebels intended to leave Brownsville for Corpus Christi. This news apparently inspired Barrett to mount a mission to retake Brownsville. Lacking any other reasonable explanation for the expedition, it appears the Union officer hatched the plan simply as an attempt to gain glory.

When Barrett ordered troops to the mainland for the attack on May 11, 1865, with about 250 men, there were some 190 Confederate cavalry troops at Palmito Ranch. A storm hindered the Federal crossing and the soldiers ended up marching all night to reach White's Ranch, not far from Palmito Ranch, where they intended to set up a camp from which they hoped to launch a surprise attack.

There was to be no surprise, however, as troops from the French Foreign Legion in Matamoros watched the Union advance and informed the Confederates. Other accounts say it was civilians who spilled the beans; still others say it was rebel soldiers who spotted the Yankees. In any event, their presence was known to the Confederates at Palmito Ranch.

Rather than allowing the soldiers to rest and recover from the all-night march, Union officers ordered the troops on toward Brownsville. They met the Confederates at Palmito Ranch and the overwhelmed rebels retreated. But, later in the day, the rebels rallied and, with perhaps as few as a hundred men, managed to force the weary Yankees off Palmito Ranch and eventually back to White's Ranch. Both forces called it a day, settled in for the night, and awaited reinforcements.

The night was a short one. Barrett arrived on the scene with more soldiers early in the morning of May 13, bringing Union strength to about five hundred. The superior Federal force again attacked and pushed the persistent rebels off Palmito Ranch, and then set fire to the scant supplies captured there.

Confederate help arrived in the afternoon, strengthening the force to some three hundred soldiers and adding half a dozen artillery guns to the mix. The outnumbered Confederates counterattacked with cavalry charges left, right, and center, and cut loose with cannon fire. While the artillery did little damage, it did surprise and scare the Union soldiers, who immediately went into retreat.

The Yankees were in such a hurry to get out of there that they outran their rear guard and, as a result, the Confederates captured numerous Federal soldiers. The rebels pressed the attack, chasing the scrambling Union troops all the way back to the crossing to Brazos Island, stopping from time to time to unlimber the artillery and toss a few shells toward the enemy. Darkness halted the attack and allowed the retreating troops to cross to the island, which they accomplished before the morning of May 14.

The Civil War—at least the fighting part of it—was over.

As is usually the case, casualty figures are uncertain. Barrett reported the loss of 115 Union troops: 1 dead, 9 wounded, 105 captured. Other reports indicate 8 killed, 24 wounded, 202 captured; 30 killed or wounded; 4 killed and 12 wounded; or 30 dead, including some drowned in the crossing and others shot from across the river by French Foreign Legionnaires. Reports of Confederate losses range from no deaths and 5 or 6 wounded to as many as 30 deaths and a few dozen wounded.

A private soldier from Indiana, John J. Williams, is believed to be the last man killed at the Battle of Palmito Ranch and, as such, the last Civil War combat death.

In addition to being the final battle of the Civil War, Palmito Ranch may well have been the most ethnically diverse. Union troops included white as well as black soldiers, and the Confederates deployed white, Hispanic, and Indian troopers.

Even as fighting was underway at Palmito Ranch, governors of the Confederate states in the Trans-Mississippi Department were in the process of telling General Edmund Kirby Smith to surrender his army, which he did on June 2, 1865. Several Confederate officers and soldiers who fought at Palmito Ranch immediately crossed into Mexico, fearing charges of treason would be brought against them.

However, the only charges resulting from the Battle of Palmito Ranch came on the Union side. Stung by criticism over his inept handling of the fight, Colonel Barrett filed charges against one of his subordinate officers. In an attempt to shift blame, he accused Lieutenant Colonel Robert G. Morrison of neglecting his duty, disobeying orders, abandoning his colors, and other charges. During the court-martial the defense called one of the Confederate officers engaged in the fight, who testified it was Barrett who had cut and run before a force less than half the size of his own. Morrison was found innocent of all charges.

Even the Battle of Palmito Ranch and the surrender of the Confederate armies did not bring an official end to the Civil War. More than a year later, when President Andrew Johnson declared the end of the rebellion on April 2, 1866, he excluded Texas because the Lone Star State had yet to form a government. When that was finally accomplished on August 20, the Civil War was finally, formally, officially at an end.

First Blood: Showdown in the Street

1865—Missouri

Some folks called him "Little Dave"—regional vernacular for Dave Junior, as he was named for his father, Davis Tutt. But his father was no more, the victim of an Ozark Mountains hillbilly feud of Hatfield-McCoy proportions, the Tutt-Everett War, which raged when Little Dave was but a boy.

The hostilities between the factions commenced in 1844 in Yellville, Arkansas, over political disagreements, and seethed for six years, with regular gunfights and other violent altercations. The combat climaxed on July 4, 1849, with a lengthy gunfight that burned powder until both sides ran out of ammunition, and then continued with hand-to-hand fighting, with some of those hands wielding clubs and knives. When the dust cleared, five lay dead, including Davis Tutt, Little Dave's father.

Local law enforcement, outnumbered and ineffective in stopping the fight, called in help from outside, and it took the militia from a neighboring county days to round up and arrest several suspects. A jailbreak, the assassination of Little Dave's grandfather (Hansford Tutt), relocation to more peaceful climes, and deaths from natural causes finally ended the feud.

The fracas has nothing to do with this story, except to establish the fact that Davis Tutt came from a long line of boisterous toughs prone to use gun violence to settle scores. When the entire nation took up arms in an even bigger feud, Tutt joined an Arkansas infantry regiment in 1862 and fought for the Confederate army for the duration.

After the war Tutt landed in Springfield, Missouri, where he would have a brief brush with fame. Brief, because his name is not well known today. But the incident for which Tutt is remembered—by some—involved one of the most famous names the Old West ever produced: James Butler Hickok.

Known to history as "Wild Bill," Hickok was born in 1837 in Illinois. A violent altercation over a girl sent Hickok packing at age eighteen, and he made his way to Kansas to join the Red Legs, a band of abolitionist vigilantes. Hickok joined the Union army during the Civil War and served as a scout.

Hickok, like Tutt and hordes of other veterans of both armies, found himself in Springfield after the war. George Ward Nichols visited the city in 1865 and wrote a lengthy and admiring article about Wild Bill. The story, published in *Harper's New Monthly Magazine* in 1867, was instrumental in creating Hickok's fame and establishing him as the original dime-novel hero of the Old West.

Nichols wrote of the many veterans infesting Springfield: "These men were temporary or permanent denizens of the city, and were lazily occupied in doing nothing." The writer showed his bias where northern solders were concerned: "Here and there upon the street the appearance of the army blue betokened the presence of a returned Union soldier, and the jaunty, confident air with which they carried themselves was all the more striking in its contrast with the indolence which appeared to belong to the place."

Nichols must have ranked former Union scout Hickok among the "jaunty," for he wrote of their meeting, "I and the drowsing city were roused into life by the clatter and crash of the hoofs of a horse which dashed furiously across the square and down the street. The rider sat perfectly erect, yet following with a grace of motion, seen only in the horsemen of the plains, the rise and fall of the galloping steed." The smitten scribe then said, "As I looked at him I thought his the handsomest physique I had ever seen," and went on to describe his subject at length:

Bill stood six feet and an inch in his bright yellow moccasins. A deerskin shirt, or frock it might be called, hung jauntily over his shoulders, and revealed a chest whose breadth and depth were remarkable. These lungs had had growth in some twenty years of the free air of the

Rocky Mountains. His small, round waist was girthed by a belt which held two of Colt's navy revolvers. His legs sloped gradually from the compact thigh to the feet, which were small, and turned inward as he walked. There was a singular grace and dignity of carriage about that figure which would have called your attention meet it where you would. The head which crowned it was now covered by a large sombrero, underneath which there shone out a quiet, manly face; so gentle is its expression as he greets you as utterly to belie the history of its owner, yet it is not a face to be trifled with. The lips thin and sensitive, the jaw not too square, the cheek bones slightly prominent, a mass of fine dark hair falls below the neck to the shoulders. The eyes, now that you are in friendly intercourse, are as gentle as a woman's.

Despite the author's florid description and obvious admiration, Hickok was reputed to have been something of a rowdy in Springfield. There are reports of drunkenness, riding horseback on sidewalks and into buildings, and otherwise living up to the "Wild" in his nickname. Among his fellow rounders in Springfield was Davis Tutt. The two were said to have been drinking and gambling buddies.

But Hickok and Tutt had a falling out. Some reports claim Wild Bill had impregnated Tutt's sister. Others say Tutt's relationship with a lady friend of Wild Bill's was too close for comfort. Still others lay it off to gambling disagreements. Whatever the case, it seems Tutt was better with a deck of cards than Hickok and, as a result, Wild Bill was in his debt, unhappy about it, and at some point refused to play against him.

There are various accounts of what lit the short fuse that eventually exploded into violence between the two. What seems to have happened, more or less, is that Hickok was engaged in a card game that his former friend and now nemesis witnessed. Tutt apparently offered free advice and lent money to one of Hickok's rivals in an attempt to see Wild Bill beaten. But Hickok won more than his share of the stakes, accumulating some $200 in the process.

According to the story in *Harper's*, author Nichols heard about the card game from someone he called "Captain Honesty" and reported it in his source's words. The captain claimed Tutt said, "Bill, you've got plenty

Frontiersman James Butler "Wild Bill" Hickok participated in the first documented Old West showdown in the street. COURTESY OF THE CITY OF DEADWOOD HISTORICAL PRESERVATION COMMISSION

of money, pay me that forty dollars yer owe me in that horse trade." Captain Honesty added, "And Bill paid him."

That did not satisfy Tutt. "'Yer owe me thirty-five dollars more; yer lost it playing with me t'other night.' Dave's style was right provoking; but Bill answered him perfectly gentlemanly: 'I think yer wrong, Dave. It's only twenty-five dollars. I have a memorandum of it in my pocket down stairs. Ef its thirty-five dollars I'll give it yer.'"

Sitting on the poker table was Hickok's fancy gold pocket watch. Captain Honesty reported that Tutt told Hickok, "I'll keep this yere watch till yer pay me that thirty-five dollars," and stuffed the ticker in his pocket.

Hickok had no choice at the time, surrounded as he was by Tutt's cohorts, but to absorb the body blow to his pride. He advised Tutt not to wear the watch in public or he would kill him. Tutt supposedly replied that he fully intended to wear the watch and to be anything but subtle about doing so.

No matter what led Hickok and Tutt to this round of threats and intimidation, there seems to be little doubt that it was the Waltham Repeater pocket watch and the pride associated with it that pushed the two into what is believed to be the first, and one of the few, actual faceoff-in-the-street gunfights that ever occurred in the frontier West.

Movies, television, and shoot-'em-up western stories have taught generations of Americans—and people around the world—that walk-down, quick-draw gunfights were a commonplace and accepted method of settling disputes, blowing off steam, and just plain raising hell in the Old West. Who can count the millions of impressionable minds that watched the spectacle of the quick-draw shootout that opened the 635 weekly episodes of *Gunsmoke*, America's purportedly longest-running prime-time live-action television drama? That gunfight certainly parrots the pattern—the steely eyed Matt Dillon steps into the street to confront a man likewise posed in the near distance. That man, of course, is in dark attire, furthering the formula. Dillon waits, and waits, a tense few seconds that stretch longer in the imagination, until the "bad guy" makes his move, at which point the "good guy" draws his revolver with lightning speed—the blink of an eye faster than his opponent—and returns fire with deadly accuracy.

Whether on *Gunsmoke* or elsewhere, even the casual fan of the western has seen and read of similar gunfights countless times.

But did it happen like that?

No doubt, there is a history of men facing off, pistols in hand, in duels in both America and Europe, since at least the eighteenth century (and even before that, using swords). But those were more often a social occasion and showy defense of honor than they were killing contests. Some participants died, for sure, but often duelists deliberately shot wide or high. Honor was just as satisfied by facing death as meting it out or suffering it.

As for the Old West walk-down shootout? Most historians say such a thing seldom occurred.

Gunfights were usually confused, close-quarters combat in chaotic situations. Despite the insult to our notions of frontier fair play, many men were killed from ambush by concealed shooters. Even what may be the most famous shootout of all, the gunfight at the O.K. Corral, was a muddled affair that doesn't fit the mythical pattern of a quick-draw contest. Some pistols were already in hand, others in pockets rather than holsters, and Doc Holliday carried a short double-barreled shotgun. And it was never established after the melee involving the nine men who, for certain, shot whom with what.

That entire incident was triggered by those on the side of the law attempting to disarm the others, who were carrying sidearms and long guns in violation of city ordinances. Similar laws were not uncommon in the frontier West, further limiting opportunities for quick-draw showdowns in the streets.

All that aside, there is no doubt that a showdown, representative in many ways of the myth, occurred between Wild Bill Hickok and Dave Tutt in the town square of Springfield, Missouri, on July 21, 1865.

Following Tutt's seizure of Hickok's timepiece, friends of the Southerner reportedly hounded Hickok and urged a confrontation, and it seems Tutt was willing. Captain Honesty claims to have warned Wild Bill. "'Don't you bother yerself Captain,' says he. 'It's not the first time I have been in a fight; and these d—d hounds have put on me long enough. You don't want me ter give up my honor, do yer?'"

The day after the card game, or, according to some, later the same day, or even a few days later according to other accounts, Wild Bill entered the town square. As Captain Honesty told it to Nichols for *Harper's*:

Just then Tutt, who war alone, started from the court-house and walked out into the squar, and Bill moved away from the crowd toward the west side of the squar. 'Bout fifteen paces brought them opposite to each other, and 'bout fifty yards apart. [Seventy-five yards between the men is the more commonly reported distance.] Tutt then showed his pistol. Bill had kept a sharp eye on him, and before Tutt could pint it Bill had his out. At that moment you could have heard a pin drop in that squar. Both Tutt and Bill fired, but one discharge followed the other so quick that it's hard to say which went off first. Tutt was a famous shot, but he missed this time; the ball from his pistol went over Bill's head. The instant Bill fired, without waitin' ter see if he had hit Tutt, he wheeled on his heels and pointed his pistol at Tutt's friends, who had already drawn their weapons. "Aren't yer satisfied, gentlemen?" cried Bill, as cool as an alligator. "Put up your shootin' irons, or there'll be more dead men here." And they put 'em up, and said it war a fair fight. . . .

Bill never shoots twice at the same man, and his ball went through Dave's heart. He stood stock-still for a second or two, then raised his arm as if ter fire again, then he swayed a little, staggered three or four steps, and then fell dead.

Nichols reported his own later conversation with Hickok himself:

I had a curiosity, which was not an idle one, to hear what this man had to say about his duel with Tutt, and I asked him: "Do you not regret killing Tutt? You surely do not like to kill men?"

"As ter killing men," he replied, "I never thought much about it. The most of the men I have killed it was one or t'other of us, and at sich times you don't stop to think; and what's the use after it's all over? As for Tutt, I had rather not have killed him, for I want ter settle down quiet here now. But thar's been hard feeling between us a big while. I wanted ter keep out of that fight; but he tried to degrade me, and I couldn't stand that, you know, for I am a fighting man, you know."

A cloud passed over the speaker's face for a moment as he continued:

"And there was a cause of quarrel between us which people round here don't know about. One of us had to die; and the secret died with him."

"Why did you not wait to see if your ball had hit him? Why did you turn 'round so quickly?"

The scout fixed his gray eyes on mine, striking his leg with his riding-whip, as he answered, "I knew he was a dead man. I never miss a shot. I turned on the crowd because I was sure they would shoot me if they saw him fall."

Hickok, of course, was not shot and he did not fall. He was tried, and acquitted, for killing Davis Tutt. For more than two decades afterward he lived a colorful life in the frontier West. He hunted buffalo, served as a scout for the Seventh Cavalry, was a lawman in Kansas cow towns, made an attempt at showmanship but fled the footlights, and gambled. Along the way he associated with other legendary figures of the western frontier, including Buffalo Bill Cody, George A. Custer, John Wesley Hardin, and "Calamity Jane" Canary.

Wild Bill Hickok met his death in a gunfight, of sorts, in the mining boomtown of Deadwood in Dakota Territory on August 2, 1876. But rather than face Wild Bill in the streets in one of those mythical Old West showdowns, his assailant, Jack McCall, stole up behind Hickok while the unwary man was engaged in a card game and shot him in the back of the head.

Jacob Brodbeck: First Flight, First Crash?

1865—Texas

Most history books would have us believe a pair of bicycle mechanics were the first men to go airborne in sustained flight in a heavier-than-air powered machine. They say it happened on Kill Devil Hill near Kitty Hawk on North Carolina's Outer Banks on December 17, 1903. Wilbur and Orville Wright's contraption got off the ground midmorning and stayed aloft for twelve seconds, covering 120 feet with Orville as pilot. Later, Wilbur took the controls and flew 175 feet. Orville took off again and landed 200 feet later. Neither brother rose more than 10 feet off the ground.

No one at the time cared much or paid much attention. Despite a public relations effort by the Wright Brothers, what little interest they managed to generate in their accomplishment soon waned.

Today, however, Wilbur and Orville Wright and their wooden aircraft are widely celebrated. But few—very few—people sing the praises of a man who may well have bested the brothers by nearly forty years.

That man was Jacob Brodbeck.

Born in Germany in 1821, Brodbeck emigrated in 1846 and settled in Fredericksburg, Texas, in 1847 among many of his countrymen. He taught school and was county surveyor, school district supervisor, and county commissioner. Brodbeck later lived in San Antonio and Luckenbach.

Most of all, it seems, Brodbeck was a tireless tinkerer. He built a self-winding clock, a machine to make ice, a washing machine driven by a windmill, and flying toys powered by rubber bands.

Apparently his interest in flying wasn't confined to toys, for Brodbeck himself wrote in an August 7, 1865, article in the *Galveston Tri-Weekly*

News (which also may have appeared elsewhere), "For more than twenty years I have labored to construct a machine which should enable a man to use, like a bird, the atmospheric region as the medium of his travels." Brodbeck said of the project:

> *I studied the flight of birds, examined the mechanical laws, govern-ing these wonderful structures, and observed the various peculiari-ties of air, and so in the year 1863, I was at last able to construct a machine which, requiring comparatively little power, imitates the flight of birds. Inasmuch as it makes use of the same peculiarities of air, and moves with the same celerity in every direction, with the wind and against it, not resembling, however, in form a bird, but being constructed like a ship, which has caused me to call it "Air-Ship."*
>
> *A small model constructed that year proved by successful experi-ments the correctness of my principles; later experiments, with some improvements in the model, resulted still more favorably.*

He went on to tell how the Civil War and blockades of the South delayed his work, then got to the main point of the article: "The con-struction of a large Air-Ship requires more means than I possess, but this surely should not be an insupportable difficulty. Should I not be justified to call upon the aid of my fellow-men who will be all, directly or indi-rectly, benefitted by the result of my invention!"

But begging for funds wasn't Brodbeck's purpose. Instead, he offered shares by subscription in his endeavor, promising a payoff from the sale of patent rights or air-ships. He then went on to educate potential investors in the fineries of forthcoming flight in his air-ship.

> *When the air-ship is in motion, the aeronaut has to each hand a crank, one to guide the ascending and descending motion, the other the lateral steerage. Immediately before him is the compass, while a barometer with a scale made for the purpose, shows him the approximate height. Another apparatus, similar to the ball regulator of a steam engine, shows him the velocity, as well as the distance passed over. It is self-evident that the speed of the air-ship depends upon the motive power*

and on the direction and force of the winds; according to my experiments and calculations it will be from 30 to 100 miles per hour.

It worked.

The fund-raising effort, that is.

Brodbeck assembled enough money from investors to build his airship. His description of the craft offers some—but not much—idea of what it looked like:

> *The AIR-SHIP consists of three main parts.*
>
> *1. The lower suspended portion, formed like a ship with a very short prow to cut the air; it serves to hold the aeronaut, as also the power producing engine with all the steering apparatus. This portion is shut up all around to prevent the rapid motion from affecting the breathing of the man within. . . .*
>
> *2. The upper portion, or flying apparatus, which makes use of the resistance of the air, consists of a system of wings, partly moveable, partly immovable, presenting the appearance of horizontal sails, but having functions entirely different from the sails of vessels.*
>
> *3. The portion producing the forward motion consists of either two screws, which can be revolved with equal or unequal motion, so as to serve the purpose of lateral steering, or of wings of a peculiar construction. The preference to be given to one or the other depends on the force of the motive power. Another apparatus controls the ascending motion.*
>
> *The material is so selected as to combine the greatest strength with the least weight.*

But would it fly? Brodbeck and a few others—including some of the investors—got together September 20, 1865, for a test flight. Just exactly where is unclear. Various reports place the test near Boerne, at Fredericksburg, or in San Antonio. But most accounts agree it was in an open field near Luckenbach where the aeronaut made—or failed to make—history.

Apparently, Brodbeck and his air-ship temporarily defied gravity to a height of twelve feet above the ground and flew some one hundred feet

This mangled heap is believed by many to be the wreckage of an airplane that took flight decades before the Wright Brothers. DAUGHTERS OF THE REPUBLIC OF TEXAS LIBRARY

before coming back to earth. Marginally higher, but not quite as far, as Orville Wright's first flight some forty years hence.

But there was no second attempt. The air-ship crashed into a chicken coop, hit a live oak tree, or simply made a hard landing. In any event, it was in no condition to fly again. So, if Brodbeck was the first to achieve powered flight in history, he was, by definition, the first involved in an airplane crash. He was not seriously injured.

The "force of the motive power" for Brodbeck's craft came from a clockwork-type mechanism—essentially a large windup spring that spun the propeller or propellers as it unwound. Once the spring wound down, of course, the air-ship had no more "motive power" and had to land. One account speculates there were two mechanisms, the first with a spring to wind the propellers and wind up a second spring as it wound down, after which the second spring would take over to propel the plane and rewind the first spring, and so on. If this were, in fact, the case, the account speculates, the two springs would, during the process, reach a point of equal tension and the whole system would simply stop. Whether that is the case, or the air-ship was powered by a single spring that simply wound down and stopped, is difficult if not impossible to say.

As is what happened next. Again, reports disagree.

The most melodramatic account says Brodbeck set fire to his invention and never gave flying a second thought. Given his devotion to the notion for "more than twenty years," that seems unlikely. Another story says it was his investors who were disheartened, and refused to front any more money for the enterprise, forcing the inventor to tour the country in an attempt to raise funds, during which his plans and papers were pilfered. Another account adds detail to the theft, saying it occurred in 1900 while Brodbeck was buttonholing prospects at the World's Fair in St. Louis.

Whatever the circumstances, there is no record of Brodbeck attempting again to use "the atmospheric region as the medium of his travels." In fact, there is no indisputable record that proves beyond doubt that he did it the first time. While there are secondhand and hearsay reports of the flight, no accounts or documents by those on the scene have been preserved, or located if they exist. Nor are there any known drawings, blueprints, schematics, or other designs.

On the other hand, there are stock certificates issued to one of the inventor's investors, as well as "detailed specifications written by Jacob Brodbeck of an airship made by him," according to a note attached to a lengthy typewritten document held at the Daughters of the Republic of Texas Library. The note says the typescript originated from detailed written plans "in the handwriting of the late Jacob Brodbeck prior to the construction of his airship which worked successfully as far as it would at that time. It was translated from German to English by his granddaughter, Miss Annie Brodbeck."

The library also has an antique photograph of a jumbled heap of what certainly looks like a crashed flying machine of some kind. Many believe it is Brodbeck's air-ship. And while there is no way to prove it is, there is no way to prove it isn't.

Apparently the US Air Force lends some credibility to aeronaut Jacob Brodbeck and his air-ship, as it recognized his contributions to flight in a 1985 ceremony at Fort Sam Houston in San Antonio honoring, among others, Brodbeck's descendants. And there is a bronze bust of Brodbeck on display in San Antonio's San Pedro Park.

The aeronaut lived out his years on a ranch near Luckenbach, Texas, until January 8, 1910, and is buried there.

Mass Murder: Circleville Massacre

1866—Utah Territory

On September 11 a group of religious zealots, whipped into a paranoid frenzy by fanatical leaders fearing the corrupting influence of outsiders, launched an unprovoked attack against innocent men, women, and children. When the killing ended, these adherents to a religion that preached peace had perpetrated the worst mass murder America had ever seen.

The year: 1857. The place: a rest stop in Utah Territory along the southern trail to California called Mountain Meadows. For a century the massacre was shrouded in obscurity, buried so deep that only rumors and whispered reports spoke of its occurrence. Eventually, the persistent poking around of a few historians brought the incident to light. Over the past half century or so, other interested historians studied and published on the subject until the Mountain Meadows Massacre found its rightful place in the blood-soaked annals of western history. And while that unfortunate bloodbath was the worst mass murder committed by Utah Mormons by a wide margin, it was not the only one. Nine years later, the worst killing of Indians in Utah would spill blood on the ground of a small town called Circleville.

The Sevier River, as it meanders along in a generally northward direction through southern Utah, passes through Circle Valley. The valley, confined by the Tushar Mountains and Sevier Plateau, is a small, generally level basin where the East Fork of the Sevier River pours into the main branch. Mormon Church leader Brigham Young sent settlers to the valley in 1864, and by the spring of the next year, a meetinghouse for church and school gatherings stood among some forty to fifty small houses, most built of logs, where a few hundred—perhaps as many as six hundred—people lived. Twenty-seven miles of bad road to the south led to the town of Panguitch; to the north lay Marysvale, just over twenty miles away on a better road.

The timing of the settlement couldn't have been worse. Just as Circleville was putting down roots, Ute Indian chief Black Hawk launched a lengthy war against the Mormons, plundering communities, rustling livestock, and killing settlers in the towns and valleys throughout the region. The Indians in Circle Valley and nearby areas, however, were Southern Paiutes, mostly a branch of that tribe called Piedes.

Unlike their Ute neighbors, the Piedes—and the Southern Paiutes in general—tended to be peaceful and attempted to coexist with white settlers. Their culture was more attuned to the desert, while the Utes shared some characteristics of the Plains Indian cultures. The Utes owned many horses, which gave them mobility for big-game hunting and war, while the Paiutes kept few horses and tended to migrate seasonally through smaller areas, relying on small game, plants, roots, seeds, and trade with other bands for their living. In fact, the Utes and Paiutes did not get along, as the Utes often raided Paiute villages and took captives to sell as slaves or keep for menial servants.

As the Black Hawk War heated up through 1865 and into 1866, both the Piedes and Mormons in Circle Valley would be affected by the hostilities.

On orders from church leaders, the people of Circleville formed a militia unit, as did settlers in virtually every community. Established for protection against Indian attacks, the volunteer soldiers in Circleville and in neighboring Marysvale were poorly suited for the task. Despite persistent beliefs that frontier settlers in the Old West were well armed, such was certainly not the case in Circleville, Marysvale, Panguitch, and many other communities in Utah Territory. A report from a Mormon leader to the head of the territorial militia said the Marysvale group could produce only "16 men, 13 guns and some revolvers." A similar survey in Panguitch turned up about forty men with a few revolvers and twenty-two long guns, about half of which were essentially useless owing to type or state of disrepair.

The men in Circleville were so bereft of firearms that they would beg the Piedes to lend them their guns. One Circleville settler, Oluf Larson, wrote, "Our arms were also of an inferior kind. I had none, but was lucky enough to get an old shotgun barrel and lock which I cleaned, oiled, and made a stock for. It was little better than a broomstick."

A band of Utes, likely some of Black Hawk's raiders, followed the East Fork of the Sevier River into Circle Valley on November 26, 1865, and attacked Circleville. While some of the Indians terrorized the town, riding through the streets firing their guns and raising a racket, others gathered cattle from the surrounding rangelands. When the Utes left they took with them most of the settlers' livestock and left behind four dead Mormons—two men and two teenage boys caught out in the fields with the cattle. Several other settlers barely escaped with their lives.

The settlers set out to build a stockade around the center of town and meetinghouse after the attack, but it is unclear how much of it was completed. Fortunately, there were no other attacks on Circleville through the winter.

The spring of 1866 did bring a sniff of protection from another source, however. Territorial militia leaders ordered construction of Fort Sanford, some seventeen miles south of Circleville and ten miles north of Panguitch. Fifty men from communities to the west across the Tushar Mountains built and served at the fort. However, given the state of the road and the terrain, it would take hurried riders from Fort Sanford at least an hour to reach Circleville, so any comfort the fort offered was cold.

Black Hawk's raiders entered Circle Valley again in April. The Utes stole herds of cattle from communities along the Sevier River some fifty miles downstream from Circleville and were chased through the night of April 22 by settlers. The Indians hid out near Marysvale and attacked when their pursuers arrived near dawn. One settler was killed and three others were wounded, one of whom later died from his wounds.

The Utes absconded and the Mormon militiamen took up the trail once they got organized in the morning. They trailed the stolen cattle to Circle Valley and up the East Fork of the Sevier River, where the pursuers were joined by men from the Circleville militia. The combined force sat atop a ridge and watched the Utes drive the cattle along the river and up the canyon; then, deciding any further action ill-advised, the citizen soldiers went home.

While all that was happening, two Indians were hanging about across the river from the newly built Fort Sanford. When apprehended by suspicious militiamen on April 22, they turned out to be Piedes who claimed to be carrying a message from Black Hawk to a militia officer from Panguitch, who they claimed to—and, in fact, did—know. The Indians attempted to leave, but the soldiers were having none of it. They shot and killed one Piede, one of the Mormons was wounded, and the other Indian escaped. Later, a band of Piedes near the fort was rounded up, disarmed, and taken to the fort. Another group, near Panguitch, grew suspicious when a militia group showed up and started shooting. After the gun smoke cleared, one white man was wounded and two or three Piedes were dead.

Exaggerated reports of the ruckus at Fort Sanford reached Circleville and added to the anxiety. Seemingly increased comings and goings at the Piede village nearby heightened suspicions. So, never mind the fact that they had always enjoyed friendly relations with the Piedes in Circle Valley, just to be on the safe side the Mormons decided to lock up their neighbors.

On April 23 a delegation visited the Piede camp and invited them to come to town for a visit with William Allred. Allred was the Mormon bishop in Circleville, and in Mormon communities of the day, that put him in charge of all religious, political, social, and military activity, along with anything else of consequence in the community. Some of the Indians rose to the bait and came to town. Allred herded them into the meetinghouse, where they were joined by militia members. The bishop read a letter, apparently sent from Fort Sanford, saying the settlers wanted the area to remain peaceful and offered to help protect the Piedes—but the Indians would have to give up their guns, which, reportedly, the militia badly needed.

Some of the Indians complied; others were reluctant. A little strong-arming on the part of the Circleville men proved persuasive, and all the Piedes were soon disarmed—and tied up with their hands behind their backs.

With those Indians neutralized the Circleville militia surrounded the rest of the Piedes in their camp and forced their surrender. One Piede man attempted a getaway and was gunned down. He either got a shot off before dying or his gun discharged when he fell. In either event, one of the militia members was slightly wounded, and the Indian bullet apparently shot the barrel off another man's rifle.

The captured Indians were disarmed and driven to town, where the men were tied up with the others in the meetinghouse; women and children were forced into the cellar beneath an unfinished construction project. While there is no record of exact numbers, reports indicate there were at least sixteen men and a similar number of women and children.

Guards were posted to keep an eye on the prisoners, and a letter was drafted for Colonel William H. Dame, militia commander over the Circleville regiment, at his headquarters across the mountains in Parowan, informing him of the situation and seeking guidance on what to do with the imprisoned Piedes.

Ironically, Dame was the militia commander who most likely ordered the attack on the wagon train camped at Mountain Meadows in 1857. He gave no such command to the Circleville militia in this instance, however. His superior officer, Brigadier General Erastus Snow, was with Dame at the time and the response came from him. "I left instructions with Col. Dame to see that those prisoners were treated kindly and such only retained in custody as were found hostile or affording aid to the enemy," Snow said later.

Those orders did not arrive in time.

What, exactly, happened next is unclear. Circleville leaders, in later reports, gave conflicting accounts, and much of the information they contained was demonstrably false. They gave reports of confessions of Piedes aiding the Utes in their depredations, including supplying ammunition— although there was no ammunition found in the Piede camp. Information the Piedes supposedly provided about the location of Black Hawk and his raiders was also clearly incorrect. Even the suggestion that the Piedes intended to join the Utes in a larger war against the white settlers was unlikely in light of the mutual dislike between the tribes.

Whatever excuse Circleville leaders cooked up after the fact, it did not justify the slaughter soon to come.

It seems the Piedes were discontent with their imprisonment and managed to untie one another and were "ready to make their escape as soon as it was dark," according to the account of Oluf Larson. "I had just been released and the new guard placed and had not proceeded far when the shooting began. I went back to the meetinghouse and the Indians were all shot and in a dying condition."

Another account suggests only a few of the Piedes were killed when they rushed the guards in the escape attempt, and that a dozen or so were still in the meetinghouse. Those men, apparently, were taken out one by one, were knocked over the head, and had their throats cut—supposedly to save scarce bullets or to prevent upsetting the other Indians with the sound of gunfire.

By whatever method, the men—about sixteen of them—were dead. It is possible that two young Piede men managed to bolt out of the meetinghouse door and run away. Militia guards missed in their attempts to gun them down (although one of them might have been wounded) and failed to capture them.

That left an unknown number—eleven, based on one report—in the cellar. However many there were, they, like their menfolk, died one at a time. Led out of the cellar, bashed on the head, throats opened by knife blade, the Piede women and children bled out on the ground of Circleville. A few small children, perhaps four, thought too young to tell what happened, may have been spared.

No one was ever punished for the murders. Mormon Church president Brigham Young did condemn the town for the massacre, saying, "The curse of God rested upon Circle Valley and its inhabitants."

A few months later, as the Black Hawk War continued, Mormon leaders in Salt Lake City ordered Circleville residents to abandon the town and seek shelter in other communities. On June 20, 1866, the head of the Utah militia showed up with a military force to see to and assist with the evacuation. Only a few of the original settlers would ever return. Marysvale was likewise abandoned.

Resettlement of Circle Valley started with a few families drifting in in 1873; the town was officially reestablished in 1874.

The small town enjoys some measure of recognition in western history today, but not for the Circleville Massacre. In 1879 the Parker family moved to a small ranch a mile south of town. The oldest child, a boy named Robert LeRoy, was about thirteen years old at the time. In later years he would earn notoriety as the outlaw Butch Cassidy.

Black Hawk's Last Ride: Reconciliation

1869—Utah Territory

Unlike many wars, the Black Hawk War in Utah Territory took a long time to get started and a long time to get finished. There was no shot heard 'round the world, no siege at the Alamo, no bombardment of Fort Sumter or the like to touch off hostilities. Instead, there were years of difficulties between Ute Indians and Mormon settlers, starting almost as soon as the religious refugees set foot in the Salt Lake Valley in 1847, that simmered until finally boiling over.

The Mormons, under leader Brigham Young, voiced a policy of coexistence with the Indians of the Territory, of feeding, rather than fighting, them. But it was a strategy more often violated than adhered to, for the Mormons, like all settlers, were hungry for land and often hungry themselves. So it was only a matter of months before the killing started.

Settlements spilled over the edge of Salt Lake Valley by 1848 into neighboring Utah Valley with the establishment of Fort Utah, which grew into the city of Provo, encroaching on traditional homelands and fisheries of one of the many bands of Ute Indians who populated the mountain valleys east and south of the Great Salt Lake. The following year, settlements sprouted in Sanpete Valley farther to the southeast, disturbing the native lands of other Utes.

While Ute leaders were sometimes cooperative, agreeing to allow Mormons to share their fertile valleys, they had no idea what the Mormon presence would come to mean. The game and the fish they relied on, the plants and their roots and seeds they harvested, and the streams that watered it all were killed or driven off, plowed under, diverted for irrigation, and otherwise disturbed and disrupted. Tensions based on nothing more than attitudes of racial and cultural superiority also caused problems.

The Utes took livestock for food and demanded more of other promised foodstuffs than Mormons could or would provide. Soon, there was bloodshed on both sides, sometimes in isolated incidents and at other times erupting into serious confrontations. In the spring of 1849, a group of Mormon militia members out to recover stolen horses and cattle pursued a band of Utes up what came to be called Battle Creek Canyon, where they killed four or five of them.

Young sent a militia force south from Salt Lake City in February of 1850 to relieve settlers at Fort Utah and touched off a bloody series of battles. The Mormons there complained of livestock thefts and intimidation by Utes, and were fearful of retaliation for the murder of a Ute by some of their own. For two days the Mormons and the Utes fought it out at the fort with little effect. The Indians retreated, with some seeking refuge in nearby Rock Canyon and most fleeing across the ice of Utah Lake to a benchland called Table Mountain. Mormons found and annihilated both groups, killing some seventy or eighty Indians. A gruesome scene at Table Mountain saw the frozen corpses of many of the Utes beheaded and the heads hauled away in the interest, supposedly, of medical science.

The bloody incidents at Battle Creek and Fort Utah were witnessed by a young and impressionable Ute who saw the violent deaths of family members. Called Nuch by his people, but Black Hawk by the Mormons, his retaliation would come later.

The next several years saw continued fighting. From 1853 through 1854 a series of raids and skirmishes were known at the Walker War. The Tintic War raged in 1856, along with other sporadic conflicts and clashes over the years, all of which contributed to the deadliest series of confrontations of them all: the Black Hawk War.

Although the fuse that ignited the Black Hawk War was long and slow burning, one particular incident is often credited with triggering open hostilities. It happened April 9, 1865, near the town of Manti, in the Sanpete Valley. A group of Mormons and a group of Utes met to talk about stolen livestock. The conversation became heated, and one of the Indians, called Jake Arapeen or Yenewood, fitted an arrow to his bowstring. One of the white men, John Lowry, reportedly drunk, pulled Arapeen off his horse, then dismounted, and the two proceeded to fight. Cooler heads prevailed and pulled the men apart, and everyone went home—more hostile than when they arrived.

Lowry later explained his side of the altercation:

> *I agreed to meet with them at Manti about the eighth of April and talk the matter over of their killing our cattle. Accordingly, the council took place. It appeared the difficulty would be settled amicably, but a certain young Indian . . . continued to halloo and make demonstrations. . . . I told him a time or two to let me finish my talk. Just then someone called out "lookout, he is getting his arrows!" I rode up to him and turned him off his horse, and pulled him to the ground. The bystanders interfered and we separated. . . . I believe they started hostilities sooner than they would have done had not the incident above mentioned occurred. But the trouble would have come just the same. . . . I have patiently borne the stigma placed upon me, for I knew the facts, and to those who still persist in looking upon me as guilty of precipitating the Black Hawk War I will say this, that I appeal from their decision to a higher court—Our Creator, who will ultimately judge all men.*

Black Hawk was, by then, a young but respected leader among the Utes. He formed a loose-knit confederation of Utes from various bands and recruited allies among the Paiute, Navajo, and Apache nations. The network allowed Black Hawk and his followers to move livestock gathered in raids southward to markets as far flung as Santa Fe and Los Angeles.

While the Indians killed Mormons whenever they caught them out, rustling livestock was their biggest aim. Through the remainder of 1865 Black Hawk and his bands killed more than thirty settlers in Sanpete Valley and Sevier County just to the southwest, and made off with more than two thousand cattle and horses.

Mormon militia groups mustered out in response to the raids chased Indians hither and yon throughout central and southern Utah, mostly to no avail. A militia group overran a Ute camp in Grass Valley in July, and some one hundred Mormons fought about a dozen Indian men and boys for hours and killed most of them. Several women and children were wounded in the battle, and some of the women continued to harass the attackers and were killed. This frightened the other women into a mad stampede, resulting in the killing of many and earning the incident the name "Squaw Fight."

Raids continued through the following year and grew so intense that the Mormons abandoned numerous small towns and forted up in a few of the larger communities. In April of 1866, during an attempt to disarm a group of Paiutes wrongly suspected of taking part in raids against the settlers, Mormon militia members in the town of Circleville killed an entire band of some twenty-seven Piedes, including women and children, except, perhaps, for a few young children and two young men who managed to escape.

A reinforced militia in his favored raiding areas sent Black Hawk farther afield in his marauding, and in June he and approximately one hundred of his followers launched an attack against the small town of Scipio. The raiders killed two residents and rounded up and made off with around 350 cattle and seventy-five horses. Militiamen from several communities in the area pursued the Utes and fought them at Gravelly Ford on the Sevier River. During the fight Black Hawk's horse was killed by gunfire and he was shot in the stomach, a wound that troubled him for the rest of his life.

Other battles were fought at Thistle and Diamond Fork, but the settlers were learning that strength in numbers—in their communities and livestock herds as well as their militia units—was paying off against the Ute raiders. So far as is known, the last raid led by Black Hawk himself happened near the southern Utah towns of Paragonah and Parowan in July of 1867, but the raid was unsuccessful owing to the strength of the guard holding vast herds of cattle and horses.

And so, in August of 1867, Black Hawk and several of his followers made their way to a Ute reservation in the Uintah Basin and spread the word they were ready to talk peace. "We had the pleasure of meeting Superintendent Head [F. H. Head, newly installed superintendent of Indian Affairs in Utah] on Wednesday evening, who had arrived from the Uinta Indian Reservation, where he had met and had a talk with the notorious Black Hawk," the *Deseret News* reported on August 28, 1867. "He expressed a desire for peace; said he could control and would be answerable for his band; and believed he could get the others with him, as they all looked to him as the head chief."

The report said Black Hawk would attempt to arrange peace talks as soon as he could gather other scattered bands of Utes.

"As an earnest of his sincerity, he stated that he had made a covenant, when he commenced to fight, that he would not have his hair cut . . . but now that he was going to have peace, he wished to have it cut, and requested the Superintendent to shorten his locks for him, which was done after finding that he was anxious to have it so." Almost exactly a year later, on August 26, 1868, the same Salt Lake City newspaper reported:

Indian Treaty–Col. F. H. Head, Superintendent of Indian Affairs, and Major Dimick Huntington, Indian interpreter, returned to the city yesterday afternoon from Strawberry Valley, Uinta, where a "big talk" had been held on Wednesday with the Indians and a treaty concluded with those who have been continuing depredatory visits to our settlements in Sanpete. Black Hawk was present, and it is claimed that he has faithfully observed the treaty made last year, and has not been engaged in any raid on the whites since.

Black Hawk made the news again September 16 when the *Deseret News* said it had received a copy of a telegram to church president Brigham Young from the leader of a local Mormon congregation in Springville, in Utah County: "Black Hawk and wife arrived at my house last evening; he wishes me to ask you if he is at liberty to travel as usual, and all be right." Apparently, by that time the Ute leader felt himself either under the protection of the Mormon leader or, perhaps, under his thumb.

His reputation among the Mormons was still evident the following summer, according to a story in the June 2, 1869, *Deseret News* that said, "Dymock B. Huntington, Indian Interpreter, informs us that, on the evening of Friday last, he had a visit from the notorious Chief, 'Black Hawk,' who has been the prime mover in the Indian disturbances for the last few years in the southern portion of this Territory." However, the story went on to report Black Hawk's continued work in bringing groups of Indians in for peace talks. "'Black Hawk' has kept his promise to keep the peace, given two years ago." The Ute chief also reported horses stolen by Indians near Payson, in Utah County, and that "he thinks more vigilance is necessary in that neighborhood."

And so on. A *Deseret News* report on July 7, 1869, had "Brother D. B. Huntington" at Fort Ephraim in Sanpete Valley, meeting a band of "Shib-er-ech and Pi-ede Indians who have been brought in by 'Black Hawk' . . . and are tired and want peace." A week later, on July 14, the *Deseret News* reported the citizens of Manti in Sanpete Valley "feel jubilant over the prospects of peace with the Indians. . . . Black Hawk said he had buried the hatchet and meant to keep it buried. He had found his heart and it was good."

Another story in the same edition reported further on Black Hawk's activities, including word on a growing relationship with whites that is unusual, if not unique, in the annals of Indian-White history: "Repentant Indians.–Brother Dimick B. Huntington [this is the same Indian interpreter whose name was spelled "Dymock" and called "Brother D. B." in earlier reports] reached this city from Sanpete on Monday evening and brings with him a good report of the Indians. He met and had a talk with about 120 of them at Fort Ephraim, about noon last Saturday."

Black Hawk reportedly brought the Indians in and was present at the talks, where: "Five of the principal men spoke on the occasion, expressing themselves very humbly and penitently over their past deeds, and asking what they must do to be saved. 'Black Hawk' said that for four years they had had no heart, but now they had got heart, eyes and ears, and could both see and hear." Furthermore, the repentant Indian leaders "agreed to protect the settlers, and give them warning when mischief was threatened by marauding Indians, and also agreed to bring in all Indians they could who are still marauding and bent on mischief."

Black Hawk's repentant and forgiving attitude toward his former enemies was not a one-time thing or passing fancy. Nor, it seems, was it a scheme to escape punishment or a ploy to put the settlers at ease while he planned future raids. The Ute leader, still suffering the ill effects of the gunshot wound he received at Gravelly Ford and now racked by lung disease—probably tuberculosis—set out on a long ride through the country he had raided over the last two years and more. He rode through the abandoned villages and farms his raids had depopulated, visiting the communities where the Mormons were forted up, seeking safety from the attacks he led. Along the way he publicly apologized, asked forgiveness, and promised peace.

The January, 5, 1870, *Deseret News* carried a letter from Parowan, a community in southern Utah, dated December 22, 1869:

> *Dear Brother Cannon [George Q. Cannon, editor]:–On the 16th instant, we had a big visit from Black Hawk, his brother Mountain, and quite a number of his band. Black Hawk and Mountain talked to the people in the meeting house in the evening, bro. Shelton, from Beaver, being the interpreter. Black Hawk made great declarations of friendship and said he wanted a big peace and a long peace. . . . He said he wished to see the settlements on the Sevier River established again, and promised that they should not be disturbed by the Ute Indians.—Black Hawk's consumptive look and hollow cough indicate that he cannot last long. . . .*

As is often the case with history when Indians are involved, there is little available to give the Ute perspective. But Black Hawk and his long, last ride still figure prominently in the collective memory of the Ute tribe. As with any man who approached greatness, the Ute chief's legacy is, and was, a mixed one among his people. Forrest Cuch served as director of the Utah Division of Indian Affairs and is a Ute Indian born and raised on the Uintah and Ouray Ute Indian Reservation in northeastern Utah. In an interview covering the history of the Ute tribe, he had this to say about Black Hawk:

> *There are some of our people who view Nuch as a sellout, because after he declares peace and cuts his hair he goes around to Mormon settlements throughout the state and he essentially apologizes. And he talks*

to them about peace, and he talks to them about how we should live together. . . . And while that can be viewed as a form of weakness, most of us know that it takes courage to apologize. And most of us know that there is strength in humility . . . and it takes a true warrior to express those sentiments sincerely. So, to me, Nuch is definitely a great hero of our people. He was a powerful warrior and he had fought his war— he didn't talk about it, he executed it. His fight was over. When he cut his hair that was it. . . .

When Nuch exercised his compassion and his forgiveness, and his apology to the Mormon settlers for the depredations, he doesn't just do it to one group. . . . I believe he travels as far as Cedar City, which is the southernmost part of the state. On his way back he's meeting with communities, he's apologizing, he's talking about peace, he's talking about relationships and the future. . . .

By this time he was skin and bone and he finally makes his way back to his homeland, Spring Lake, the place where he was born. And that is the place where he passes on out of this world. His work is complete, he has fought the good fight, and he has ended his life in peace. All the world was not kind to Nuch, but Nuch was kind to his people, and to his land, and in the end he was kind to his victors. He was a great man.

By the end of September, the end was near for Black Hawk. The *Deseret News* of September 28, 1870, carried this report:

Black Hawk.—As President [Brigham] Young and party were coming past Payson on Friday last, Mountain and Joe, two Indians, the first-named being Black Hawk's brother, called upon the President and informed him that the notorious Black Hawk, who achieved such unenviable distinction as the leader in thieving and murderous raids on the people of Sanpete Valley and other settlements a few years ago, was dying. He had lost his sight and speech. He and the Indians with him are encamped at the little spring creek, three miles from Payson.

Then, from the Correspondence column of the October 5, 1870, *Deseret News*:

Spring Lake Villa, Sept. 27th, 1870.

Editor Deseret News:—*Dear Sir,—I hasten to tell you that Black Hawk, the Indian desperado, is dead. He has been living here in camp with his brother "Mountain," together with "Joe" and his band for some days. We knew he was sick, but did not think of so sudden a demise. This morning, before sun up, the Indian wail was heard in their camp, and soon was seen an Indian squaw with, two horses heavily packed, on their way towards the foot of the mountain. Stopping at a small ravine within sight of our door, they killed one of the horses and proceeded to put away the body of the great Black Hawk. This is the place of his birth. Here he commenced his depredations, and here he came to die. . . .*

The Métis: Gone the Way of the Buffalo

1869—Prince Rupert's Land, United States and Canada

Not long after the Bois de Sioux River defines the southernmost junction of the states of North Dakota and Minnesota, it is joined by the Otter Tail River. The result is the Red River, or, more properly in this context, la Rivière Rouge.

The Red River flows on northward, defining the remaining length of the border between North Dakota and Minnesota; enters Canada; and, 550 miles from the confluence of the Bois de Sioux and Otter Tail and 255 miles after crossing the international boundary, pours into Lake Winnipeg. The land it drains along the way, the Red River Valley, was once part of Prince Rupert's Land, belonging to Hudson's Bay Company. The whole of the claim encompassed all of today's Manitoba, most of Saskatchewan, a broad swath of southern Alberta, portions of northern Ontario and Quebec, and, in what is now the United States, all the land in the Red River watershed in Minnesota and North Dakota and small slices of Montana and South Dakota.

The Red River Valley is also the ancestral homeland of the Métis, perhaps the most influential people in the history of the fur trade, buffalo hunting on the northern plains, and all manner of commerce in the region, as well as farming. While concentrated in the Red River Valley, the Métis also spread into Montana, Michigan, and Wisconsin, and into Illinois and Indiana. Their influence in what is now Canada was likewise widespread.

As early as the seventeenth century, and continuing into the eighteenth and nineteenth centuries, French and Scottish fur traders in numbers took wives from the Algonquian, Cree, and other tribes. Families were formed and communities created. A language—Michif, primarily developed from French and Cree, but including words from other native dialects and English—was born, a new culture evolved, and a new people emerged: the Métis.

Originally affiliated with the North West Company and antagonistic to the expansion of Hudson's Bay Company, the Métis early on established themselves as suppliers of pemmican, the food that fueled the fur trade. Dried meat, pounded into tiny pieces and then mixed with fat and often berries, was packed into parfleches for storage and transport. Long-lasting and nutritious, pemmican accompanied explorers, traders, trappers, and most everyone on the western frontier. The Métis were renowned for the quality of the pemmican they produced and enjoyed a virtual monopoly in supplying the provender for the North West Company and later Hudson's Bay Company.

Summer and fall would find the Métis buffalo hunters on the northern plains in large numbers. The squeal of the wheels of their Red River carts—the music of the "North West fiddle"—announced their presence. The carts, built solely of wood and rawhide and leather, with no metal parts, were pulled by horses or oxen and could carry half a ton of buffalo hide, meat, trade goods, or whatever needed hauling. Wooden wheels, turning on unlubricated wooden axles, created the cacophonous wail. For reasons of efficiency and protection, the Métis hunted in groups, with hundreds, sometimes more than a thousand, carts rolling out onto the plains in pursuit of buffalo, which they hunted from horseback.

Besides pemmican, fresh meat—particularly from the cooler autumn hunt—hides, and tongues were also harvested in the buffalo hunts, which continued from around 1820 until the late 1870s, when the herds were all but gone.

Disappearing buffalo herds were not the only challenge threatening the Métis. The nation of Canada, created in 1867, had its eyes on the Hudson's Bay Company's Prince Rupert's Land with the intention of acquiring the territory for its fledgling state. The threat became real in 1869 when Canada purchased Prince Rupert's Land, including the Métis homeland in the Red River Valley.

Land titles were of special concern to the Métis, as land ownership among them was based on the irregular surveys of the French system, centered on watersheds and natural features, while the Canadians preferred the English system of straight lines and right angles. Canadian officials sent surveyors to the region before the transfer from Hudson's Bay Company was complete. The Métis turned them back, postponing the transfer.

To counter perceived threats associated with the Canadian acquisition, the Métis formed a provisional government in November 1869, in an attempt to protect their land and other rights, as well as their culture and very existence. Leading the charge was Louis Riel. A list of rights to be honored as a condition of union with Canada, drawn up by Riel and other members of the Métis government, demanded representation in parliament, bilingual government officials, recognition of existing land rights, and other concessions. The Métis also seized and occupied Fort Garry, where the city of Winnipeg is now located.

While most—including the English-speaking supporters of Canada—agreed with the demands, Riel's government was not without opposition. The Canadian Party, as it was called, formed a militia to oppose the Métis and their supporters. One of the leaders of the opposition group was arrested, tried, and executed by the provisional government on March 4, 1870. As a result, Riel was charged with treason.

Continuing unrest in the Red River Valley led the Canadian government to send a military expedition to restore order—and get rid of Riel. Rather than submit to what seemed to him certain death, Riel fled to Montana. The "Red River Rebellion" was over. During his exile in Montana, Riel worked as a trader and interpreter, married a Métis woman named Marguerite Monet dit Bellehumeur, fathered three children, became a US citizen, dabbled in politics, and taught school.

While many of their demands were honored by the Canadian government, the Métis were not satisfied with what they viewed as limited and tenuous protection of their rights. Riel, even though in exile in the United States, was elected to represent the Métis in parliament three times.

Many Métis left the Red River Valley and migrated west to Saskatchewan and Alberta. There, they faced similar problems with land and rights when increasing numbers of settlers arrived. Others in the region, including the Indian tribes and white farmers, were also dissatisfied with the Canadian government. For the Cree, Blackfoot, Blood, Piegan, and Salteaux tribes, the government seemed unwilling to honor treaty obligations. White farmers, living a tenuous existence on the isolated plains, also sought support from the government and weren't getting it.

The Métis saw Riel as the answer, and in 1884 they sent a delegation to Montana to lure him back to Canada. He agreed to lead the resistance and attempted, with limited success, to unite the Métis, the Indians, and the white settlers. As he had done in the Red River Rebellion, he drew up a list of demands to present to the government. In March of 1885 Riel again formed a Métis provisional government; he was appointed leader, with Métis hunter Gabriel Dumont over the military. Dumont and his militia occupied Duck Lake and on March 26 skirmished with the North West Mounted Police there, killing three policemen and nine volunteers and wounding many others.

Over the next few weeks, Canada poured soldiers into the area, and a force of more than five thousand was soon in the field. Some nine hundred of the soldiers met about 150 Métis fighters at Fish Creek on the South Saskatchewan River near Batoche on April 24. The Métis, entrenched in a ravine, ambushed the soldiers, killing six and wounding nearly fifty, at a cost of four of their own. The Canadian soldiers were also fending off attacks by Indians in the area, taking more casualties and seeing their strategies and tactics disrupted.

Dumont and his troops again engaged the Canadians at Batoche on May 9. The fighting went on for days, with the government forces eventually overwhelming and overrunning the Métis. The Canadians claimed losses of eight soldiers, with fifty of the Métis rebels killed.

This time, Dumont fled to Montana. Riel surrendered May 15. What came to be called the North West Rebellion ended June 3, when the North West Mounted Police killed four Cree warriors at Loon Lake.

Louis Riel faced trial for high treason. His lawyers claimed he was insane, driven by irresistible political and religious zeal. Riel disagreed and articulated his beliefs at trial so well that many were swayed to his point of view. But few, if any, believed him insane. The verdict came back guilty, but the jury asked for mercy. The judge ignored their plea and sentenced Riel to death. After several delays and appeals, the hangman finally stretched his neck on November 16, 1885. Eight Indians were likewise tried and executed for their participation in the rebellion.

Along with Gabriel Dumont, many of the most steadfast Métis leaders were in exile in Montana. Others were in jail. A general amnesty later freed the prisoners and allowed the exiles to return. The aftermath of the Red River and North West rebellions disrupted and disorganized the Métis for decades. But throughout the twentieth century, the resilient Métis agitated for rights and recognition in Canada and were eventually recognized as an aboriginal people.

The Métis in the United States did not fare so well, lost in a governmental requirement to declare themselves either "white" or "Indian," though they were neither. Most assimilated and lost their cultural traditions and heritage. Only in isolated areas near the Canadian border was any semblance of Métis identity or community maintained. There are whispers today of a reemerging Métis identity in the Red River Valley and elsewhere.

Making Barbwire Famous:
The Frying Pan Ranch

1881—Texas

The ranch that made barbwire famous suffers a case of mistaken identity. Established in 1881 with the acquisition of ninety-five sections of the Texas Panhandle, that geographical identification gave the ranch its brand—a circle representing a pan with a bar for a handle: the Panhandle Ranch.

But the name didn't take. As cowboys are wont to do, the hands hired to herd the twelve to fifteen thousand head of cattle that stocked the ranch saw things their own way. They decided the brand looked more like a frying pan, and that's what they called it. Soon enough, rather than the Panhandle Ranch, the place became the Frying Pan Ranch.

Henry B. Sanborn, a salesman, put the place together in partnership with his boss, Joseph F. Glidden. Glidden is one of only a few men, and perhaps the only one, who single-handedly changed forever the history of the American West.

He's the man who invented barbwire. Sort of. Sanborn was one of his salesmen.

The story of the Frying Pan Ranch and the "devil's rope" that encircled it started around 1873 when Glidden went to the county fair in his hometown of DeKalb, Illinois, where he was a farmer. (Glidden was born in Charlestown, New Hampshire, in 1813 and later lived in New York, but moved to Illinois in 1843.) On display at the fair was a new kind of fence built by one Henry Rose. Hanging along a typical, ineffective smooth wire fence was a wooden rail with the points of nails poking out all along its length to discourage cattle and other livestock from leaning against, breaking, and trampling down the wire.

The sight set Glidden to thinking.

He fiddled around with various ideas to create a wire fence with barbs. He cut short lengths of wire at an angle to create sharp points. He modified a coffee grinder to twist the short bits into a loop, or coil, with protruding ends. He strung those "barbs" along a length of smooth wire, then stretched another wire along beside it. He tied off one end of those wires and hooked the other ends to hooks fastened to the axle on a grindstone. He turned the crank on the grindstone, twisting the strands of wire together, securing the barbs. He called it barbed wire and filed a patent in 1874.

He has been known ever since as the inventor of barbwire.

But, really, he did not invent it.

According to the Antique Barbed Wire Society, one of the first, if not the first, patents for recognizable barbwire was awarded to Louis Jannin in 1865 in France.

Credit for the first patent awarded for a barbwire fence in the United States goes to Lucien Smith of Ohio in 1867.

That same year, William Hunt of New York won a patent for a rowel-type barb cut from sheet metal.

A year later, Michael Kelly, also of New York, patented the first metal ribbon barbed fence.

In 1871 Lyman Judson, again of New York, used the word barb for the first time in his patent for a fence.

But none of those patented barbwire designs was practical or affordable for a fence of any length. Joseph Glidden wins that honor for his fence, patented in 1874. The patent was tied up in court for years, challenged by other inventors, but the Supreme Court declared Glidden's process worthy of the patent in 1892, by which point it was too late anyway—Glidden's wire had already won in the court of public opinion and the marketplace.

Glidden and a partner, Isaac Elwood, established the Barb Fence Company in 1874 and cranked out five tons of wire their first year, with continuous improvements in the manufacturing process, increasing production to six hundred thousand pounds the next year. In 1876 Glidden sold his half of the company to Washburn & Moen Manufacturing, pocketed a hefty sum for the sale, and then proceeded to get rich off the royalties from his invention.

Meanwhile, back at the Frying Pan Ranch. . . .

Glidden and Sanborn's notion in 1881 to fence in an entire ranch with barbwire to demonstrate the effectiveness of the fencing material was no more original an idea than Glidden's wire. It was simply a scaled-up version of a dramatic demonstration cooked up years earlier—in 1876—by Sanborn's predecessor in Texas, a salesman who would become famous as John "Bet-A-Million" Gates.

Gates, an Illinois native born in 1855, signed on with Washburn & Moen to sell barbwire when he graduated from college in 1876. Upon arriving in San Antonio, he realized it would take something extraordinary to overcome skepticism concerning the wire. Some couldn't imagine the flimsy strands would hold half-wild range cattle; others feared the barbs would slice and shred the animals. So, the salesman rented out Military Plaza, a public square established by Spain in 1722 and since surrounded by the city, as was the Alamo, just a half mile away.

The resourceful salesman built a corral of fenceposts strung with barbwire in the plaza and filled it with Texas Longhorn cattle, allowing them to mill around and go about their business in full public view. The barbwire fence held the cattle fast without causing any discernable harm to the critters. Gates's point was well made, and he wrote up orders for more wire than the factory could produce.

Believing himself due a partnership in the company, which the firm refused to offer, Gates went to work for a competing manufacturer and, despite a long and colorful career in a number of fields, disappears from this story.

The Frying Pan Ranch, then, was essentially the same idea writ large. It took 120 miles of four-wire barbwire fence to enclose the ranch, at a cost of $39,000. The wire was hung on cedar posts cut in nearby Palo Duro Canyon and the breaks of Sierrita de la Cruz Creek.

Glidden, used to verdant, water-rich Illinois, was taken aback when he first visited his ranch in 1884. He is supposed to have said the country

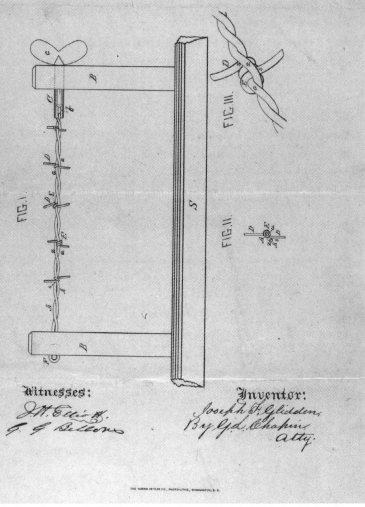

Patent drawings for Joseph Glidden's barbwire, which encircled the Frying Pan Ranch and changed the American West. WIKIMEDIA COMMONS

didn't grow enough grass to feed a goose. But there must have been enough to feed cattle, for the Frying Pan Ranch raised and shipped thousands and thousands of the animals over the years, and then even more as the ranch grew in size.

The big ranch was cut in half by the railroad when it arrived in the Panhandle in 1887. A town site that would become Amarillo was established near the ranch, but Sanborn developed an alternative site a mile or so away, bordering the ranch, and that's the one that took hold. Around the same time, Sanborn and Glidden parted ways, with Sanborn taking ownership of business interests in town and twenty-five thousand more acres and Glidden holding on to the rest of the ranch.

But he did not hold it for long. Within a few years the cattle herd was dispersed and the land divided into leased pastures. Glidden's son-in-law, William Henry Bush, took title in 1898. He later hired his brother James to run the place. As of 2014 descendants of the Bush family continue to operate parts and pieces of the Frying Pan Ranch.

Surviving a Lead Storm: Elfego Baca

1888—New Mexico Territory

Some men attract legends the way alfalfa blossoms attract honeybees. Such a man is Elfego Baca.

The legends start with his birth. As the story goes, his soon-to-be mother jumped into the air for a fly ball while playing in a February 10, 1865, softball game and when she hit the ground, so did baby Elfego. Then there's the one about his being kidnapped a year or so later by wayward Navajos who soon returned the child—after bathing him in boiling oil and slamming him against a rock—because he proved more than they wanted to deal with. And they say that many years later, a fully grown Baca (all five feet, seven inches of him) stole a pistol from Mexican rebel Pancho Villa, who put a price on his head for the theft. And there's a story that while Baca was practicing law in Albuquerque, a would-be client charged with murder in El Paso asked for representation. The attorney is said to have responded by wire: "Leaving at once with three eyewitnesses." Baca claimed to have represented thirty people charged with murder, only one of whom ended up in prison.

Legends and tales are one thing; the truth is an altogether different animal. But in the case of Elfego Baca, the facts are often as outlandish as the fiction. The reputation he earned as a lawman, whether a self- or duly appointed one (both may have been true at various times), was sometimes sufficient to prompt outlaws to surrender on request—by mail, no less: "I have a warrant here for your arrest," the letter said. "Please come in by _____ and give yourself up. If you don't, I'll know you intend to resist arrest, and I will feel justified in shooting you on sight when I come after you." Baca once said in an interview, "I never wanted to kill anybody, but if a man had it in his mind to kill me, I made it my business to get him first."

Still, the most incredible incident in Baca's career has more to do with his getting shot at than shooting.

Congressman Bill Richardson, representing New Mexico in the United States House of Representatives in 1995, read out a tribute to Elfego Baca on the House floor. "It is still a mystery why Baca travelled to San Francisco [a community in Socorro County] Plaza in October, 1884, but his confrontation with some Texas cowboys is what made him a legend," Richardson said.

It seems likely that Baca heard reports from Pedro Sarracino, sheriff of Lower Frisco, of cowboys and other newcomers to the booming area abusing and terrorizing native New Mexicans. Baca, unlike the sheriff, decided to do something about it. Baca may have been deputized, or he may have pinned on a mail-order badge of his own accord. But he traveled to Frisco determined to confront the cowboys.

On October 29 a saloonkeeper asked Baca to restrain a rowdy cowboy named Charlie McCarty (or McCarthy) who was shooting up the place. Baca disarmed and arrested the cowboy, a rider for the Slaughter Ranch, upsetting his fellow cowboys in the process. The local magistrate at first refused to hear the case, being afraid of the cowboys, so Baca held McCarty in a house while deciding what to do.

A band of armed and angry cowboys rode up, a dozen or so according to reports, and demanded McCarty's release. Baca ordered them to leave or he would start shooting. They didn't and he did. McCarty's boss, a cowboy named Young Parham, led the mob and in the ruction his horse—perhaps shot—reared over backwards and crushed Parham, killing him.

That ended things for the time being. McCarty was tried the next day and fined five dollars. Baca refused to return the man's pistol, instead rushing out a side door after the trial and taking shelter in a nearby jacal, or small shack. The cowboys were not amused. They congregated in numbers, with eighty or so being the most commonly cited number, to avenge the death of Parham and the arrest of McCarty. Surrounding the jacal and concealing themselves as well as possible, they set into perforating the hut's thin walls—made of cedar stakes and mud—with lead.

As townsfolk gathered on the hills above to spectate, the cowboys continued laying down fire, with Baca inside throwing lead back at them through gaps in the walls. What the outside shooters did not know was that the floor of the jacal was a foot to a foot and a half below ground level, so as long as the besieged Baca laid low, he could return fire while bullets zipped by overhead. He managed to kill at least one of the cowboys and wound another. Other accounts, including Baca's, say he killed four of the attackers and wounded another eight, but some historians say those accounts do not stand up to scrutiny.

New Mexico miracle man Elfego Baca huddled in a stick-and-mud jacal and survived a thirty-three-hour gunfight. 000-742-0005, PICT 000-742, CENTER FOR SOUTHWEST RESEARCH, UNIVERSITY LIBRARIES, UNIVERSITY OF NEW MEXICO

The gunfight roared on throughout the day. Come nightfall, attempts were made to set fire to the jacal's roof, made of branches covered with dirt. A piece of the roof caved in as a result. But Baca weathered that storm as well, and morning found him making tortillas on the small cookstove in the hut.

Morning also brought the law, and with a guarantee of protection and safe passage Baca agreed to surrender himself, but not his weapons. He arrived safely at the courthouse in Socorro, despite harassment along the way by mounted cowboys and planned ambushes lost in confusion when each of two groups sent out to lay the trap thought the other successful and abandoned their attempt. Locked in a cell for four months,

Baca withstood two attempts to convict him of murder, just as he had withstood the hail of gunfire.

All told, the siege and gunfight lasted some thirty-three hours. Estimates of the number of bullets fired at Baca range from four hundred to one thousand to four thousand. The jacal's flimsy door, hauled into court for Baca's trials, had at least 367 and perhaps more than 400 bullet holes punched through it. Kitchen utensils were said to have been mangled by gunfire in the assault, and even a skinny stick of a broom handle suffered eight wounds.

Elfego Baca, however, was untouched.

He went on to be elected Socorro County sheriff and served as county clerk, mayor, school superintendent, district attorney, and US marshal. Despite his popularity among the Hispanic population, he lost a run for Congress. Along the way Baca studied law and was admitted to the bar in 1894. He also worked at various times as a private investigator, political organizer, and newspaper columnist.

He died quietly in 1945.

Representative Bill Richardson told Congress, "The story of Elfego Baca demonstrates a man's will to preserve justice in a land and time of rampant corruption and bullying. Baca's bravery instilled hope to the native New Mexican people who upheld the laws of the land and refused to succumb to racial injustices."

The Birth of the Modern World: Electricity

1891—Telluride, Colorado

Of all the "things" that make our modern world work, you could make a pretty good argument that none of them is more ubiquitous or essential than electricity.

Even a brief power outage makes the point. No light. No refrigerator. No freezer. No furnace. No air conditioner. No computer. No Internet. No television. No radio. No washing machine. And, for many, no clothes dryer or stove or water heater. And that's just at home. Chances are, your workplace would shut down as well, leaving you with nothing to do but wait for the power to come back on and start the world turning once again.

Electricity has become such an indispensable part of life that we seldom contemplate that it did not even exist in any useable form until late in the nineteenth century—barely a blip ago on the timeline of history.

And few people remember, or even know, that we owe the electricity running through our lives to a man, a mine, and a mountain stream near Telluride, Colorado.

The victory achieved in Telluride proved to be the final battle in the "War of Currents," fought in the 1880s with the man who ran the world's most prolific invention machine, Thomas Edison, on one side and Nikola Tesla and George Westinghouse on the other. Allied with Tesla and Westinghouse was the man on whose battlefield the war was won, Telluride businessman Lucien Lucius (L. L. for short) Nunn.

When the harnessing of electricity was in its infancy, Edison fought for transmission of direct current. It worked well with the incandescent light bulb he invented, and producing light was electricity's biggest benefit at the time. Direct current worked well with machines and motors and batteries, too. It was stable, economical, and reliable. Also figuring into Edison's support was the fact that many of his patents and inventions were compatible with direct current, and should that transmission system be adopted on a large scale, the rewards would be tremendous.

The big disadvantage of direct current lay in the fact that the power flowed only one way and was tied to a particular voltage, and a low one at that, which could not be changed easily. The result was that transmission distance was severely limited. If we lived in a direct current world, there would be hundreds, thousands, millions of generating stations scattered throughout our towns and cities, as direct current's reach is barely beyond the bounds of your neighborhood.

Tesla, on the other hand, worked out a way to generate and transmit electricity via an alternating current. Edison and Tesla were well acquainted, Tesla having worked for the famous inventor after arriving in America from Serbia. The two inventors parted company over disagreements about compensation. Tesla was something of a genius, every bit as inventive, if not more so, than Edison. But it seems he lacked the discipline and business sense of his former employer, and was even a bit eccentric.

And it may be that Tesla would have lost the war in a rout had not George Westinghouse joined the fight. Westinghouse was an engineer and the inventor of the compressed-air braking system for trains. His studies in the infant field of electrical transmission led him to believe Edison's low-voltage direct-current system was doomed by its inability to move electricity over long distances. He started tinkering around with alternating current, using transformers imported from Europe.

Westinghouse wired up an experimental alternating-current power network in Massachusetts, using a hydroelectric generator to whip up power at five hundred volts, then boost it with a transformer to a much higher voltage for more efficient and powerful transmission, then run it through another transformer to down-convert it to one hundred volts, which would light up an Edison incandescent bulb.

Westinghouse and his partners started building small, mostly experimental electrical lighting systems and by 1889 were operating in several towns. An integral part of Westinghouse's plans were several patents purchased or licensed from Tesla, including an electric motor that operated on alternating current, which overcame one of direct current's few remaining advantages. Alternating current's superiority was becoming evident.

Edison fought back. He fired off salvo after salvo to back his claim that alternating current was dangerous—a killer, in fact. Edison's troops traveled from town to town using alternating current to electrocute cats and dogs and horses and cattle and sheep. And, in one instance that showed what a circus the whole thing was becoming, they zapped a rogue show elephant from Coney Island with alternating current. In a particularly brutal demonstration, Edison built an electric chair and used it to execute a criminal with alternating current in a New York state prison.

Tesla counterattacked, arranging demonstrations during which he grasped live wires and allowed low-voltage alternating current to pass through his body with no ill effect.

But it was L. L. Nunn who demonstrated once and for all that alternating current could work in the real world.

Lucien Lucius Nunn was born in Ohio in 1853 and answered the call to "Go West" at age twenty-seven, after obtaining considerable education at universities in America and Germany. He and a partner hiked into the high-country mining town of Telluride in 1881 and went to work at a variety of jobs. According to some accounts, they were handy with carpentry tools and built a number of cabins—and Telluride's first bathtub.

Nunn dabbled in real estate, practiced law, operated a newspaper, and ran the only bank in the county. That bank, by the way, launched Butch Cassidy's life of crime (outside of rustling livestock) when he and a pair of saddle pals robbed it of more than $20,000 on June 24, 1889.

But it was the mining business that brought Nunn and alternating current together to create the future. Nunn collected and consolidated a number of mining and milling enterprises around Telluride, among them the Gold King Mine—which looked to be the downfall of the young entrepreneur. The mine's location was so rugged and isolated—Telluride itself is 8,750 feet above sea level—as to be nearly inaccessible, some 3,000 feet higher and more than three miles from town. All the ore from

This generator and switchboard at the Ames Power Plant near Telluride, Colorado, led the way in large-scale electrical generation. LIBRARY OF CONGRESS

the Gold King had to be hauled out muleback to be milled, which was altogether too inefficient and expensive. But obtaining power for a mill at the mine site proved a problem.

Steam power was out of the question, as the forests around Telluride were already ravished, offering no possibility of fuel for the necessary fires. Hauling in coal would be as inefficient as hauling out ore, as well as prohibitively expensive. Hydropower was the answer, and the South Fork of the San Miguel River had the water and the fall to create more than enough power to run the mill. The river, however, was nearly three miles away, two thousand feet lower in elevation than the mill site, and at the bottom of a gorge.

Nunn's search for a solution led him to investigate alternating current, and he convinced shareholders in the Gold King Mine to go all in for the new, even experimental, technology. That was no easy task. Several engineers reported the foolishness of the enterprise and predicted it would fail. There were gaps of knowledge about the kinds of equipment that would be required to make a high-voltage, alternating-current system work, and a good deal of uncertainty about how Mother Nature—in the form of ice, snow, cold, wind, water pressure, and lightning storms—would affect the scheme.

Somehow, Nunn prevailed and went to work putting the pieces together. Tesla was, at the time, living and working in Colorado Springs, and although he never visited Telluride, the job of designing the system was his. Equipment, and the expertise to install it, came from Westinghouse in the form of the largest matching generator and motor available, along with a one-hundred-horsepower alternator and all manner of other gadgets, devices, and contraptions. The generator, housed in a wooden shack built beside the San Miguel River at a place called Ames, was connected to a six-foot water wheel in the river and wired to the motor at the mill, more than two and a half miles away. The two strands of copper wire reportedly set the enterprise back only about $700. The cost of wire to transmit direct current in the same situation was estimated to be nearly one hundred times as much.

The water wheel started turning on June 19, 1891, generating electricity and pumping it up the power lines to the Gold King mill.

That was the day, arguably, the modern world was born.

While primitive by today's standards, the system was complex, cobbled together from materials as disparate as paraffin, shellac, motor oil, mahogany, walnut, commutators, coils, transformers, fuses, alternators, switchboards, cables, copper, and so on. And the Ames Power Plant grew and expanded from there, soon providing power to mines throughout the region.

But the system, while workable and reliable, required babysitting. Fifteen to twenty trained operators were on duty at all times, often in dangerous conditions. To avoid grounding and electrocution, reports say switchboard operators worked with one hand in their pocket. Without mechanical circuit breakers, circuits had to be broken manually, which resulted in an electric arc. Small arcs could be blown away with the breeze from a waving hat. Larger arcs, when disconnecting the generator, were said to snake and sizzle and stretch as far as eight feet and became something of an entertainment attraction for local folks, who often visited the plant out of curiosity. Other workers patrolled the power lines to prevent and repair problems. Still others walked the flumes that fed water to the wheel that worked the generator, plugging leaks.

Nunn devised a system of keeping track of his workers, using pins stuck in a map to chart their locations. Soon, Nunn's people were known as "pinheads." The training and education necessary for a steady supply of pinheads proved of great interest to Nunn, and he set up programs to teach and train the bright young men he recruited to keep the power network running. The Telluride Institute, as the program became known, trained workers for other power plants Nunn established, including one in nearby Ilium and others in Utah, Idaho, Montana, Canada, and Mexico.

It seems Nunn's devotion to education overtook his interest in mining and electrical generation, and his partners relieved him of his management position. He continued experimenting with educational programs and eventually established Deep Springs Collegiate and Preparatory School, now Deep Springs College, on the isolated Swinging T Ranch in California near the Nevada border, and was integral in the school's operations until his death in 1925.

Although the power plant at Telluride proved the feasibility of commercially produced and distributed alternating current electricity and essentially won the "War of Currents," there was still some mopping up to do.

Niagara Falls had long been recognized as a tremendous source of power, but harnessing it was the subject of debate and competing proposals. Edison and his General Electric company proposed a direct current system, while Westinghouse proposed using Tesla's polyphase alternating current. Nunn contributed his expertise and experience to the Westinghouse proposal. A commission headed by William Thomson—Lord Kelvin of Great Britain—and including luminaries of the day such as John Jacob Astor IV, J. P. Morgan, and Lord Walter Rothschild, studied the competing proposals and awarded the project to Westinghouse and alternating current. But it took the 1893 World's Fair in Chicago to finally convince the commission—and the public.

The Columbian Exposition, celebrating the four-hundredth anniversary of Columbus's voyage to the New World, was the first electrified

World's Fair. General Electric offered to do the job for $1 million, with much of the money paying for the miles and miles of copper wire it would take to distribute direct current. Westinghouse offered to illuminate the "White City" for half as much, using alternating current. Westinghouse and Tesla got the job.

Their alternating current lit up one hundred thousand incandescent lights when President Grover Cleveland flipped the switch on May 1, 1893. In the Hall of Electricity at the fair, Tesla and Westinghouse created a display showing how rotating magnets generated electricity and alternating current to perform work. Even the twelve working generators that supplied the power for the World's Fair were on display in the Hall of Machinery. The Fair attracted twenty-seven million visitors. The brightly lit fairgrounds and electrical displays fascinated most of them, no doubt, and created an appreciation for the value of the emerging power source. The more technically inclined among them gained an understanding of alternating current and its superiority.

Construction on the Niagara Falls Power Plant was completed in 1896, and on November 16 Westinghouse's generators, operating with Tesla's alternating current, sent power down the line to industrial plants at Buffalo, New York—a scheme that had already proved its worth at L. L. Nunn's Ames Power Plant at Telluride, Colorado.

Bibliography

Head 'Em Up and Move 'Em Out: Trail Driving (1546–1865—North America)

Dary, David. *Cowboy Culture: A Saga of Five Centuries.* Lawrence: University Press of Kansas, 1981 and 1989.

Dillon, Richard H., ed. "California Trail Herd: The 1850 Missouri-to-California Journal of Cyrus C. Loveland." http://freepages.genealogy.rootsweb.ancestry .com/~crow2000/california_trail_herd_intro.htm. Accessed 10/1/14.

"Florida Cattle Ranching." Florida Memory, www.floridamemory.com/photographic collection/photo_exhibits/ranching. Accessed 10/1/14.

Leigh, Phil. "Florida's Cattle Wars." *New York Times*, December 19, 2013.

Link, Ed. "Illinois Cattle Drives." www.illinoiscattledrives.com. Accessed 10/1/14.

"The Shawnee Trail." www.theshawneetrail.com. Accessed 10/1/14.

Skaggs, Jimmy M. "Cattle Trailing." Handbook of Texas Online, www.tshaonline.org/ handbook/online/articles/ayc01. Accessed 10/1/14.

Alexander Mackenzie: Crossing the Continent (1792–1793—North America)

"Alexander MacKenzie, 1762–1820." The Oregon History Project, www.oregonhistory project.org/articles/biographies/alexander-mckenzie-biography. Accessed 10/1/14.

"Alvar Nunez Cabeza de Vaca: Explorer." Enchanted Learning, www.enchantedlearning .com/explorers/page/d/devaca.shtml. Accessed 10/1/14.

"Alvar Nuñez Cabeza de Vaca." The West Film Project and WETA, www.pbs.org/weta/ thewest/people/a_c/cabezadevaca.htm. Accessed 10/1/14.

Mackenzie, Alexander. *Voyages from Montreal through the Continent of North America.* New York: A. S. Barnes and Company, 1903.

"Sir Alexander Mackenzie (1764 – March 1820)." Bella Coola Grizzly Tours, www .bcgrizzlytours.com/index.asp?p=102. Accessed 10/1/14.

"Sir Alexander Mackenzie." Canada History, www.canadahistory.com/sections/eras/british %20america/Mackenzie.html. Accessed 10/1/14.

Zebulon Pike: Lost in the Louisiana Purchase (1806–1807—Western Frontier)

Crutchfield, James A. *It Happened in Colorado*. Guilford, CT: TwoDot, 2008.

"Zebulon Pike: Hard Luck." *National Park Service Museum Gazette*, January 1996. www
.nps.gov/jeff/historyculture/upload/pike.pdf. Accessed 10/1/14.

Maximilian and Bodmer: Science and Art in the Old West (1833–1834—Missouri River)

Crutchfield, James Andrew. *It Happened in Montana*. Guilford, CT: TwoDot, 2008.

Ferguson, Stuart. "From the Rhine to the Wild West." *Wall Street Journal*, February 2, 2011.

"An Illustrated Expedition of North America: Bodmer and Maximilian in the American West." National Agricultural Library, http://specialcollections.nal.usda.gov/
bodmer-exhibit. Accessed 10/1/14.

Kimberling, Clark. "Maximilian zu Wied-Neuwied (1782–1867)." http://faculty.evansville
.edu/ck6/bstud/princemax.html. Accessed 10/1/14.

Noll, Michael G. "Maximilian, Prince of Wied-Neuwied (1782–1867)." Encyclopedia
of the Great Plains, http://plainshumanities.unl.edu/encyclopedia/doc/egp.ea.027.
Accessed 10/1/14.

"Corralled for Defense": Indian Attacks on Wagon Trains (1840–1860—Emigrant Trails)

Brooke, Bob. "Oregon Trail: Wagon Tracks West." *Wild West*, April 2000.

Clayton, William. *The Latter-Day Saints' Emigrants' Guide*. Tucson, AZ: Patrice Press,
1983.

Czajka, Christopher W. "Hardship without Glory: Life on the Trail." Frontier House,
www.pbs.org/wnet/frontierhouse/frontierlife/essay3.html. Accessed 10/1/14.

"Frequently Asked Questions." National Historic Oregon Trail Interpretive Center,
Bureau of Land Management, www.blm.gov/or/oregontrail/history-faqs.php.
Accessed 10/1/14.

Hastings, Lansford W. *The Emigrants' Guide to Oregon and California*. Bedford, MA:
Applewood Books.

Jefferson, T. H. *Map of the Emigrant Road, Independence Mo. to San Francisco, California.* New York: published by author, 1849.

Madsen, Brigham D. "The 'Almo Massacre' Revisited." *Idaho Yesterdays,* Fall 1993.

Marcy, Randolph B. *The Prairie Traveler.* 1859. Reprint, Bedford, MA: Applewood Books, 1993.

Morelock, Jerry D. *Review of Circle the Wagons!,* by Gregory F. Michno and Susan J. Michno. *Armchair General,* March 2009. www.armchairgeneral.com/circle-the-wagons-book-review.htm. Accessed 10/1/14.

Muncrief, Dennis. "The Warren Wagon Train Massacre—Indian Version." Oklahoma GenWeb, www.okgenweb.org/~okmurray/Murray/stories/warren_massacre02.htm. Accessed 10/1/14.

Muncrief, Dennis. "The Warren Wagon Train Massacre—White Man's Version." Oklahoma GenWeb, www.okgenweb.org/~okmurray/Murray/stories/warren_massacre01.htm. Accessed 10/1/14.

"Native Americans on the Oregon Trail." The Oregon Trail, www.america101.us/trail/Native.html. Accessed 10/1/14.

"Site of Utter Party Massacre." Idaho State Historical Society Reference Series, http://history.idaho.gov/sites/default/files/uploads/reference-series/0233.pdf. Accessed 10/1/14.

"The Snake River Massacre—Account by One of the Survivors." *Oregon Argus,* November 24, 1860.

"Trail Basics: Indians." National Oregon/California Trail Center, www.oregontrailcenter.org/HistoricalTrails/Indians.htm. Accessed 10/1/14.

Unruh, John D. *The Plains Across.* Urbana: University of Illinois Press, 1979.

Porter Rockwell: God's Gunfighter (1840–1878—Western Frontier)

Kelly, Charles, and Hoffman Birney. *Holy Murder: The Story of Porter Rockwell.* New York: Minton, Balch & Company, 1934.

Schindler, Harold. *Orrin Porter Rockwell: Man of God, Son of Thunder.* Salt Lake City: University of Utah Press, 1983.

Van Alfen, Nicholas. *Orrin Porter Rockwell: Mormon Frontier Marshal and Body Guard of Joseph Smith.* Salt Lake City: Deseret Book Company, 1974.

Van Wagoner, Richard S., and Steven C. Walker. *A Book of Mormons.* Salt Lake City: Signature Books, 1982.

Edward Fitzgerald Beale: A Frontiersman for All Reasons (1846—California)

Bonsal, Stephen. "Edward Beale: A California Pioneer." *Out West: A Magazine of the Old Pacific and the New III (December 1911 to June 2012).*

Bonsal, Stephen. *Edward Fitzgerald Beale: A Pioneer in the Path of Empire, 1822–1903.* New York and London: G. P. Putnam's Sons, 1912.

"Brigadier General Edward Fitzgerald Beale." The California State Military Museum, www.militarymuseum.org/EdBeale.html. Accessed 6/7/12.

"California Explorers: Edward Fitzgerald Beale." Needles Field Office, Bureau of Land Management, www.blm.gov/pgdata/etc/medialib/blm/ca/pdf/pdfs/needles_pdfs/brochures.Par.79254.File.dat/Beale.pdf. Accessed 10/1/14.

Camp, Charles L. "Kit Carson in California: With Extracts from His Own Story." *California Historical Society Quarterly* 1 (October 1, 1922).

"Edward Fitzgerald Beale." *Snowy Range Reflections: Journal of Sierra Nevada History & Biography,* Winter 2013.

"Ned Beale Dead." *San Francisco Call,* April 23, 1893.

Walker, Dale L. *El Dorado: The California Gold Rush.* New York: Forge Books, 2003.

Weiser, Kathy. "Old West Legends: Beale's Wagon Road from New Mexico to California." Legends of America, www.legendsofamerica.com/we-bealeroad.html. Accessed 10/1/14.

Weiser, Kathy. "Old West Legends: Edward Fitzgerald Beale—Blazing the West." Legends of America, www.legendsofamerica.com/we-edwardbeale.html. Accessed 10/1/14.

The Free and Independent State of Deseret (1847—Great Basin)

Bigler, David L. "The Elephant Meets the Lion: Gold Rush Conflicts in the Great Basin." Address given at the Oregon-California Trails Association Trails Symposium, Salt Lake City, UT, April 14, 1999. http://user.xmission.com/~octa/symposium_bigler.htm. Accessed 10/1/14.

"Constitution of the State of Deseret, with the journal of the convention which formed it, and the proceedings of the legislature consequent thereon (1850)." https://archive.org/details/constitutionofst00dese. Accessed 10/1/14.

Poll, Richard D. "Deseret." Utah History to Go, http://historytogo.utah.gov/utah_chapters/pioneers_and_cowboys/deseret.html. Accessed 10/1/14.

"The State of Deseret—Appendix: Constitution and Ordinances (1849–1851)." *Utah Historical Quarterly* 8, nos. 2, 3, and 4 (1940).

"Utah Becomes a State." I Love History, Utah Division of State History, www.ilove history.utah.gov/topics/statehood/index.html?utm_source=twitterfeed&utm_medium=twitter. Accessed 10/1/14.

Samuel Brannan: The Man Who Started the Gold Rush (1848—California)

"The Apostate Mormon." California Missions Resource Center, www.missionscalifornia.com/stories/apostate-mormon.html. Accessed 10/1/14.

Bagley, Will. "Latter-day Scoundrel: Sam Brannan." *Wild West*, August 2008.

Campbell, Eugene E. "The Apostasy of Samuel Brannan." *Utah Historical Quarterly XXVII* (1959): 157–67.

"Samuel Brannan." American Experience: The Gold Rush, www.pbs.org/wgbh/amex/goldrush/peopleevents/p_brannan.html. Accessed 10/1/14.

"Samuel Brannan." The West Film Project and WETA, www.pbs.org/weta/thewest/people/a_c/brannan.htm. Accessed 10/1/14.

Before Civil Rights: The Chinese in America (1849—California)

"An act to execute certain treaty stipulations relating to the Chinese, May 6, 1882." Enrolled Acts and Resolutions of Congress, 1789–1996; General Records of the United States Government; Record Group 11; National Archives.

Chang, Iris. *The Chinese in America: A Narrative History.* New York: Viking Press, 2003.

"Examples of Legislation Affecting the Rights of Chinese Immigrants." The Chinese Experience in 19th Century America, http://teachingresources.atlas.illinois.edu/ chinese_exp/resources/resource_2_3.pdf. Accessed 10/1/14.

"'The Heathen Chinee' by Bret Harte." The Chinese Experience in 19th Century America, http://teachingresources.atlas.illinois.edu/chinese_exp/resources/resource_1_5 .pdf. Accessed 10/1/14.

"'Our Misery and Despair': Kearney Blasts Chinese Immigration." History Matters, http://historymatters.gmu.edu/d/5046. Accessed 10/1/14.

"Proposed Amendment to the Constitution." California State Archives (page 18), www .sos.ca.gov/archives/collections/1879/archive/F3956-87.pdf. Accessed 10/1/14.

"Some Mid-19th Century American Attitudes." The Chinese Experience in 19th Century America, http://teachingresources.atlas.illinois.edu/chinese_exp/resources/ resource_1_2.pdf. Accessed 10/1/14.

"Some State of California and City of San Francisco Anti-Chinese Legislation and Subsequent Action." The Chinese Experience in 19th Century America, http:// teachingresources.atlas.illinois.edu/chinese_exp/resources/resource_2_4.pdf. Accessed 10/1/14.

"Yick Wo v. Hopkins (1886)." The Chinese Experience in 19th Century America, http://teachingresources.atlas.illinois.edu/chinese_exp/resources/resource_2_5.pdf. Accessed 10/1/14.

Dear Sir: Corresponding via the Jackass Mail (1851–1860—California and the Great Basin)

Chorpenning v. United States—94 U.S. 397 (1876). Justia, US Supreme Court, https:// supreme.justia.com/cases/federal/us/94/397. Accessed 10/1/14.

McLaughlin, Mark. "Snowshoe Thompson: Sierra's Skiing Mailman." Tahoe Nuggets blog, http://thestormking.com/tahoe_nuggets/Nugget_47/nugget_47.html. Accessed 10/1/14.

"Overland Mail to California in the 1850s." United States Postal Service, https://about .usps.com/who-we-are/postal-history/overland-mail.htm. Accessed 10/1/14.

Ships of the Southwest Desert: Camels Join the Army (1856—Texas)

"Camels in Texas—1856." Lone Star Junction, www.lsjunction.com/facts/camels.htm. Accessed 10/1/14.

Carroll, Charles C. "The Government's Importation of Camels: A Historical Sketch." National Agricultural Library, www.nal.usda.gov/awic/pubs/camelimport.htm. Accessed 10/1/14.

Emmett, Chris, and Odie B. Faulk. "Camels." Handbook of Texas Online, www.tsha online.org/handbook/online/articles/quc01. Accessed 10/1/14.

"Lieutenant William H. Echols, 'Report' to United States Thirty-sixth Congress, Second Session, Senate Executive Document, No. I (Washington, 1861), 37–50." The Texas Camel Experiment, www.qsl.net/w5www/camel.html. Accessed 10/1/14.

Weiser, Kathy, ed. "Camel Caravans of the American Deserts, by James M Guinn." Legends of America, www.legendsofamerica.com/we-camelcaravans.html. Accessed 10/1/14.

Weiser, Kathy. "Ghost Camels in the American Southwest." Legends of America, www .legendsofamerica.com/we-ghostcamels.html. Accessed 10/1/14.

Zentner, Joe. "Camels in America's Southwest: The Desert Camel Experiment." Desert USA, www.desertusa.com/mag05/sep/camel.html. Accessed 10/1/14.

American Royalty: Emperor Norton I (1859—San Francisco)

Cowan, Robert Ernest. "Norton I, Emperor of the United States and Protector of Mexico." *Quarterly of the California Historical Society*, October 1923.

Gazis-Sax, Joel, ed. "Norton I, Emperor of the United States and Protector of Mexico, Welcomes You to His Archives." www.notfrisco.com/nortoniana. Accessed 10/1/14.

Moylan, Peter. "Emperor Norton." Encyclopedia of San Francisco, www.sfhistory encyclopedia.com/articles/n/nortonJoshua.html. Accessed 10/1/14.

Root Hog or Die: The Pig War
(1859—San Juan Island)

Oldham, Kit. "San Juan Island Pig War." HistoryLink: The Free Online Encyclopedia of Washington State History, www.historylink.org/index.cfm?DisplayPage=output .cfm&file_id=5724. Accessed 10/1/14.

"The Pig War." San Juan Island National Historical Park, National Park Service, www .nps.gov/sajh/historyculture/the-pig-war.htm. Accessed 10/1/14.

Randolph B. Marcy: Tour Guide for the Westward Emigration
(1859—Emigrant Trails)

Marcy, Randolph B. *The Prairie Traveler. 1859*. Reprint, Bedford, MA: Applewood Books, 1993.

The Comstock Lode: A Silver-Lined Mountain
(1859—Utah Territory)

Branch, Edgar Marquess, Michael Barry Frank, and Kenneth M. Sanderson, eds. *Mark Twain's Letters, Volume 1: 1853–1866*. Berkeley and Los Angeles: University of California Press, 1987.

Bush, Don. "The History of the Crookedest Short Line in America, the Virginia and Truckee Railroad." www.vcnevada.com/history/Vnthist.htm. Accessed 10/1/14.

Bush, Don. "History of Virginia City, Nevada and the Comstock Lode." www.vcnevada .com/history.htm. Accessed 10/1/14.

"Closing the Western Frontier: The Comstock Lode and the Mining Frontier." Digital History, www.digitalhistory.uh.edu/disp_textbook_print.cfm?smtid=2&psid=3149. Accessed 10/1/14.

Colton, Roger. "More History of the Crookedest Short Line in America." www.vc nevada.com/history/Vnthist_RC.htm. Accessed 10/1/14.

"Comstock Lode." Online Nevada Encyclopedia, www.onlinenevada.org/articles/ comstock-lode. Accessed 10/1/14.

"Digging Deeper into the Comstock." Nevada Bureau of Mines and Geology Educational Series E-48, 2009, www.nbmg.unr.edu/dox/e48.pdf. Accessed 10/1/14.

Weiser, Kathy. "Nevada Legends: Comstock Lode—Creating Nevada History." Legends of America, www.legendsofamerica.com/nv-comstocklode.html. Accessed 10/1/14.

Weiser, Kathy. "Nevada Legends: Virginia City and the Comstock Lode." Legends of America, www.legendsofamerica.com/nv-virginiacity.html. Accessed 10/1/14.

Barney Ford: From Runaway Slave to Wealthy Businessman (1860—Colorado)

"Barney Ford Biography." Denver Public Schools, http://ford-elementary-archive.wiki spaces.dpsk12.org/Barney+Ford+Biography. Accessed 10/1/14.

"Barney Ford House Museum." Summit Historical Society, www.summithistorical.org/barneyfordhouse.htm. Accessed 10/1/14.

"Business: Barney Ford." Colorado State Archives, www.colorado.gov/pacific/sites/default/files/Business.pdf. Accessed 10/1/14.

Cleary, Brooke. "Barney L. Ford: Runaway Slave, Denver Pioneer." History Colorado, http://games.historycolorado.org/kids/Barney%20Ford.pdf. Accessed 10/1/14.

Crutchfield, James Andrew. *It Happened in Colorado*. Guilford, CT: TwoDot, 2008.

Jessen, Kenneth. "Former Slave Barney Ford Became a Colorado Millionaire." *Reporter-Herald* (Loveland, CO), February 26, 2012.

Battle of Glorieta Pass: The Gettysburg of the West (1862—New Mexico Territory)

"The Battle of Glorieta Pass." The American Civil War, www.mycivilwar.com/battles/620326a.htm. Accessed 10/1/14.

"Battle of Glorieta Pass." Pecos National Historical Park, National Park Service, www.nps.gov/peco/historyculture/copy-of-battleofglorietta.htm. Accessed 10/1/14.

Bryan, Susan Montoya. "Gettysburg of the West: Glorieta Battlefield Trail Allows Access to Pivotal Civil War Site." *Deseret News* (Salt Lake City, UT), October 11, 2009.

"Glorieta Pass New Mexico: American Civil War, March 26–28, 1862." AmericanCivil War.com, http://americancivilwar.com/statepic/nm/nm002.html. Accessed 10/1/14.

Hickman, Kennedy. "American Civil War: Battle of Glorieta Pass." About.com, http:// militaryhistory.about.com/od/civilwar/p/glorietapass.htm. Accessed 10/1/14.

Nagle, P. G. "History of the Glorieta Battlefield: The Civil War in New Mexico." http:// glorietapass.org/history.html. Accessed 6/7/12.

Massacre at Bear River: First, Worst, Forgotten (1863—Washington Territory)

Madsen, Brigham D. *The Shoshoni Frontier and the Bear River Massacre.* Salt Lake City: University of Utah Press, 1985.

Miller, Rod. *Massacre at Bear River: First, Worst, Forgotten.* Caldwell, ID: Caxton Press, 2008.

Adobe Walls: Ruins of a Way of Life (1864 and 1874—Texas)

Anderson, H. Allen. "Adobe Walls, Texas." Handbook of Texas Online, www.tshaonline .org/handbook/online/articles/hra10. Accessed 10/1/14.

Venturino, Mike. "The Battle of Adobe Walls Myth vs Reality: The Facts Have Been Twisted over the Years, but the Real Story Is Still Astounding." *Guns,* June 2005. http://milpas.cc/rifles/ZFiles/Articles/History/Battle%20of%20Adobe%20 Walls%20myth%20vs%20reality.html. Accessed 10/1/14.

The End of the Civil War: Battle at the End of Texas (1865—Texas)

Hunt, Jeffrey William. "Palmito Ranch, Battle of." Handbook of Texas Online, www .tshaonline.org/handbook/online/articles/qfp01. Accessed 10/1/14.

"Thornton Affair." A Continent Divided: The U.S.–Mexico War, University of Texas Arlington Center for Greater Southwestern Studies, http://library.uta.edu/us mexicowar/topic.php?topic_id=7. Accessed 10/1/14.

Weaver, Mark. "Battle of Palmito Ranch." American Civil War Story, www.american civilwarstory.com/battle-of-palmito-ranch.html. Accessed 10/1/14.

First Blood: Showdown in the Street (1865—Missouri)

Holcombe, R. I., ed. "Killing of Dave Tutt by 'Wild Bill.'" *In History of Greene County, Missouri.* St. Louis: Western Historical Company, 1883.

Leonard, Carl. "The First Western Showdown Between Wild Bill Hickok and Davis Tutt Took Place at the Market Square of Springfield, Missouri Today in 1865." Now We Know Em, http://nowweknowem.com/2013/07/the-first-western-showdown-between-wild-bill-hickoc-and-davis-tutt-took-place-at-the-market-square-of-springfield-missouri-today-in-1865-now-we-know-em. Accessed 10/1/14.

Lubet, Steven. "Slap Leather! Legal Culture, Wild Bill Hickok, and the Gunslinger Myth." *UCLA Law Review* 48, no. 6 (2001).

Nichols, Colonel George Ward. "Wild Bill." *Harper's New Monthly Magazine* 34, no. 201 (February 1867).

"Shoot Out with 'Wild Bill' Hickok, 1869." EyeWitness to History, www.eyewitnessto history.com/hickok.htm. Accessed 10/1/14.

Trimble, Marshall. "How Far Apart Were Wild Bill Hickok and Dave Tutt in Their Famous 1865 Showdown in Springfield, Missouri?" *True West*, April 2003.

Wood, Larry. "Wild Bill Hickok & Dave Tutt." Ozarks History blog, http://ozarks-history.blogspot.com/2009_11_01_archive.html. Accessed 10/1/14.

Jacob Brodbeck: First Flight, First Crash? (1865—Texas)

Eckhardt, C. F. "First to Fly." Texas Escapes, www.texasescapes.com/CFEckhardt/First-to-Fly-Jacob-Brodbeck.htm. Accessed 10/1/14.

"First Flight: The Brodbeck Airship, 40 Years Before Wright Bros." Texas Less Traveled, http://texaslesstraveled.com/brodbeck.htm. Accessed 10/1/14.

Jent, Steven A. *Browser's Book of Texas Quotations.* Plano: Republic of Texas Press, 2001.

Kohout, Martin Donell. "Brodbeck, Jacob Friedrich." Handbook of Texas Online, www.tshaonline.org/handbook/online/articles/fbr63. Accessed 10/1/14.

"Was a Texan the First Man to Fly in an Airplane?" Inside the Gates blog, http://drt library.wordpress.com/2009/09/30/was-a-texan-the-first-man-to-fly-in-an-airplane. Accessed 10/1/14.

Mass Murder: Circleville Massacre (1866—Utah Territory)

Newell, Linda King. *A History of Piute County.* Salt Lake City: Utah State Historical Society and Piute County Commission, 1999.

Reeve, W. Paul. "Circleville Massacre, A Tragic Incident in the Black Hawk War." Utah History to Go, www.historytogo.utah.gov/utah_chapters/american_indians/circleville massacre.html. Accessed 10/1/14.

Black Hawk's Last Ride: Reconciliation (1869—Utah Territory)

Forrest Cuch interview by Phil Gottfredson, 2009. Black Hawk Productions, transcript in author's possession.

Newell, Linda King. *A History of Piute County.* Salt Lake City: Utah State Historical Society and Piute County Commission, 1999.

The Métis: Gone the Way of the Buffalo (1869—Prince Rupert's Land, United States and Canada)

"Anger in the West: Fury with Ottawa Creates Shaky Alliances on the Prairies." Le Canada: A People's History, www.cbc.ca/history/EPISCONTENTSE1EP10CH 4PA1LE.html. Accessed 10/1/14.

"Are You Métis?" Métis Nation of Indiana, http://usmetis.weebly.com. Accessed 10/1/14.

"The Fate of Louis Riel: Madman or Hero? The Trial of the Metis Leader." Le Canada: A People's History, www.cbc.ca/history/EPISCONTENTSE1EP10CH4PA4LE .html. Accessed 10/1/14.

"Métis." The Canadian Encyclopedia, www.thecanadianencyclopedia.ca/en/article/ metis/. Accessed 10/1/14.

"The Metis Rebellion." Peace and Conflict, www.histori.ca/peace/page.do?pageID=233. Accessed 10/1/14.

"The North West Rebellion: The Uprising Is Short but Its Legacy Continues Today." Le Canada: A People's History, www.cbc.ca/history/SECTIONSE1EP10CH4LE .html. Accessed 10/1/14.

"Return From Exile: Louis Riel Comes Home to Lead His People." Le Canada: A People's History, www.cbc.ca/history/EPISCONTENTSE1EP10CH4PA2LE .html. Accessed 10/1/14.

Making Barbwire Famous: The Frying Pan Ranch (1881—Texas)

Anderson, H. Allen. "Frying Pan Ranch." Handbook of Texas Online, www.tshaonline .org/handbook/online/articles/apf03. Accessed 10/1/14.

"Barbed Wire." The Great Idea Finder, www.ideafinder.com/history/inventions/barb wire.htm. Accessed 10/1/14.

"Barbed Wire Overview." Antique Barbed Wire Society, www.antiquebarbedwiresociety .com/overview.html. Accessed 10/1/14.

"Brief History of Barbed Wire." Antique Barbed Wire Society, www.antiquebarbedwire society.com/historical.html. Accessed 10/1/14.

"Frying Pan Ranch Historical Marker." Amarillo Public Library Photoarchive Collection, http://images.amarillolibrary.org/cdm4/item_viewer.php?CISOROOT=/Phot oArchiv&CISOPTR=383&CISOBOX=1&REC=1. Accessed 10/1/14.

"Joseph F. Glidden." The Rise of Barbed Wire and Its Transformation of the American Frontier, http://xroads.virginia.edu/~CLASS/am485_98/cook/develp3.htm. Accessed 10/1/14.

"Joseph Farwell Glidden." The West Film Project and WETA, www.pbs.org/weta/the west/people/d_h/glidden.htm. Accessed 10/1/14.

Joseph Glidden entry in The Writer's Almanac podcast transcript, January 18, 2013, http://writersalmanac.publicradio.org/index.php?date=2013/01/18. Accessed 10/1/14.

Surviving a Lead Storm: Elfego Baca (1888—New Mexico Territory)

Elfego Baca interview by Janet Smith, July 13, 1936. Transcript in the Library of Congress, http://lcweb2.loc.gov/ammem/wpa/20040209.html. Accessed 10/1/14.

Hardin, Jesse Wolf. "The Guns of Elfego Baca." www.thefreelibrary.com/ The+guns+of+Elfego+Baca.-a0102274458. Accessed 10/1/14.

Hardin, Jesse L. "Old West Legends: Elfego Baca & The 'Frisco War.'" Legends of America, www.legendsofamerica.com/WE-ElfegoBaca.html. Accessed 10/1/14.

Santana, David, Melissa Ann Villela, Rosalynn Torres, and Michael Telles. "Elfego Baca Lived More Than Nine Lives." *Borderlands* 22 (2003).

"Tribute to Elfego Baca—Hon. Bill Richardson, in the House of Representatives, Wednesday, May 10, 1995." *Congressional Record*, Government Printing Office.

The Birth of the Modern World: Electricity (1891—Telluride, Colorado)

"The Founder: L. L. Nunn." Deep Springs College, www.deepsprings.edu/about/founder. Accessed 10/1/14.

Michaels, Daniel. "Long Dead Inventor Nikola Tesla Is Electrifying Hip Techies." *Wall Street Journal*, January 14, 2010.

"Milestones: Ames Hydroelectric Generating Plant, 1891." IEEE Global History Network, www.ieeeghn.org/wiki/index.php/Milestones:Ames_Hydroelectric_Generating _Plant,_1891. Accessed 10/1/14.

Nunn, P. N. "Pioneer Work of the Telluride Power Company." *In Power Transmission: Second Volume*; A Series of Papers and Discussions Presented at the International Electrical Congress in St. Louis, 1904. New York: McGraw, 1906.

Switzer, Caitlin. "Let There Be Light . . . L.L. Nunn and the Ames Power Plant." *Montrose* (CO) *Mirror*, January 16, 2013.

"Telluride Colorado History." Mont Maison, www.montmaisontelluride.com/telluride history.html. Accessed 10/1/14.

Underhill, Wendy. "Technology in Telluride: Nerds, Pinheads and Geeks, This Is Your Town!" *Nexus*, July/August 2010.

"Why Telluride?" Telluride Tech Festival, www.techfestival.org/why-telluride. Accessed 10/1/14.

INDEX

About the Author

Rod Miller is the winner of Western Writers of America Spur Awards for short fiction and poetry, the Westerners International Award for poetry, and the Academy of Western Artists Award for best poetry book. He is the author of five novels, three poetry books, and three other books of history, and he writes for magazines. Miller is a lifelong resident of the American West, and the people, places, and happenings of his homeland are the subjects of his writing. Visit him online at www.writerRodMiller .com.